W9-DED-040

Can Workers Have a Voice?

Can Workers Have a Voice?

The Politics of
Deindustrialization in Pittsburgh

Dale A. Hathaway

The Pennsylvania State University Press

University Park, Pennsylvania

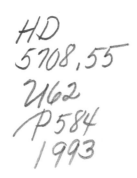

Library of Congress Cataloging-in-Publication Data

Hathaway, Dale A., 1951–
    Can workers have a voice? : the politics of deindustrialization in
    Pittsburgh / Dale A. Hathaway.
        p.   cm.
    Includes bibliographical references and index.
    ISBN 0-271-00924-1
    1. Plant shutdowns—Pennsylvania—Pittsburgh Region—Case studies.
    2. Unemployment—Pennsylvania—Pittsburgh Region—Case studies.
    3. Steel industry and trade—Pennsylvania—Pittsburgh Region—Case
    studies. I. Title.
    HD5708.55.U62P584   1993
    338.6'042—dc20   92–32477
                                                                                CIP

Published by The Pennsylvania State University Press,
Barbara Building, Suite C, University Park, PA 16802-1003

It is the policy of The Pennsylvania State University Press to use acid-free paper
for the first printing of all clothbound books. Publications on uncoated stock
satisfy the minimum requirements of American National Standard for Information Sciences—Permanence of Paper for Printed Library Materials, ANSI
Z39.48–1984.

Contents

List of Figures and Tables

FIGURES

TABLES

Preface

Because I am convinced of the need for thoroughgoing political change in the United States, the subject of political change has long been of great interest to me. During the early 1980s, my attention was drawn to what appeared to be a nascent uprising of steelworkers in the Pittsburgh region. Workers there had been laid off by the tens of thousands, with dreadful consequences for them and their communities.

I particularly noticed three dramatic acts of resistance to this industrial holocaust. A group of workers were organizing to prevent destruction of one of the steel mills. A clergyman was arrested and hauled out of his church, apparently for speaking too vigorously in defense of unemployed workers. Yet another group of workers forced the sheriff to stop foreclosure on the homes of unemployed people.

Putting these small bits of information together with my general knowledge of the wave of plant shutdowns and massive layoffs that had been sweeping the nation, I naively concluded that we might be on the verge of some real political change—that previously fairly conservative workers might be changing their minds about what they were willing to put up with. Yet as I looked more deeply into the matter, I found that the few activists I learned of in Pittsburgh were distinct exceptions to the rule of dejected acceptance that better typified the response of workers nationally to the distinct decline in the fortunes of the industrial middle class.

My goal then became to explain why so few workers showed any overt resistance to the losses they were so frequently suffering. For reasons described in the Introduction to this book, I chose to focus primarily on three groups of Pittsburgh workers, in order to better understand the balance of power between industrial workers and corporate executives. Members of each group took time to teach me about Pittsburgh and about their histories, and I was repeatedly impressed by their sincerity and the ingenuity they showed in very difficult circumstances.

While this book is based mostly on events that happened in Pittsburgh in the 1980s, its concerns are larger and more immediate. Just as US Steel eliminated nearly 30,000 jobs in Pittsburgh in the 1980s, General

Motors has announced that it will eliminate 75,000 jobs in the near future. Some suggest that number will be much higher. The end of the cold war brings mixed blessings to communities with many jobs based around weapons production. The nation is moving toward elimination of trade barriers with Mexico, a move likely to send hundreds of thousands of additional jobs south of the border. Real wages for most workers have been declining for nearly two decades now. Many people are concerned about the future.

This book is really about our ability as a society to respond to the pressures of the global economy that are rapidly transforming communities all over the United States. Currently, a small class of corporate executives is being allowed to make the decisions that determine how we as a society will reorganize our lives to face the future. Good executives are skilled at determining what needs to be done to advance the interests of their own corporations, but we cannot expect them to be as concerned with what is important for the lives of the people they employ or for the community that surrounds them.

Yet these executives make most of the decisions, and for a country that prides itself on being a democracy, I see this as a distinct problem. The fact that so few workers responded to the massive industrial shutdowns of the 1980s is a symptom of this problem. Finding out why workers have had so little voice can tell us about the social dynamics that prevent most people from having a say in the decisions that are being made now and that will affect the vitality of their communities and the quality of their lives for decades to come.

This book is talking about the voice industrial workers like those who lost their jobs in Pittsburgh's Monongahela Valley have in the face of industrial shutdowns. But it is also about most of the rest of us too—who work in large corporate or government organizations. Most of us work for a living in environments that we do not really control. Most of us have little say over the major economic decisions that create or destroy jobs. In that sense, most of us are or have been or will be workers. What stands between us and having a voice in shaping our futures? To answer this question, we need to study why workers had so little say in the 1980s.

The argument is that the balance of power between corporate leaders and ordinary workers explains, better than anything else, why so few workers chose to resist the economic onslaught they confronted in the 1980s. In confronting the power of Pittsburgh's corporate elites, none of the groups studied succeeded in besting Goliath. The balance of power in Pittsburgh was decidedly in favor of the executives.

The failure of the worker groups to succeed in challenging the monopoly corporate elites have on decision-making power is described here not primarily to provide a historical record of the groups' activities but rather to show how a small class of wealthy executives dominate economic decision-making. However, this limited purpose is not entirely satisfactory. Having gotten to know the people involved in these groups, I cannot leave it at that. In each case study I have also described some of the ideas and tactics that contributed to the small but important successes each group had along the way.

My conclusion is that the vast majority of workers were not foolish for refusing to take on the awesome power of U.S. Steel, Westinghouse, or Mellon Bank. But this book celebrates those whose bravery or foolishness encouraged them to try, because the small victories recorded here may someday be built on by others foolish enough or determined enough to take on apparently awesome elite power.

If workers are to have a voice in shaping the futures of their communities as they confront shutdowns in the auto or aerospace industries or in other sectors of our volatile, global economy, they will have to be brave enough to try challenging those who seem so invincible. That is what wise fools like shipbuilder Lech Walesa or playwright Vaclav Havel did in the 1980s. Despite a history that excluded people like them from having much voice in their societies, they imagined that things could change. They imagined it because they felt it had to be. They were convinced that those making decisions made bad decisions because they excluded ordinary people from the decision-making process.

The world was amazed at the speed of change in Eastern Europe when workers demanded a voice. When we look at decisions reshaping communities in the United States as we approach the twenty-first century, it is important to ask: Can workers have a voice in shaping the future?

Acknowledgments

Writing a book is both a solitary and a communal activity. Writing is solitary in that no one else in the world understands what one is really doing, no one else must put in the long hours and years of research, writing, revision, frustration, and small triumphs. It is communal in that it would be impossible to make it through the solitary struggle without the help and support of a great many people. I want to acknowledge some of that support now, conscious that I may leave out many who have helped. To all of you, thanks too.

Theodore J. Lowi, who guided this project in its earliest stages, has been a frequent source of intellectual inspiration, offering analytical insights like my matrices and numerous ideas on organization and emphasis. But even more important has been his steady encouragement. Others have been inspirational too. Jaroslav Vanek got me to Cornell to study labor-managed economics and supported me when I deserted the sterile discipline of economics for a more humane approach to some of those same concerns. Eldon Kenworthy gave me my first written critique of an early chapter and provided much-appreciated guidance over a glass of wine in my early days at Cornell. Michael Goldfield has amazed me with how much writing it is possible to do while also teaching. His presence helped keep me honest on my left.

I appreciate all those who have read various drafts. In this category I have two special thanks, one for Peter Bachrach, whose hard-nosed critique made me rethink some central concepts and grow in the process, and one for the Indy 500 Writers Group, who helped me finish the job.

I must not neglect the essential nonacademic help I received from such people as those who picked me up when I had to hitchhike between Ithaca and Pittsburgh; Malik Baker, who provided affordable housing and friendship in Pittsburgh, members of various Friends Meetings, who have held me in the light; fellow graduate students and our janitor, Al, who made the basement of McGraw Hall a home away from home; and especially members of the Nicaragua Affinity Group (NAG), who shared with me an exploration of direct political action, and much love as well. On a more personal side, I thank my parents for early inspiration and continual support.

Finally I must acknowledge the valor, courage, persistence, intelli-gence, imagination, and sincerity of the workers I met in Pittsburgh who took the time to teach me about their struggles. Their dedication, their willingness to find ways to stand up while others gave up, will stay with me always. I wish them well in this changing world.

Abbreviations

ACCD	Allegheny Conference on Community Development
ACHD	Allegheny Conference on Human Development
DMS	Denominational Ministerial Strategy
HUD	U.S. Department of Housing and Urban Development
IUMSWA	Industrial Union of Marine Shipbuilding Workers of America
JTPA	Job Training Partnership Act
LCA	Lutheran Church in America
MVUC	Mon Valley Unemployed Committee
NUN	National Unemployed Network
PUP	Philadelphia Unemployment Project
RIDC	Regional Industrial Development Corporation of Southwest Pennsylvania
SEIU	Service Employees International Union
SVA	Steel Valley Authority
UE	United Electrical Workers
USS	United States Steel Corporation and later a division of USX
USWA	United Steelworkers of America
USX	USX Corporation, new name for more diversified USS
WABCO	Westinghouse Air Brake Company

INTRODUCTION

Early in the 1970s, the United States began to lose its position as unquestioned leader of the world economy. Many industrial sectors began to feel the strain of international competition. By the early 1980s, massive plant shutdowns became common. It was clear that the United States was in the midst of a major economic transformation. This transformation was frequently discussed in books, journals, and the electronic media, but, more important, it was experienced in the communities across the land whose fortunes rose or fell as the shape of the economy shifted.

Pittsburgh experienced both the rise and the fall of the 1980s as a time of triumph and cataclysmic collapse. While its corporate headquarters and high-tech sectors experienced healthy growth, its steel industry shed 90 percent of its employees in a few short years. Nearly 100,000 industrial jobs were lost in the greater Pittsburgh region, and many of the communities once sustained by those jobs instantly fell into decay. While Pittsburgh is a particularly dramatic example of the dislocations experienced in the decade, dozens of other communities around the nation experienced similarly sudden declines. Some, like Pittsburgh, also experienced the euphoria of postindustrial expansion. And the process continues.

The change the United States is currently undergoing may be as fundamental as the metamorphosis of the late nineteenth century when the nation's economy was rapidly evolving from primarily agricultural and locally based to primarily industrial and nationally based. It is clearly as significant as the dramatic period of the 1930s and 1940s, which saw the collapse and reconstitution of U.S. capitalism, the establishment of a limited welfare state, and the achievement of global hegemony. We cannot yet predict the outcome of our current evolution, but we know it is driven by the transformation of technologies and the globalization of nearly all markets.

As in previous periods of economic transformation, there are and will be both winners and losers, not only among individuals and economic sectors, but also among communities and regions and classes. This transformation is often thought of in terms of the economic forces driving it. Yet because it is a process that results in winners and losers, that involves a redistribution of power in our society, it must also be seen as a decidedly political process.

In the United States, a country that makes much of its claim to be a democracy, one is tempted to ask whether these decisions are being made in a democratic way. Yet regardless of one's interest in democracy, any serious student of politics is obligated to ask questions about interests. Whose interests are being considered, denied? advanced, destroyed? With stakes as high as these, we would expect the fights among groups with conflicting interests to be a central concern of our political process. And we would expect those with the most to lose to be putting up obvious resistance.

Previous economic transformations have always provoked large-scale political resistance. The upsurge of the farm-based People's Party in the 1880s and 1890s, as well as the militant labor struggles of the 1930s, were key elements in the political life of their times. Yet no comparable movement has emerged to resist the dramatic social and economic dislocation caused by our current transformation.

This study is motivated by the simple question, "Why?" Why was there no major political response to factory shutdowns that often cast thousands of workers at a time out of the ranks of the middle class into the ranks of the unemployed, where they faced few options and had to scramble for low-wage, low-status jobs in the new and burgeoning service sector? To speak of the situation in terms of thousands, however, substantially understates the problem. If one recognizes the connection between the decline of wages and employment in the industrial sector, and the problem of unemployment, underemployment, and low-wage employment throughout the economy, then one is speaking of a problem that affected 20 to 80 million workers, depending on the definition one uses. When dependents are included, the problem encompasses approximately half the country's population.[1] Clearly one would expect the issue to have been a more salient political topic than it was in the 1980s or is now in the 1990s.

The experience of the 1890s and the 1930s strongly suggests that those who are damaged by dramatic economic transformation normally attempt, in some form we might broadly call political, to protect themselves from further damage, if not to restore themselves to their previous position. The period from 1870 to the election of 1896 was marked by ever-increasing efforts of Americans to organize in their communities, in their places of work, and through formal political channels to resist the damage being inflicted on them by the increasing concentration of economic power. Farmers formed marketing cooperatives and captured several state legislatures, while industrial workers conducted the first industry-wide strikes. The political movement known most generally as populism resulted in two serious attempts to capture the Presidency.[2]

Americans responded to the collapse of industrial capitalism in the 1930s in a variety of ways. Industrial workers struggled and sometimes died in their ultimately successful effort to gain legal recognition of their unions. The hungry marched on Washington, ransacked grocery stores, resisted eviction and foreclosure, staged general strikes that stopped most production in San Francisco and Minneapolis, and briefly took over many of the municipal services in Seattle. The economically disadvantaged also formed the basis of a major electoral realignment by providing the massive base of President Franklin Roosevelt's new coalition.[3]

1. These estimates are from Bertram Gross, "Rethinking Full Employment," *The Nation*, January 17, 1987, p. 46.
2. For a thorough discussion of both economic and political efforts of farmers' activities, see Lawrence Goodwyn, *The Populist Moment* (Oxford: Oxford University Press, 1978). An excellent treatment of both farm and labor political roles in the 1890s is in Walter Dean Burnham, *Critical Elections and the Mainsprings of American Politics* (New York: Norton, 1970). While there are many available labor histories of the period, three of the best are Richard O. Boyer and Herbert M. Morais, *Labor's Untold Story* (New York: United Electrical, Radio & Machine Workers, 1955); Jeremy Brecher, *Strike!* (Boston: South End Press, 1972); and Melvyn Dubovsky, *Industrialism and the American Worker, 1865–1920* (Arlington Heights, Ill.: AHM Publishing, 1975).
3. Both Boyer and Morais (*Labor's Untold Story*) and Brecher (*Strike!*) provide discussions of the labor struggles. Broad-ranging treatments of the efforts of labor, farmers, and the unemployed are found in Francis Fox Piven and Richard A. Cloward, *Poor People's Movements: Why They Succeed and How They Fail* (New York: Vintage Books, 1979); Jack Salzman, *Years of Protest: A Collection of American Writings of the 1930s* (Indianapolis: Bobbs-Merrill, 1967); and David A. Shannon, *The Great Depression* (Englewood, N.J.: Prentice-Hall, 1960). The political history of the period is treated in Burnham, *Critical Elections*; Mike Davis, "The Barren Marriage of American Labor and the Democratic Party," *New Left Review* 124 (November–December 1980), 43–84; Alonzo Hamby, ed., *The New Deal:*

In the 1980s, workers offered but a dim shadow of the protests of earlier eras. Rather than increasing their mobilization in response to declining fortunes, they continued to fade into the background. Union membership dropped below 16 percent of the work force—less than half what it had been twenty years earlier. Yes, the workers faced a determined "capitalist offensive"[4] led by a union-busting President in the 1980s, but workers in earlier periods had faced guns and clubs of both business and government.

Why were workers in the 1980s apparently so unwilling to defend their interests? I argue that the process of economic decision-making has taken on forms that discourage workers from playing any role in the process. A process that excludes workers more effectively than all the guns of the nineteenth-century Pinkertons is a reflection of firmly entrenched, antidemocratic power.

The Decision-Making Process: A Reflection of Power

A crucial part of understanding how certain decisions are made involves understanding who gets to be involved in making those decisions. Each state in the United States has its own rules about who is allowed to vote in elections—one of our more celebrated decision-making processes. Once officials are elected, the U.S. Constitution specifies that the President, with the advice and consent of the Senate, will decide whom he will appoint to the Supreme Court and that the House of Representatives will be first to decide what new taxes to introduce. In these and in many other cases, there are clear rules about who gets to decide, because determining who gets to decide is likely to affect the outcome of decisions.

The above cases, while formally accurate, offer only superficial descriptions of the decision-making processes. Any casual student of elections knows that those who manipulate the images in political campaigns must also be considered in the decision-making process. So too must those who give the money to pay the image manipulators. And while the House has the formal authority to introduce new tax legislation, we all know that a plethora of interest groups weigh in heavily on

---

Analysis and Interpretation (New York: Longman, 1981); and William E. Leuchtenburg, *Franklin Roosevelt and the New Deal* (New York: Harper & Row, 1963).

4. Michael Goldfield, *The Decline of Organized Labor in the United States* (Chicago: University of Chicago Press, 1987), argues that a "capitalist offensive" has been going on since the 1950s.

any such decisions. We also know that average citizens, as individuals, have relatively little influence over such decisions.

In every decision-making process there are insiders and outsiders, and some actors clearly have more say than others. There is a hierarchy of decision-making power that those who have the most power guard jealously, and in the process reinforce the barriers between insiders and outsiders. While the debates among insiders may be fierce, insiders often have more in common with each other than they do with outsiders. What they agree on most is preserving the basis of their own power. Even in spheres thought of as beyond the realm of business, that power is often tied to established patterns of power rooted in the economic system. According to Richard Hofstadter,

> The fierceness of political struggles has often been misleading; for the range of vision embodied by the primary contestants in the major parties has always been bounded by the horizons of property and enterprise. However much at odds on specific issues, the major political traditions have shared a belief in the rights of property, the philosophy of economic individualism, the value of competition; they have accepted the economic virtues of capitalism as necessary qualities of man.[5]

Another word for insiders is "elites."[6] In Washington the decision-making elites include the elected officials, their top appointees, and those whose positions of economic power and/or social connections give them considerable influence. The trouble with the idea of elites is that it violates the notion of democracy. It means that in a nation of supposed equals, some people are more equal than others. Unlike earlier feudal societies, in which the noble elite were celebrated and openly demonstrated their privileges, power, and splendor, the United States celebrates equality. Its elites often hide their abundant power, pretending to be "just plain folks." Only in this context can we understand billionaire

5. Richard Hofstadter, *The American Political Tradition* (New York: Knopf, 1948), p. viii.

6. The literature on elites and elite theory is extensive. C. Wright Mills, *The Power Elite* (New York: Oxford University Press, 1959), was a first major attempt (after Charles Beard, that is) to describe how the democratic structures of the United States could be controlled by an elite. Following in Mills's footsteps, G. William Domhoff, *Who Rules America* (Englewood Cliffs, N.J.: Prentice-Hall, 1967), made a frontal attack on Dahl and other pluralists of the 1960s. Domhoff's *Powers That Be: Processes of Ruling-Class Domination in America* (New York: Random House, 1978), is an attempt to go beyond a description of the elite to the process of their rule. His *Who Rules America Now?* (Englewood Cliffs, N.J.: Prentice-Hall, 1983) is an update of earlier work.

Ross Perot's claims to represent "the common man" in the 1992 elections. Reality is disguised, but the power of elites is not significantly limited. While the notion of elites may be troubling, only the most naive would deny that they exist.

But who are they? Who is and is not elite depends on the particular decision-making context. In this study I am concerned primarily with decisions that reshaped the economy of the Pittsburgh region and that in the process reshaped the lives of hundreds of thousands of people and their communities. Defining the decision-making process allows us to determine who were the insiders and who were the outsiders.

The elites with which we are most concerned comprise a group of major economic power holders, who are described in some detail in Chapter 5, and many of whom are listed by name in Table 2. Their power comes largely through ownership—both personal and corporate—of major assets. In Pittsburgh, these elites made the decisions that reshaped the city. They sometimes cooperated with each other, and sometimes competed. They worked with various community planning bodies and with politicians at a variety of levels, but they rarely allowed their autonomy to be diminished by those contacts. Politicians also acted to shape Pittsburgh's evolution, but their actions were nearly all reactions to decisions made by the corporate elite. Public officials proved nearly irrelevant in most important decisions.

I also look at decisions made beyond the sphere of what is normally thought to be the world of private economic decision-makers—decisions made within churches and academic institutions. Clearly there is a hierarchy of power within churches. While each church member has a small part in shaping church policy, ordained priests and ministers have much more power. But bishops, archbishops, and their close associates have the most power and are therefore the elites. In the academic realm a similar hierarchy exists. Yet because each of these institutions is to a significant extent dependent on private donations, we often find that those with elite status in the economic realm also exercise significant power within churches, academic institutions, and in fact in most institutions throughout society, based on their ability to make monetary contributions.

Of the leading nations in the world, the United States is the most ardently capitalistic and has the least-developed public sector. Capitalism divides society into two classes of people (not very neatly): those who own and/or control sufficient amounts of capital that their income derives primarily from capital; and the rest of us, whose income is based primarily not on what we own but on what we do. Those who own large amounts of capital have power both over their own economic resources but also, through investment and grants, over a variety of decision-making spheres throughout society. The economic elite in many cases become the elite of the elite. Some of these elites are powerful only within a small community, others are powerful within a region or a nation, and for some the globe has become their only limit. Thus, there are hierarchies of elites within different decision-making arenas and at different levels of geopolitical reach. On some issues, those with political authority have more power than those whose power is primarily economically rooted. On other issues, the situation is reversed. Therefore, the question "Who makes up the elite?" depends on (1) the issues being decided and (2) who exercises the most power.

It may be useful to distinguish briefly between elites and an elite. Above we have talked primarily of "elites"—individuals who exercise large amounts of power. An elite, however, is a group of people who by their position in society have exceptional amounts of power—for example, a class of people such as the owners and top management of Pittsburgh's largest corporate entities. The important distinction is that when discussing an "elite" one is talking about persistent social structures rather than about the activities of individuals.

A world run by a coherent elite is a world with little possibility for democracy. In Pittsburgh it is tempting to discuss corporate elites as a unified elite. One of the groups studied here sees Pittsburgh's most powerful actors in such terms. I also see the economic elites of Pittsburgh as clearly the dominant participants in most policy areas and as quite unified. However, my research does not show them to be as omnipotent or as monolithic. There is some room for democratic influence in Pittsburgh, in spite of the desires of elites. The groups described in this book have managed to force elites to take account of them despite their lowly position in the hierarchy of power. They have insisted on the possibility of democracy, that even workers should have a voice.

Generalizing from the case of Pittsburgh, I argue that the elites who are shaping the economic transformation of the United States are not elected representatives of the people, but wielders of the tremendous private economic power held by corporations. Politicians play only secondary roles in the process. Common citizens like the steelworkers of Pittsburgh are distant outsiders. This constitutes the hierarchy of decision-making power.

In that hierarchy, the barrier between insiders and outsiders is maintained by the power of the insiders. Rules, laws, customs, and assumptions all work to create decision-making systems that make access automatic for some and nearly impossible for others. The rules are made by those with sufficient power to make them—the relevant elite for each arena of power. The very structure of those systems then tends to perpetuate the exercise of power by specific groups over time to such an extent that people accept such systems as natural. It is important for our purposes to see that what appears natural is actually the result of the exercise of elite power.

In order to gain insight into how this power is used, I draw heavily on the theoretical underpinnings offered by John Gaventa in his *Power and Powerlessness: Quiescence and Rebellion in an Appalachian Valley*.[7] As its title suggests, Gaventa's book has a goal similar to mine: explaining political quiescence when objective circumstances might lead one to expect rebellion. The author argues that the exercise of power by elites creates the apparent quiescence of the nonelite. To observe this process of preventing dissent, Gaventa looks at three dimensions in which power is exercised. I use those three dimensions of power in examining the ability of Pittsburgh's elites to make the region's most significant decisions.

The first of these dimensions is the most obvious and most readily observed. It often consists of overt contests of power between insiders. Different factions use their various resources to obtain a desired result. The winner of the contest is frequently recognized as the result of a vote. The resources of power may include, for example, constituent support, money, charisma, and political know-how. This dimension also includes overt uses of power against outsiders, such as acts of war, arrests, and the use of bulldozers.

Most political scientists writing on politics in the United States employ a first-dimensional approach that ignores most actors who are not within the formal political process. The classic example of a first-dimensional approach is Dahl's early attempt to answer the question "Who governs?"[8] by looking at three different types of decisions made by the New Haven City Council. Dahl found that the resources necessary to influence political decisions were fragmented but not equally distributed, so no one powerful individual or group could dominate all the others in all or even most key decisions.[9] He therefore concluded that a rough approximation of democracy existed in New Haven.

Peter Bachrach and Morton Baratz introduced the second dimension of power to social scientists in their classic discussion entitled "The Two Faces of Power."[10] According to Bachrach and Baratz, whose conclusions

7. Urbana: University of Illinois Press, 1980.

8. Robert A. Dahl, *Who Governs? Democracy and Power in an American City* (New Haven: Yale University Press, 1961).

9. Ibid., p. 227.

10. Peter Bachrach and Morton Baratz, "The Two Faces of Power," *American Political Science Review* 56 (1962), 947–52.

were based on a study of Baltimore, the second dimension of power prevents issues from reaching the formal decision-making arenas. It is used to try to block outsiders at the gateways of the polity. In many ways, to study the second dimension is to study "nondecisions."

> Non-decision-making is a means by which demands for change in the existing allocation of benefits and privileges in the community can be suffocated before they are voiced, or kept covert; or killed before they gain access to the relevant decision-making arena; or, failing all these things, maimed or destroyed in the decision-implementing stage of the policy process.[11]

Nondecisions would not show up at all in a study like Dahl's. In fact, if someone other than Bachrach and Baratz had studied the politics of Baltimore paying attention only to the insiders, they might have found that Baltimore looked roughly as democratic as New Haven. By looking at how elites used the second dimension of power to exclude outsiders, Bachrach and Baratz found a profoundly antidemocratic politics to be the real determinant of what did and did not get decided.

Looking beyond the first dimension of power is more complex than staying within it, but it produces better analysis simply because it excludes less of reality. However, the differences are more than analytic differences. The elite largely determine the rules governing the formal political arena, and because most of them have followed the rules, they have achieved their power within the bounds of legitimacy as they have defined it. Analysis within this realm tells us about conflicts between elites. Analysis beyond the first dimension of power exposes the basis of that power. As such, it is more likely to be subversive of it. Thus, the decision to look beyond the first dimension of power is not merely an analytical one but a political one as well.

Nondecisions are extremely important in relation to the topic at hand. They can also be difficult to observe because they are either nonresponses or very oblique responses to challenges from outsiders. They do not directly engage the substance of the challenge. Nondecisions can be employed at a variety of points in a political encounter. For instance, groups of irate unemployed workers can be delegitimated by labeling them Communist, or they can be co-opted by getting them to participate in a labor-management public relations scheme or a committee to facilitate the distribution of welfare benefits to fellow sufferers. They can

11. Peter Bachrach and Morton Baratz, *Power and Poverty: Theory and Practice* (New York: Oxford University Press, 1970), p. 44.

be listened to with all due consideration and have their concerns referred to a study commission. They can have their demands for plant-closing legislation redirected into the more "politically realistic" job-training legislation. If at this point workers and their allies have rallied sufficient first-dimensional power to obtain passage of such legislation, the training programs can nonetheless be controlled by the local business elite who managed previous shutdowns, and jobs selected for training can turn out to be low-paying or not in demand. These and other forms of non-decision-making can ward off a variety of challenges in a way that greatly reduces the visibility of the process of challenge and response.

The third dimension of power is the least visible of the three but the most important one in my analysis.[12] It operates through a variety of mechanisms to prevent potential challengers from envisioning any alternative to "the way things are"—or, if they somehow envision an alternative, to convince them that the process of challenge would be futile and potentially dangerous. When it is functioning well, this type of process works as an auto-censorship device within the mind of a potential challenger. The result is apparent quiescence, and the exercise of elite power is unobserved.

This third-dimensional power is created in part by consistent elite victories in the first and second dimensions. Such victories can deprive people of alternative visions. The United States is remarkable for its lack of socialist political organization and for its weak labor movement.[13] One cause of this weak left wing is the series of elite victories, such as the imprisonment of the early twentieth-century socialist Eugene Debs while he campaigned for President, the extralegal deportation of thousands of left-wing activists during the 1919 Palmer raids, the passage of the Taft-Hartley amendment, which included provisions to purge labor unions of left-wing members, and the cold-war anticommunist fervor that branded

---

12. The third dimension is introduced to social science by Steven Lukes in *Power: A Radical View* (London: Macmillan, 1974). This trilogy of authors and dimensions, as well as the times and political perspectives from which they were introduced, provides the basis for an article waiting to be written. Each dimension carries as much political as analytic weight.

13. Writings in response to the question posed by Werner Sombart in the title of his book, *Why Is There No Socialism in the United States?* (Armonk, N.Y.: M. E. Sharpe, 1976), are vast. A good sampling would include: J. Laslett and S. M. Lipset, eds., *Failures of a Dream? Essays in the History of American Socialism* (Garden City, N.Y.: Doubleday, 1974); S. M. Lipset, "Why No Socialism in the United States?" in S. Bialer and S. Luzar, eds., *Sources of Contemporary Radicalism* (Boulder, Colo.: Westview Press, 1977); Louis Hartz, *The Liberal Tradition in America* (New York: Harcourt Brace & World, 1955); and Theodore J. Lowi, "Why Is There No Socialism in the United States? A Federal Analysis," *International Political Science Review* 5, no. 4 (1984), 369–80.

any left-leaning individuals as traitors. One result of these elite class victories is that few U.S. citizens have been exposed to alternative ideas about how society might be organized. When jobs and communities are threatened by the need to protect corporate profits, they have little but their emotions to tell them that things might be done another way.

Consistent elite victories give rise to the common saying "You can't fight City Hall." This attitude of powerlessness needs to be seen as a reflection of elite power. Every defeat that is observed by potential challengers teaches them the likely futility of challenging entrenched power. The effects tend to be cumulative and to increase over time. Elite power is also reinforced by consistent messages taught by schools, the media, churches, and other institutions, which reinforce the unquestioned hierarchy of power produced by contemporary capitalism. One such message is that one should not rock the boat. "Troublemakers" are routinely frowned on, regardless of the issue at hand. Most ideas critical of the power of corporations are likely to be branded as "socialistic" or "communistic," labels even worse than "troublemaker." The result is that the established concentration of power is strengthened.

The permeation throughout society of such intentionally but unselfconsciously narrow-minded attitudes creates a culture that reinforces the power of those who have already achieved elite status. Since most elites in this society owe much of their power to their economic position, the perpetuation of these attitudes can be thought of as cultural hegemony, or more specifically as the cultural hegemony of capitalism.[14]

Capitalism divides society into two classes, but we know that most people are not capitalists. Yet most people accept as normal, as common sense, as the way things are, many notions that support the power capitalists have over them. For instance, they accept that wealth connotes achievement and worth regardless of how that wealth may have been achieved. They participate in the rituals of consumerism. And though they may detest their place in it, they accept the general structure of class relations in the United States. These and a myriad other attitudes allow capitalist elites to dominate, to exercise hegemony over most significant economic and political decisions made in this country.

How is it that most people live their lives within a culture that reinforces their inferior status? Do most people deal with questions of social power by using ideas that disempower them? That often appears to be the case. Others have suggested that most people view matters of

14. The term was developed by Antonio Gramsci and articulated in his *Prison Notebooks* (New York: International Publishers, 1971). For a more accessible version of Gramsci's theories see Carl Boggs, *Gramsci's Marxism* (London: Pluto Press, 1976), esp. chap. 2.

power through a "dual consciousness"—that is, they may despise and deny the legitimacy of those who have power over them, while at the same time realizing that in most circumstances it is most practical to act passively, as though they accept that power.[15] Such people carry within them the disempowering messages of elite hegemony, but they also keep alive the seeds of resistance. If this is indeed the case, we should see the cultural hegemony of capitalism, or any other such manifestation of third-dimensional power, as always tentative, always in need of reinforcement. When such power or the pervasiveness of opposition to it is exposed to the light of day, it is weakened, just as the power of a famous emperor was weakened when a child proclaimed "He has no clothes!"

Words, Ideas, and Power

If there is such a thing as the cultural hegemony of capitalism—as this author believes—then the effort of a noncapitalist to think clearly about the use of power requires a certain amount of ideological combat. One must begin by stripping away the ideological victories reflected in everyday speech and thought to avoid having to concede defeat before beginning. How we think about such ordinary concepts as the political and the economic, the public and the private, democracy and capitalism, has great political significance.

One significant result of capitalist hegemony has been the successful creation of an apparent separation between the political and economic realms. This is of central concern for the study at hand. Corporate elites score a great third-dimensional victory whenever they are able to convince the public that a plant shutdown or major layoff is entirely the result of market forces; that their decisions are arrived at as though through scientific formulas with only one possible outcome; that if those particular decisions were not made even worse declines would result. Thus, the issue becomes classified as economic rather than political, and public debate is therefore limited.

Certainly, corporations must respond to market pressures, but most major corporations have such vast resources and such large market shares that they have the ability to shape market forces as well as respond to them. There are frequently a variety of options from which they can

---

15. Mike Yarrow, "How Good Strong Union Men Line It Out: Exploration of the Structure and Dynamics of Coal Miners' Class Consciousness" (Ph.D. diss., Rutgers University, 1982); Michael Mann, *Consciousness and Action Among the Western Working Class* (Essex, U.K.: Anchor Press, 1973).

choose to assure profitability. It is important to recall that the goal of profitability is a legal as well as economic requirement for all publicly owned corporations. Yet economists tell us that many major corporations engage not in profit-maximizing but in profit-satisficing—that is, once a certain level of profitability is assured, executives seek other goals, such as market share, prestige, and high executive salaries.[16] In fact, in the case of *Paramount v. Time-Warner* a federal judge ruled management could pursue goals other than profit maximization.[17] Thus, changes in legal requirements to establish the maintenance of employees' jobs as a goal to be pursued would not be required so long as a certain level of profitability is maintained.[18]

Corporations could make such a choice, but it is unlikely without legal pressures. Several European nations have created incentives and penalties that make it more costly not to pursue a policy of employment stabilization. In another, quite different situation, throughout the 1970s and 1980s, many Yugoslav enterprises competed in national and international markets and had to ensure a certain level of profitability in order to survive. Yet because the workers managed the firms, maintaining stable levels of employment was always a major goal. In each case, including more than just the interests of corporate elites in the decision-making process led to different, profitable responses to market pressures.

The decision to shut down a factory is an economic decision, but it is also a political one. It is certain to affect not only the shareholders but the workers and the entire community as well. A variety of choices, some more drastic than others, are usually available. It is a tremendous third-dimension victory that corporations have succeeded in convincing most Americans that there is a separation between economic and political matters. This allows the corporations, by definition, to be the only legitimate insiders and leaves workers and other community members as outsiders with no opportunity even to consider that they might have a right to influence the decisions that so centrally affect their lives.

16. Herbert Simon, "Theories of Decision-Making in Economic and Behavioral Science," *American Economic Review*, June 1959, suggests that profit-satisficing is a better model than profit-maximizing. R. Marris, *The Economic Theory of "Managerial" Capitalism* (New York: The Free Press, 1964), argues that management goals routinely supersede the goal of profit-maximization. John K. Galbraith, *The New Industrial State* (Boston: Houghton Mifflin, 1967), says management pursues corporate growth, autonomy, and technical leadership, often at cost to profit-maximization.

17. *New York Times*, July 15, 1989, p. 1:1. For a more complete discussion of this issue, see Chapter 6.

18. In fact, *quo warranto* suits could be brought to determine whether corporate officers were meeting their fiduciary obligations by choosing to shut down a plant while they may have taken other comparably "unprofitable" actions in the recent past.

Related to the artificial dichotomy between the political and the economic is the barrier between private and public. In the political culture of the United States, decisions about what is done with privately owned economic resources are generally regarded as private rather than public matters. Yet there is a significant difference between the decision of a one-person shoe repair shop to close and that of U.S. Steel to eliminate tens of thousands of jobs. One obvious way to look at that difference is to compare the scale of the impact on the public.

In each case, an individual or individuals make a decision to reallocate the private economic resources they own. Yet in the case of the shoe repair shop the impact will be limited to the few local customers, who must now find a new repair shop or perhaps buy new shoes. In the other case, whole communities are devastated. We can easily classify the first decision as having primarily private effects, but the second decision has an enormous public component to it. Yet our political culture treats the two as virtually equivalent—both are seen as private matters, not public. So political discussion is again curtailed. The corporate elites have once again kept outsiders out of decisions they prefer to make alone, regardless of the scope of public impact. This is another third-dimension victory for elite power.

The 1980s saw elites gain additional ground in their efforts to withdraw economic affairs from political discussion. Part of the "Reagan revolution" was the programmatic and ideological campaign to promote privatization while simultaneously advancing the slogan that government is the problem not the solution. The extent of the ideological victories of privatization is made shockingly plain when one realizes that Kennedy's inaugural urging "Ask not what your country can do for you, ask what you can do for your country," or Martin Luther King's common usage of the word "love" as a social force rather than a transaction between two individuals, simply would not work in the Reagan-Bush era. Even emotions have been privatized. The Supreme Court held that there was no right to free speech in privately owned shopping malls. Space for public discourse—mental, emotional, or physical space—was vastly diminished in the 1980s. As public space shrank, elite autonomy grew. If we agree that democracy means at least that ordinary citizens are able to hold elites accountable for their decisions, then we must also acknowledge that in the 1980s, under the rhetorical cover of increasing liberty for individuals, the possibility of practicing democracy was eroded in significant if invisible ways.

The briefest of comparative glances at Western Europe assures us that this separation between political and economic matters or between the private and the public realms is an artifact of the American political system rather than a fact of nature. For example, as a result of legislation in Germany, workers were entitled to a significant voice in many plant-level decisions in most corporations. In Sweden, labor unions and their associated political party act through the government to set policies affecting investment, levels of employment, working conditions, and even the potential transferral of the ownership of industrial capital from the private to the public domain. In France, when the government announced the shutdown of steel plants in the early 1980s, both unions and labor-based political parties took to the streets in massive numbers. As a result, they gained substantial economic concessions involving retraining, income maintenance, and relocation assistance.[19] European workers have no trouble seeing private economic issues as public political issues in which they should have a say.

The present study does not recognize the artificial distinction between things political and economic. While economic factors will always be considered as relevant constraints, the process in which they are evaluated will be considered political. Similarly, I argue that communities must expand their definitions of public interest and public policy if they are to be able to defend themselves against world-scale "private" corporations.

This argument to open our eyes to the political nature of economic transformation brings us to the issue of democracy. The people of the United States think of themselves as citizens of a democratic nation, yet fundamental decisions about the future of communities and about the quality of life of most citizens are routinely made in arenas that are defined as off-limits to political interference, and thus to democracy. In place of politics and democracy we are asked to trust the economically efficient decisions of the marketplace. Here again, we are asked to trust a carefully nurtured myth. Chapter 6 takes up this myth in more detail. Here I merely remind the reader that notions of efficient markets are based on the assumption of small-scale interaction among many equally powerful actors—but that assumption fits most of reality poorly. Nearly all contemporary markets are dominated by a few firms that are vastly more powerful than their consumers or their workers—most of us as individuals. We have little reason to trust that markets will produce outcomes that are efficient for anyone but the powerful firms. The myth of market efficiency should not lull us into thinking that we can afford to give up on the possibility of democracy.

As for democracy, I propose that it must mean at least that the

19. Anthony Daley, "Challenge to Labor: Job Loss and Institutional Innovation in the French Steel Industry" (Paper presented at the New England Political Science Association, Cambridge, Mass., April 7–8, 1989).

interests of a majority of citizens are not routinely ignored when decisions are made that establish policies—I call them public policies—that
will shape the future of their communities. If one thinks generally of
democratic principles, this seems a reasonable and even minimalist
proposal. Yet when we compare it with the actual process of decision-
making used to guide the transformation of our economy and our
society, the above proposal is clearly a radical departure.

A Hypothesis and Introduction to the Case Studies

We have both historical and theoretical reasons to expect that the current
economic transition, because it is replacing millions of industrial jobs[20]
with relatively lower-paying, less-secure service-sector jobs, should provoke a large-scale political response. This has not happened. To answer
the question "Why has this not happened?" I propose the following
hypothesis.

A reasonably coherent class of economic elites exists. These elites are
using their power (as best they can in the context of changing world
markets) to direct the transformation of the U.S. economy toward their
own ends. As part of this process, they must limit the ability of outsiders
to influence decision-making. One of the most effective ways to limit
outsiders is to convince them that any attempt to influence decisions
would be both illegitimate and futile. The consistent defeat of challengers
tends to teach possible future challengers that they should not even
bother to try. Quiescence is learned.

The major methodological challenge of this study is to explain a
nonevent. When something does occur, it is often difficult to determine
the cause of its occurrence. A variety of things may make it difficult to
determine which factors are real causes, which are more significant than
others, and which are mere distractions. It is even more difficult to
identify the cause of something that does not happen.[21]

When all is working well for elites, their power is sufficient to prevent
workers from making any visible challenge to their right to make policy

20. The *Economic Report of the President*, 1986 (Government Printing Office, Washington,
D.C., 1986), p. 298, shows a decline of nearly 2 million industrial jobs from 1979 through
1985 despite an increase of 7 million jobs in the economy overall. This figure underestimates
the scope of the transition because it does not show the decline in wages and security that
those reductions have caused for still-employed industrial workers.
21. Lowi, "Why Is There No Socialism in the United States?" discusses the problem of
explaining a nonoccurrence.

decisions. The exercise of power is on the invisible level—the third dimension of power as discussed above. Workers have internalized the controlling power of their economic superiors. It is contained within the "normal" functions of our society. Only those in the process of challenging elite hegemony see its control over society as anything but normal.

Only when a challenge does occur are elites forced to use their power in other, more visible ways. Thus, we can study how elite power blocks political responses to its policy decisions only where that power is insufficient to prevent a challenging political response from arising. To do so requires that we examine a deviant case, an exception to the rule of quiescence in the face of the destruction of industrial jobs.

A more ambitious study might attempt a quantitative approach to the question at hand. There are certainly enough examples of major plant closings that one would have little difficulty generating an impressively large sample. One might then attempt a statistical analysis relating level of political response, a scaler variable, to a variety of significant variables likely to influence response in either a positive or negative manner. The difficulties with such an approach, however, would be discouragingly large. The number of independent variables undoubtably would be quite large, difficult to measure with any degree of validity or reliability in different locations around the nation, frequently collinear. And, as argued above, many crucially important variables would often be unobservable.

This book adopts a more modest and, I hope, more fruitful approach. Three deviant cases—that is, three groups of workers who chose to challenge rather than to accept plant shutdowns—are examined in depth. All three cases ultimately confirm the power of elites as a force deterring meaningful participation by outsiders. Technically this does not *prove* anything about workers who did little or nothing in response to losing their jobs. Yet the fact that my findings are quite consistent with the results Gaventa found in the very different setting of Appalachian coal-mining valleys suggests that this approach is applicable to a wide variety of cases.[22] In more general terms, it suggests that we should not be fooled into thinking that the nonresponse of workers is a sign of their contentment when it may more likely be a sign of their defeat.

The case-study method allows us to give enough attention to detail to answer some questions that a more superficial quantitative approach

22. Arend Lijphart, "Comparative Politics and Comparative Method," *American Political Science Review* 65 (September 1971), 682–93, provides a discussion of different types and uses of case studies. In his typology, this study would be a "theory-confirming" case study.

would miss. In order to evaluate the hypothesis that industrial workers generally do not respond politically to plant shutdowns because they are discouraged from doing so by the power of elites, we must determine what workers might learn from the experiences of the groups we study. To do so, we ask the following questions:

1. What demands do the groups make of the elites?
2. How do elites respond to the groups?
3. Are groups able to stay mobilized?
4. Are groups able to achieve their goals?

This case-study approach allows us to examine the strategies these groups use in pressing their demands, as well as the many—often subtle—ways elites respond to them.

Elite power can be reflected in at least the following ways, which correspond to the three dimensions of power:

1. *Overt power.* Sanctions against challengers, and/or fear on the part of challengers that elites might impose sanctions
2. *Procedural power.* Belief by potential challengers and the general public in the legitimacy of the elites' monopoly on decision-making power; stalling, co-optation, or other means of sidetracking challengers
3. *Internalized power.* Lack of apparent alternatives, and/or a sense of futility in the minds of potential challengers

Elites might respond to challenging citizens in a variety of ways. A simple typology of four such responses is depicted in Figure 1.

A popular vision of the political order of the United States suggests that elites in decision-making positions facilitate the political involvement of individuals who are mobilized into interest groups, and the elites will respond seriously to their petitions. Political scientists call this form of democracy "pluralism" because it responds to the many different interests in society. Pluralism requires both that the elites be interested in responding to the political expressions of nonelite citizens and that those citizens be mobilized into groups that are pushing for such responses. This corresponds to cell 1 of Figure 1. A facilitative elite can also respond to concerns expressed through nonmobilized individuals as they do through a responsive bureaucracy (if one can imagine such a creature), as in cell 3. However, we shall not assume that elites are always eager to respond to nonelites' desires in a facilitative manner. When they respond to mobilized groups in a nonfacilitative way, they resort to types of nondecisions that may range from postponing to outright repression (cell 2). When the interests of nonmobilized individuals clash with those

Elite Orientation

	Facilitative	Non-Facilitative
Mobilized Individuals	1 Pluralist Democracy	2 Non-Decisions or Repression
Non-Mobilized Individuals	3 Bureaucracy	4 Elite Hegemony

Fig. 1.   Citizen-Elite Interaction Matrix

of a nonfacilitative elite, the individuals are virtually powerless. The result is elite hegemony and apparent quiescence (cell 4).

Gaventa's explanation of quiescence suggests that we will find that the elite generally take a nonfacilitative approach to the concerns of workers. However, we will expect that the type of elite response will be proportional to the degree of challenge posed by mobilized workers. For example, a demand for soup kitchens for the unemployed, a demand that requires the transfer of some material resources from insiders to outsiders, is likely to be granted. Rather than challenging the legitimacy of the elite decision-making process, such a concession may strengthen the insiders by increasing their legitimacy.[23] It may also co-opt the challengers into a less confrontational attitude toward the insiders.[24] On the other hand, a demand that corporations base their investment decisions on something other than internal profitability[25] is likely to provoke

23. See James O'Connor, *Fiscal Crisis of the State* (New York: St. Martin's Press, 1973), for a discussion of the importance of legitimation to the state.

24. Co-optation through elite concessions of material, not political, resources is a key theme of Piven and Cloward's *Poor People's Movements*.

25. See Dan Luria and Jack Russell, *Rational Reindustrialization* (Detroit: Widgetripper Press, 1981), for an extensive discussion of social cost accounting.

strong resistance. Such a demand would alter not only the allocation of a small share of material resources, but also the very process of making future policies and of allocating future power resources.[26]

The bulk of this study looks at the experiences of three groups who try to move from cell 4 to cell 1. My hypothesis suggests that elites will use their power to restrict the politicization of the process of economic transformation. If all groups end up in cell 4 after challenging elites, this will show that most workers have a rational basis for remaining quiescent in the face of massive job losses.

The Setting

The setting for the case studies is the steel-making community of Pittsburgh, Pennsylvania. The shutdown of Pittsburgh's steel industry, especially that located in the Monongahela River valley, is archetypical of industrial shutdowns across the country. Steelworkers were unionized and well paid. Their industry came under tremendous pressure from international competition. What was once the center of the region's economy was nearly eliminated in a few short years. In the Monongahela ("Mon") Valley more than 30,000 steelworkers—nearly 90 percent of the work force—lost their jobs in the first six years of the decade.

This economic demise caused tremendous dislocation in the communities most affected. What is distinct about Pittsburgh, however, is that the steel shutdowns produced a variety of different political responses. While participation by workers was not what anyone would want to call massive, there were enough challenges to allow us to select three appropriate deviant cases. These cases focus on specific subgroups of Pittsburgh residents affected by the shutdowns, but the theory suggests that how these groups were treated can tell us what kinds of influences were active on other area residents, most of whom did not respond politically to the shutdowns.

The Challenger Groups

Initially, membership of all three groups overlapped considerably, emerging out of the more militant segments of Steelworkers Union

---

26. This would also require altering FCC regulations on fiduciary responsibilities of corporate officers, one bulwark of entrenched elite power that must be overcome before such a change.

locals in the Mon Valley. Each of these groups worked with other church and community-based organizations. All initially sought to stop or at least slow steel-mill shutdowns and to improve the lives of those affected by layoffs. Each was conscious of the need to challenge an elite group in order to accomplish these goals. Over time, each group focused on different strategies in challenging the elite and serving other workers. Each received different responses to its efforts.

The first case chosen for this study involves a group of labor activists—the Network to Save the Mon-Ohio Valley—and a group of predominantly Protestant ministers, the Denominational Ministerial Strategy (DMS). The Network/DMS gained national attention in the fall of 1985 when one of the ministers, the Rev. D. Douglas Roth, was arrested and dragged out of his church by police after he had aroused the indignation of his bishop for his work—both inside and outside the church—on behalf of unemployed steelworkers. Many other arrests followed.

The Network/DMS made the most overt attack on the power of the Pittsburgh elite, condemning their policies of deindustrialization as immoral. They also disseminated—in a very accessible and inflammatory manner—information designed to make visible to Pittsburgh residents what they saw as the elite-dominated decision-making process.

The group that addressed the issues of production most directly is the Tri-State Conference on Steel, a collection of union members supported by intellectuals and elements of the Roman Catholic church. Working creatively, largely through the local political process, the members of this group attempted to stop specific plant shutdowns, to reopen some closed industrial facilities, and to promote a new approach to the region's economic development that would reverse the process of deindustrialization.

The third group, the Mon Valley Unemployed Committee, was concerned primarily with issues affecting the survival of laid-off workers. Working in a variety of arenas, they obtained a moratorium on home foreclosures and extended federal unemployment benefits and relief from utility shutoffs. This group of union activists won support from local corporations acting both directly and through foundations and churches.

These three groups will be used as comparative cases. Because they operate in the same environment, are responding to the same industrial shutdowns, and are confronting the same elite, the cases can be considered "most similar."[27] The comparisons will allow us to guard against the possibility that any one of the groups chosen for study could be

27. Adam Przeworski and Henry Teune, *The Logic of Comparative Social Inquiry* (Melbourne, Fla.: Kreiger, 1982).

merely a collection of irresponsible "loonies," which any community would deal with in a repressive manner. If this were the case, the response of elites to the challengers would say nothing about how those elites would respond to another group of more responsible or more normal workers, and the response of the elite would have no instructional effect on uninvolved workers who would not identify at all with the challenging group. If all three cases exhibit responses by the elite that attempt to marginalize the influence of the challenging group, then the alternative hypothesis—that elite response is driven by the unusual nature of the challenging group rather than by the usual nature of the elite—can probably be rejected.

The fact that the cases are similar in so many ways makes the possibility of valid comparisons much more likely, but it also reduces the generalizability of the conclusions. They will hold conclusively only in the Pittsburgh region, but if this study's conclusions support a theory that was previously tested in a "most different" situation—Gaventa's Appalachian valley—then the generality of that theory will have been strengthened considerably, and the lessons derived from this study can probably be applied broadly, at least within the United States.

One might reasonably ask if there were not other sorts of groups involved in challenging elite priorities in the Pittsburgh region. The only two other groups worthy of consideration in Pittsburgh in the early and mid-1980s would have to be local government and the United Steelworkers of America (USWA), the union most affected by steel's shutdown. I have already suggested that local government is very strongly influenced by Pittsburgh's economic elites, but local government did pose occasional objections to elite plans, such as when the county commissioners pressured U.S. Steel to postpone demolition of part of its Duquesne mill.

What is clear from this study is that all such actions are better seen as responses to pressures generated from the three groups already chosen than from government itself. As for the USWA, it would have been very interesting to study its efforts to challenge U.S. Steel's decision to eliminate the jobs of 90 percent of its regional membership if the union had made any significant efforts to do so. The USWA also participated in efforts to delay the demolition of the Duquesne mill, but it is doubtful that it would have taken those steps without the efforts of the smaller insurgent groups. In fact, when it did join in that project it worked to minimize the power of those groups. Later it worked to oppose the reelection of union local presidents active in those groups. Not until the late 1980s, when most jobs were already lost, did it mount a militant strike, the goals of which had more to do with wages than levels of employment. The three cases chosen for study made the most significant challenges to elite power in Pittsburgh. We shall see what became of their efforts.

Purpose, Values, and Politics

Narrowly speaking, the purpose of this book is to determine why there was so little response to the massively destructive economic transformations of the 1980s. I argue that most of those hurt by plant shutdowns, community bankruptcies, declining standards of living, and so on apparently had good reasons for doing little or nothing: either they had learned that they were virtually powerless to change the policies that were hurting them, or they could imagine no alternative to acceptance, or both. Those attitudes are a reflection of elite power operating in the third dimension.

If this book offered only an explanation for worker quiescence, it might only serve to reinforce elite power, making future challenges even less likely. What makes this problem so interesting, however, is that most people in the United States would agree that it is wrong for elites to prevent other people from having a meaningful voice in determining the future of their communities; that it violates the ethos of democracy that is such an important part of this country's self-image.

Democracy can mean different things to different people. It is as much a value as an objective fact. It is a goal, or a means to an end, more than it is something that exists as an institution. For some the key goal of democracy is order. By involving all members, at least to some extent, in the process of running a society, the legitimacy of that social order is enhanced and becomes more stable.[28] Others see the purpose of democratic procedures as being primarily about social justice. This latter group is concerned with protecting the rights and interests of all by ensuring that they are adequately expressed through society's governing processes. The goals of stability and justice are often—at least in the short run—in conflict with each other.

Proponents of these two tendencies differ markedly on how they view

---

28. This discussion of democracy being about either stability or justice draws heavily on a discussion in Carole Pateman, *Participation and Democratic Theory* (Cambridge: Cambridge University Press, 1970), esp. chaps. 1 and 2. For an excellent discussion of voting as more about stability than accountability, see Benjamin Ginsberg, *The Consequences of Consent* (New York: Random House, 1982).

elites. An advocate of the democracy-as-stability camp offered this caution about democracy:

> Once a democratic system has been established . . . the democratic ideal must be minimized. This ideal is a leveling principle that aggravates rather than provides an answer to the real problem in democracies, that of retaining verticality, i.e. the structure of authority and leadership.[29]

That writer correctly sees democratic forms as being potentially subversive to elite-dominated decision-making. What better word than "verticality" for showing that some people will rank higher than others? The defenders of verticality believe most people are either incompetent or uninterested and that therefore elites should make most decisions. For them the role of citizens is to vote periodically for officials who will make some of society's rules, and then to allow elites to run the show.

For those who advocate democracy as a means to justice, verticality and political passivity are two related problems that must be overcome for justice to be achieved. I am of this mind. Therefore, this book does not stop at merely discovering the potency of elite power; it seeks to undermine it. Exposing it at work in its hidden forms is part of that process.

If elite power and political passivity continue unabated, perhaps the elite will lead all of us to the best of all possible futures. Those unwilling to trust in that possibility are invited to read on, to learn about the efforts of three groups of ordinary citizens who—unwilling to trust Pittsburgh's economic elite with the future of their community—fought back in innovative ways. In the process, these groups teach us both about elite power and about the ingenuity and courage of people who dare to demand a voice.

---

29. G. Sartori, *Democratic Theory* (Detroit: Wayne State University Press, 1962); paraphrased in Pateman, *Participation and Democratic Theory*, p. 10.

1

DESTRUCTION OF
A STEEL-MAKING COMMUNITY
Pittsburgh's Economic Transformation

The story of Pittsburgh in the 1980s is a tale of two cities. In 1985 Rand McNally named it the most livable city in the United States. Billboards touting this fact showed its skyline of gleaming new buildings at the head of the Ohio River. Others proclaimed it "The City with a Smile." Yet for many workers there were few smiles and no glitter. For much of the decade, unemployment was well over 10 percent, and more than 50 percent in some areas. The county's population declined by 10,000 a year from 1980 to 1985. Pittsburgh's success had an ugly underbelly.

An assessment of the economic transformation of Pittsburgh requires attention to the declining sectors—primarily steel but encompassing other well-paid, unionized manufacturing jobs as well—and to the sectors on the rise: high-tech services and industries, corporate headquarters, and the rapidly growing low-wage service sector. Though the focus here is on the regional transformation, the national and international business contexts will be important as well. This chapter shows how Pittsburgh has chosen to respond to the larger context of change.

The forces driving changes throughout the national economy transformed Pittsburgh dramatically in the early 1980s. Figure 2 sums up the rapidity of these changes. As recently as 1980, Pittsburgh employed 33.7 percent of its work force in manufacturing jobs, significantly more than the national average of 31.7 percent. Yet by 1986, employment in manufacturing had dropped to only 24.8 percent of the Pittsburgh work

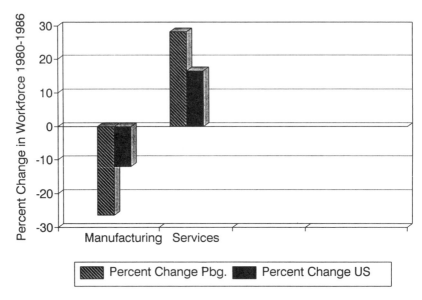

Fig. 2.   Work Force Shifts from Manufacturing to Services, Pittsburgh and the
United States, 1980–1986

force and 27.9 percent nationwide. Unemployment in the region went as
high as 16 percent. The national trend had hit Pittsburgh with a ven-
geance. What were the forces driving that transformation?

The Decline of Steel

As long as there has been a steel industry, Pittsburgh has been thought
of as its center—until recently. Workers in Pittsburgh drank Iron City
Beer, and the Pittsburgh Steelers represented the region's rough, macho
ego in the competitive world of professional football. Employment in
steel reached its peak in the late 1940s and early 1950s, when it stood at
nearly 80,000. It began a steady decline in the 1970s, nose-diving in the
early 1980s. In 1987 a journalist summed up the effects of this violent
transformation of the Monongahela Valley:

> The number of people who derived their income from steel had
> declined to less than four thousand, down from over thirty-five
> thousand in 1981 and from eighty thousand in the 1940s. The

mill towns, once so alive with the heavy throb of industry, now gave off the weak throb of welfare and retirement communities. The degree of suffering caused by lost jobs, mortgage foreclosures, suicides, broken marriages, and alcoholism was beyond calculation. Many people, especially the young, had left the valley, but middle-aged and older workers, unable or unwilling to migrate from the only home they had ever known, went through the anguish of trying to start new careers. The standard of living, boosted to a high level by the United Steelworkers, was falling steadily.[1]

Employment in steel mills throughout the Pittsburgh region followed a course of decline similar to that of the Monongahela Valley. Mellon Bank put regional losses at 60,000 jobs in primary metals, plus another 50,000 other manufacturing jobs. While the nation lost 6 percent of its manufacturing jobs between 1980 and 1986, Pittsburgh lost a wrenching 44 percent—approximately 110,000 jobs—most of them in steel and related industries.[2] After 1984, the worst had been done, but the job losses in manufacturing continued at a slower rate (see Figure 3).[3]

The shutdown of steel brought with it long-term unemployment for thousands in Pittsburgh. A nation-wide study showed that of 219,000 primary metals workers who lost their jobs between 1979 and 1983, less than half had found new employment by January 1984. Of those who had found work, 18 percent found only part-time employment. Nearly half of those who found full-time work had to accept new incomes that were at least 20 percent below their former earnings.[4]

A survey of more than 4,000 former steelworkers conducted locally late in 1989 showed little improvement. Only 40 percent had found full-time employment, and on average these fortunate ones earned only 72 percent of their former incomes. Another 20 percent were employed part-time, often at more than one job. Both groups complained of poor or nonexistent benefits, such as health care, retirement, or paid holidays.[5]

1. John P. Hoerr, *And the Wolf Finally Came: The Decline of the American Steel Industry* (Pittsburgh: University of Pittsburgh Press, 1988), p.11.

2. Figures on job losses are from Judith Leff, "United States Steel Corporation and the Steel Valley Authority" (Harvard Business School 0-386-171, 1986), p. 8; Hoerr, *And the Wolf Finally Came*, p. 11; *Mellon Economic Update: Pittsburgh*, 4th quarter (Pittsburgh: Mellon Bank, 1987).

3. Data in Figure 3 for employment in Pittsburgh are from Mellon Bank, Economic Division, May 1992.

4. U.S. Department of Labor, Bureau of Labor Statistics, "Displaced Workers, 1979–1983" (Washington, D.C., 1985).

5. Steel Valley Authority, *Final Report: Economic Development Survey, Homestead* (March 1990).

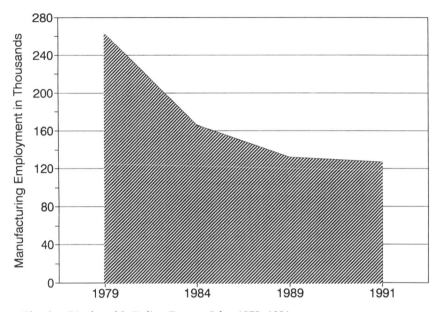

Fig. 3. Pittsburgh's Fading Factory Jobs, 1979–1991

Deindustrialization hit all valley communities hard, striking at the very fabric of their societies, challenging the institutions of local government, religion, and family. It hit some even harder than others. In East Pittsburgh, when Westinghouse cut employment from 7,000 to 1,200 in a few short years, the population declined by nearly 40 percent and tax revenues were cut in half. Clairton, home of the U.S. Steel plant that was once the world's largest coke-processing center, went bankrupt in 1985 and had to lay off the police force and turn the local schools over to the state. In Homestead, the historic U.S. Steel mill that once employed 15,000 workers has now been mostly demolished. However, the police force remained employed throughout the period. In 1985 some 93 percent of all serious crimes there were committed by unemployed people, most of them first-time offenders. Asked why he had committed the burglary that landed him in jail for three years, one former steelworker replied, "I had three kids and no benefits."[6] In the late 1980s, the building that had housed Homestead's Local 1397 of the USWA was

6. "Decline of Electric Valley," *Pittsburgh Post-Gazette*, July 31, 1986, p. 4; "Clairton Doles Out Final Checks," *Pittsburgh Post-Gazette*, September 5, 1985; Clare Ansbury, "Laid-Off Steelworkers Find That Tax Evasion Helps Make Ends Meet," *Wall Street Journal*, October 1, 1986, p. 1.

converted to a recovery center to support people overcoming drug and alcohol problems. In 1992 the economy remained so bad that even this operation looked like it must close.

While unemployment in the Pittsburgh area ranged from 8 to 16 percent in the early and mid-1980s, a door-to-door survey in three mill towns found that 55 percent of all heads of household and 46 percent of all working-age males were unemployed. Suicides in those communities were twice the national average, and divorce was up dramatically.[7]

The Pittsburgh metropolitan area was one of only five in the nation to lose population in the period 1980–84, ranking somewhat behind Detroit and Buffalo for rate of decline. In 1980 the Southwest Pennsylvania Regional Planning Commission had predicted that the county's population would increase by 50,000 in the 1980s. Five years later their spokesperson remarked: "Our forecast took into account the crunch that was expected in the primary metals industry. What we didn't know was that it would collapse so abruptly."[8]

Not everyone has been upset by the decline. In a lead editorial, the *Post-Gazette* called the 40,000 drop in county population "a blessing that should be accepted and built upon."[9] By 1990 the Pittsburgh metropolitan area had lost more than 160,000 residents—in the *Post-Gazette*'s terms, even more to build on.

By 1985, military recruiters were doing better in Pittsburgh than anywhere else in the nation. As the top Marine recruiter acknowledged, "It would be foolhardy to say unemployment played no part."[10] Texas police and prison officials who made frequent recruiting trips to Pittsburgh in the mid-1980s beamed: "Hey, that's a goldmine up in Pittsburgh. . . . You're good working people—that's all there is to it. And you're unemployed. You need jobs."[11]

Yet in the Mon Valley, few saw anything but injustice in their fate. The steelworkers resented the fact that while they, their fathers, and grandfathers had built the mills and made fortunes for the corporate elite, that same elite had now cast them abruptly aside and moved on to make more profits elsewhere. These workers also had a sense that they had done their share to build the country: making steel for roads, for buildings, for war. They had proudly fought in those wars too. Allegheny County had one of the highest ratios of combat veterans in the country. One journalist summed up the frustrations of many workers:

7. "Survey Claims 50% Jobless Rate in Valley," *Pittsburgh Press*, July 25, 1985.
8. *Pittsburgh Post-Gazette*, May 10, 1985, p. 1.
9. *Pittsburgh Post-Gazette*, May 29, 1985, p. 8.
10. *Pittsburgh Post-Gazette*, April 15, 1985, p. 1.
11. *Pittsburgh Post-Gazette*, June 18, 1985, p. 10.

War and steel were a part of the same bargain, the same obligation. Like their fathers, the young men went to war and made steel and expected a good life in return. They did their part. Now they realize, too late to make any difference, that the rest of the country has no intention of keeping its half of the bargain.[12]

Why Steel Declined

Some of the extensive discussion of what caused the decline of steel production is aimed at determining how to prevent further deterioration, but much of it is aimed at fixing the blame. While most explanations have some merit, their policy implications and their political implications are often quite different. The key explanations evaluated here show that there are a variety of possible explanations. It is essential to see, however, that the group that is able to force social acceptance of its explanations and their related policy prescription will be the group to determine who wins and who loses. Ultimately, the important choice of perspectives is more political than it is analytical.

The most common explanation for the decline of steel is foreign competition. Adding to the problem of foreign competition are two other frequently mentioned factors: overly high U.S. labor costs and poor management. The final explanation considered here will be declining demand due to technological change—that is, the substitution of plastics and other materials for steel.

Foreign Competition

The U.S. steel industry developed along with the spread of railroads and industry within the United States in the nineteenth century, continuing its rapid growth as an almost entirely domestic industry throughout the early twentieth century. After World War II, while the mills of Europe and Japan lay largely in ruins and the scope of international economic activity quickened, exports became a significant market for U.S.-made steel. In this postwar context the industry boomed. From 1940 to 1950, production of steel in the United States rose by 45 percent, while global production rose at a slower 30 percent. By 1950, the United States

---

12. William Greider, "They Had an American Dream," *Rolling Stone*, June 20, 1985, pp. 47–48.

produced 48 percent of the world's steel.[13] While U.S. wages in steel production were the highest in the world, worker productivity allowed the United States to produce steel at the world's lowest prices. Agreements between steel management and the United Steelworkers of America traded steady wage increases for a no-strike clause. Both management and labor prospered, while steelworkers led the way for American workers to climb into the ranks of the middle class.

Yet by the late 1960s the situation was changing. Imports of steel, along with textiles, autos, and other sectors of U.S. manufacturing, had clearly lost the unquestioned preeminence they had enjoyed in world markets only two decades earlier.

The reasons that foreign-produced steel was able to compete so successfully with domestic steel are many. The cost of U.S. labor and the inefficiencies of U.S. management will be discussed in some detail below. Here we mention various foreign advantages that have been labeled "unfair."

The chief "unfair" advantage is what has been known as "dumping": the sale of foreign goods within the United States at prices below the cost of production. Foreign companies have an incentive to "dump" goods in the United States in order to be able to produce at sufficiently larger volume to achieve cost reductions through economies of scale. They may also choose to "dump" goods in the United States to expand their share of U.S. markets, eventually hoping to eliminate future competition.

Another advantage denounced as "unfair" includes government subsidies received by foreign steel industries. Such subsidies may allow them to modernize at significantly lower costs. The lower required rate of profit experienced by many foreign producers has a similar effect, allowing investment of capital in steel to accelerate abroad while a similarly rewarding investment in the United States would be vetoed as not sufficiently lucrative.

The converse of "unfair" government aid to foreign steel producers is the "unfair" imposition of "burdensome" environmental regulations imposed in the United States. Steel corporations have frequently said that such costs have forced them to close certain mills. In some cases this has led communities to lobby the federal government for dirtier air. Metzgar shows that when management in Bethlehem, Pennsylvania, succeeded in focusing the community's anger on environmental regulations and government bureaucrats, they were able.to move that anger away from their corporation, which had just eliminated 5,000 jobs.[14]

13. "Iron and Steel," *World Book Encyclopedia*, 1958, p. 3896.
14. Jack Metzgar, "Plant Shutdown and Worker Response," *Socialist Review* 10, no. 5, September–October 1985.

Finally, during the decade of domestic steel's drastic decline, the U.S. dollar was said to be substantially overvalued. The effect of this overvaluation can be appreciated quite clearly after the steep decline of the U.S. dollar in 1987. As the value of the dollar fell from a value of approximately 250 yen in 1985 to approximately 125 yen in late 1987, the price of U.S. steel denominated in yen (eliminating other adjustments) fell by one-half while the dollar cost of Japanese steel doubled. Imports of steel from Japan fell from nearly 6 million tons a year in 1985 to 4.3 million tons in 1987 and 3.1 million tons in 1990.[15] Clearly the overvaluation of the dollar must have had a significant effect on the decline of the U.S. steel industry.

Some of the policy implications of diagnosing "unfair" foreign competition as the cause of the steel decline appear quite straightforward. Some of them have been implemented. As just discussed, the value of the dollar has been adjusted, largely through central bank policy. The question of why the adjustment was not made earlier is an interesting one, but it cannot be addressed here. Restrictions against "dumping" have been in effect since the Trade Act of 1974, but steel corporations only began demanding that they be seriously enforced in 1983.[16] Early in 1987, Representative Richard Gephardt began to establish himself as a contender for the Presidency by sponsoring trade legislation imposing penalties against various types of "unfair" trade practices. The political debate over how to define "unfair" opened the way for some labor constituencies to suggest that interference with the right of foreign labor to organize and participate in collective bargaining was unfair and thus deserved penalizing tariffs. In the early 1990s, discussion of unfair practices showed up in debates about the North American Free Trade Agreement being negotiated with Mexico, where it included both wages and environmental issues. Discussion of "unfair" European subsidies to agriculture stalled talks on the General Agreement on Trade and Tariffs. What is perceived as "unfair" often depends on the type of government policy one wants.

Though the advantage foreign industries have due to lower acceptable rates of profitability has been frequently discussed, there has been no serious effort to lower the definition of acceptable profitability for important industrial sectors in the United States. To do so through changes in company policy would be economically suicidal if it were attempted on a company-by-company basis. To do so through government action—though technically feasible and potentially quite benefi-

---

15. American Iron and Steel Institute, news release, February 20, 1992.
16. John P. Hoerr, *And the Wolf Finally Came*, p. 417.

cial—would be ideologically impossible because it would question the ability of capitalist markets to set investment priorities wisely. As discussed in the Introduction, a variety of mechanisms other than markets help establish investment priorities, but the myth of the impersonal market forces guiding investment decisions is one of the key legitimating factors of the economic decision-making process in the United States. It masks the personal responsibility of corporate executives.

In an effort to head off stronger congressional action, President Ronald Reagan negotiated with many countries voluntary import reductions that took effect in 1985. The goal of this program was to reduce the market share given over to imported steel from the 26 percent they had reached in 1984 to 20 percent. The program succeeded in bringing imports under 18 percent. Restraints were not renewed in 1992. Steel companies responded by suing many foreign steel-makers for dumping.[17]

Early in the Reagan administration, manufacturing industries were awarded large investment tax credits. Among those leading the lobbying effort to achieve these credits was U.S. Steel. In testimony to Congress, David Roderick, U.S. Steel's chief executive officer, persuasively argued that the money made available through such tax credits was essential if corporations like his were to modernize their plants sufficiently to meet foreign competition. But when U.S. Steel got their credits in March 1982, they promptly spent $6.4 billion to purchase Marathon Oil, and simultaneously announced the closing of 8 plants and 71 facilities and the elimination of 15,000 jobs, 3,800 of them in the Monongahela Valley.[18] Workers in the Mon Valley were outraged at this betrayal. It was an obvious sign that U.S. Steel had consigned them, their mills, and their communities to the scrap heap.

In addition to the variety of "unfair" advantages that have led to the success of foreign competition, there are two major domestic situations that may have exacerbated those advantages: poor management and overly high U.S. labor costs. As might be expected, different people blame these two factors as the root of our problems.

High Wages

Steelworkers in the United States have long had wages far above those paid by most foreign competitors. For example, while total labor costs in the United States were around $23 an hour, in South Korea they were

17. Ibid., p. 418; American Iron and Steel Institute press release, February 20, 1992.
18. Leff, "U.S. Steel and the SVA," p. 8.

a mere $3 an hour. Part of this difference was offset by high productivity in the United States and by the shipping costs incurred by foreign steel-makers. Yet with all these factors taken into consideration, labor made up 25 percent of the cost of domestic steel delivered in the United States in 1985, compared with the figures for competitors such as Japan, Korea, and Brazil, which were 11.7 percent, 5.5 percent, and 8 percent, respectively. These comparisons were even worse when, as recently as 1982, labor costs accounted for 34 percent of the total costs of domestic steel. Since that time, savings in labor costs have accounted for more than 70 percent of the reductions in the price of steel made in the United States. Layoffs and investments in more efficient technology made U.S. labor once again the world leader in output of steel per hour worked. Labor has borne the brunt of the blame and the brunt of the remedy.[19]

Clearly the major policy implication of diagnosing high labor costs as a major cause of steel's demise is the reduction of labor costs. This can be accomplished in three ways: (1) using less labor through automation and other productivity enhancements, such as changing work rules, (2) lowering wages and benefits, and (3) moving production abroad. All three ways are being used. Each of them imposes severe costs on workers.

Automation is the most apparently benign of the efforts to reduce labor costs. Jobs are eliminated in the name of technological necessity and progress. This undercuts most community opposition even though the loss in employment may be high. Workers remaining after automa-tion may feel more secure and more loyal to the corporation whose choice to modernize rather than decapitalize has saved them their jobs. It is important to point out here, however, that automation has sometimes been chosen not to save money but to eliminate labor, which manage-ment may see as more troublesome and less predictable than new machines.

Automation reduces the hours of labor required to produce a given amount of steel. This increase in productivity can be accomplished by investing in new technology. During the 1980s, however, U.S. Steel raised productivity primarily by closing its older mills—throwing out thousands of workers in the process—thus raising the average productiv-ity for the mills remaining open. In this way, the decision not to modernize plants in the 1950s, 1960s, and 1970s led to their closing in the 1980s. The figures in U.S. Steel's annual reports boasting of great

19. Data from Locker/Arbrecht Associates, "Confronting the Crisis: The Challenge for Labor," Report to the United Steelworkers of America, December 16, 1985; *Statistical Highlights, U.S. Iron and Steel Industry* (Washington, D.C.: American Iron and Steel Institute, 1987); and Irwin Ross, "Is Steel's Revival for Real?" *Fortune*, October 26, 1987.

gains in productivity carry with them the suggestion of modernization, investment, and progress.[20] In the Mon Valley, though, the rise in productivity registered in the 1980s reflected little new investment. And instead of progress, these communities saw destruction.

In 1992, with employment at slightly over 10 percent of its 1980 level, U.S. Steel did complete significant modernization of its Mon Valley Works with the completion of a continuous caster. This modernization brought U.S. Steel to world-class levels of technology, giving it an ability to produce all its raw steel with continuous casters. Modernization of furnace technology is not yet complete. U.S. Steel's total investment in modernization since the early 1980s exceeded $3 billion. In addition to eliminating most of its work force in the 1980s, U.S. Steel also eliminated several product lines. With the 1992 closing of its South Works in Chicago, it gave up its ability to produce structural steel. This combination of layoffs, closing old plants, and investing in new technology left U.S. Steel producing less than half the steel it had produced ten years earlier with approximately one-quarter of its earlier national work force.

Efforts to reduce costs by changing work rules generally have been made during contract bargaining. They are sometimes made on a plant-by-plant basis in negotiations with local union leadership. They may involve reductions in what is commonly referred to as "featherbedding"—such practices as requiring that a certain number of workers be on hand in certain plant locations even though they may all be kept busy only part of the time. Efforts may also involve changes regarding overtime employment or the use of nonunion outside contractors to perform certain tasks. Many of the changes clearly improve the technical efficiency of labor. Some of them reduce plant safety.[21] All of them require labor to concede power and income. The management of U.S. Steel has been particularly forthright in explaining that it uses decisions by local unions on work-rule concessions to determine which mills it will keep open and which it will close.[22] This allows them to play one

20. For instance, the *U.S. Steel 1985 Annual Report*, p. 54, boasts of an increase in productivity that reduced man-hours per ton of steel shipped by 20 percent in the preceding year alone.

21. A sad incident from the summer of 1985 is illustrative. A nonunion crew was called in to reline one of the furnaces at the Edgar Thomson mill in Pittsburgh. The crew was told to use fire clay rather than fire brick. A more experienced union crew with more ability to control its work process might have insisted instead on safer and more long-lasting fire brick. The fire clay bubbled and exploded, killing two men.

22. David Roderick interview, December 1983, in the film *The Business of America* (California Newsreel); also confirmed in my interview with David Higie and William Hoffman at USX headquarters, Pittsburgh, July 29, 1986.

local union off against another, sometimes eliminating locals it sees as troublesome militants in the process. In the Mon Valley, only the mill with the most compliant union leadership—the Edgar Thomson Works—was left operating at anywhere near capacity. In the process of weeding out plants, this strategy of favoring compliant union local officers became a major factor in union local elections.

Lowering costs through the direct reduction of wages and benefits has been a solution used throughout the industry. The last industry-wide steel contract, signed in 1983, reduced labor costs by $2.19 an hour.[23] After that contract, the union negotiated additional concessions with steel companies on a company-by-company basis. For a time, however, labor costs continued to rise, reflecting not a rise in wages but increased costs of pensions from the early retirements brought on by many job-elimination agreements.

The clearest example of reducing labor costs through production abroad is the choice of U.S. Steel to close its mill in Provo, Utah. The mill sold most of its raw steel to a U.S. Steel finishing mill in Pittsburg, California, near San Francisco. The California mill would stay open but would get its raw steel from a joint venture of U.S. Steel with Pohang Steel in Korea. At the time the deal was announced, the Pohang mill was run by a former Korean army general. No union had ever been formed there, and labor militancy was considered almost criminal. Workers earned about $2.50 an hour and worked fifty-two-hour weeks. Furthermore, in Korea, unlike most Third World countries, there were 40,000 U.S. troops stationed nearby to help ensure stability.[24] This is a dramatic example of what U.S. Steel's management apparently considers more favorable labor relations.

Poor Management

A share of the blame for steel's decline is often attributed to poor management. Historically, the U.S. steel industry was dominated by a few very large companies. Until foreign competition became a major factor, the oligopolistic nature of the industry allowed management to raise prices whenever profits were threatened. A more competitive industry would have had to innovate to cut costs. When competition

23. Hoerr, *And the Wolf Finally Came*, p. 385.
24. Tim Shorrock, "A New Phase in Korean-American Relations: U.S. Steel's Pohang Strategy," *AMPO-Japan Asia Quarterly Review* 17, no. 3 (1985), 2–13. See also Hoerr, *And the Wolf Finally Came*, p. 489.

became a real threat, these corporations asked for protection, and they usually got it.[25]

Major criticisms of management build on the fact that managers in the United States have based their decisions largely on short-term profit-maximizing criteria rather than on long-term strategic planning. In recent decades, top management has become more concerned with financial performance than with the manufacture of a specific product line such as steel. U.S. Steel, the largest steel-maker, was one of the leaders in the trend to diversification away from steel. When foreign competition was minimal, executives saw no need to modernize manufacturing facilities. When real estate offered a better rate of return, they invested in land, shopping malls, and office buildings, rather than steel. Meanwhile, foreign competition was building new, large, state-of-the-art plants. Management did not respond to this threat until it was perhaps too late. By the mid 1970s, the U.S. steel industry had fallen significantly behind world standards for modernization of production facilities. For example, in 1975 the United States still produced nearly 20 percent of its steel in inefficient open-hearth furnaces. Meanwhile, the world average was approximately 16 percent and Japan's was only 1.1 percent. The United States produced only 9.1 percent of its steel with the new energy-efficient, laborsaving continuous casters, while Japan cast more than 30 percent of its production.[26] From this point on, the flood of imports surged.

Major modernization attempts were not begun until the late 1970s. Wheeling-Pittsburgh Steel Corporation led the modernizers with half a billion dollars of investment. Yet given the oversupply of steel and the resultant downward pressure on prices, this only led them to bankruptcy. U.S. Steel Corporation chose to diversify away from steel. On July 8, 1986, the corporation changed its name to USX, with steel operations being only one of three operating divisions. In the previous year, steel had produced only one-third of the corporation's revenues, while oil and gas had produced more than half.[27] As recently as 1979, steel had brought in 70 percent of revenues.[28] One study suggests that, during the years of diversification away from steel, management chose to continue granting major wage increases to workers as a way to keep them from asking questions as it invested steel profits elsewhere. This

25. This critique of management is presented persuasively in Mark Reutter, *Sparrows Point: Making Steel—The Rise and Ruin of American Industrial Might* (New York: Summit Books, 1988).

26. International Iron and Steel Institute, *World Steel in Figures, 1976*, pp. 6–8.

27. *U.S. Steel 1985 Annual Report*, p. 1.

28. *Pittsburgh Post-Gazette*, February 12, 1986, p. 11.

strategy also provided executives with a "blame the overpaid workers" excuse when steel mills began to fold.[29] The profitable National Steel Corporation saw the handwriting on the wall in 1984 and decided to sell out its financially troubled West Virginia mill to its employees. The new employee-owned company opened as Weirton Steel. Its first years were profitable, but by the early 1990s employment had fallen by 25 percent. As a worker-owned enterprise, Weirton was keenly interested in retaining as many jobs as possible. It invested heavily in modernizing its production facilities and developing new product lines, and it entered the 1990s as the nation's seventh largest steel company. Its employment will probably stabilize at this new level, but workers and managers are both asking the state for help in developing other jobs in the region for sons and daughters who might otherwise have found jobs in the mill.

When profits were high and international competition was developing, management did not invest enough to prepare for what was coming. When the competition arrived, most steel management, in addition to calling for protection by the government, either cut and ran, or overinvested in a struggle to keep up.

Changes in Demand

In response to the energy crisis of the early 1970s and the ensuing flood of imported cars, the auto industry looked for ways to make cars lighter and thus more fuel-efficient. They began making smaller cars and substituting plastic or fiberglass for steel. Clearly, imported cars are not made with domestic steel. The shift from steel to aluminum cans and plastic bottles ate into another share of the market. Modern structural materials such as carbon filaments promise to eat still further into demand. An overall measure of how much steel is consumed relative to the size of the national economy fell by 45 percent between 1970 and 1985.[30]

The above picture of declining demand for steel is incomplete. It ignores the potential demand for steel that would be created if the nation chose to rebuild its crumbling infrastructure. Investment banker Felix Rohatyn notes:

29. Collin Lawrence and Robert Lawrence, "Manufacturing Wage Dispersion: An End-Game Interpretation," The Brookings Institution, Washington, D.C., 1985.
30. Thomas O'Boyle, "Industry Seeks Radical Cures," *Wall Street Journal*, April 16, 1985.

A major domestic reconstruction program for such facilities as railroads, bridges, waterworks, roads and school buildings must be undertaken soon. It will be more labor intensive than a continued military buildup, and it will be a better long run investment for the country. It cannot be financed without changes in our priorities.[31]

One group in this study, the Tri-State Conference on Steel, has devoted considerable attention to trying to bring the issue of infrastructure to the forefront of the discussion about whether there is a future for steel production in Pittsburgh. Clearly the effort has not yet been successful. As Rohatyn points out, priorities must change first. Those who set our nation's investment priorities (on the basis of short-term profit rather than long-term viability) are evidently not willing to withdraw sufficient resources from their investment in manufacturing abroad, and in the military apparatus they feel necessary to sustain it, to make a serious commitment to rebuilding the infrastructure. At some point, as the transportation systems, utilities, and schools required to operate our economy continue to deteriorate, this calculation may change. At this point one can only speculate about how much of the domestic steel industry will be left to meet the expanded demand at that time. Meanwhile, wear and corrosion continue. The Spring 1992 flood in Chicago's Loop shows some of the potential cost of neglecting repairs to basic infrastructure.

The issue of contracting or expanding demand once more brings home the point that the messages the market gives to guide investors depends enormously on major decision-makers, not solely on impersonal, uncontrollable mysteries. Cars no longer require as much steel as they once did, and an enormous amount of steel is required to rebuild the bridges and roads that the newer, lighter cars will drive on. The choice of decision-makers to respond to only one of these two changes in the demand picture is not one determined by economic necessity.

Policy Responses to the Decline of Steel

Clearly the causes of the decline of steel are myriad and complex. In some way, each of the aforementioned causes—foreign competition, high U.S. wages and poor management, and the changing structure of

31. Felix Rohatyn, "On the Brink," *New York Review of Books*, June 11, 1987, p. 3.

domestic demand—and their many variants have contributed to the decline. Our concern in this discussion is not to determine the "real cause" but to look at how decisions about how to respond to the decline have been made. Obviously, what one sees as the problem's cause should influence the decision on how to respond to it. Yet the various actors involved with the problem are likely to be biased in their diagnosis of the causes. Labor is not likely to blame excessively high labor costs, nor is management likely to blame poor management. The two other causes—foreign competition and changing demand—are equally available to both management and labor, yet the remedies corresponding to these causes are not as easily affected by either of them. Given this situation, it is reasonable to expect that each of these two key actors—labor and management—will blame the other as cause, and that they may attempt to use the other two causes as ploys to press their case. As it turns out, management has played this approach more effectively than labor has, and the management at USX has played it best of all.

As U.S. Steel closed down one mill after another in the Mon Valley, they loudly blamed foreign competition and excessive labor costs for forcing them to lay off workers in groups of several thousand at a time. They negotiated on a plant-by-plant basis for work-rule concessions. Finding the most compliant union leadership at the Edgar Thomson Works, they concentrated production there. On the chain-link fence surrounding the Thomson Works, they placed a banner nearly one hundred feet long. Emblazoned on it in red, white, and blue beneath a waving flag was the message "Help Curb Imported Steel. Write Your Congressman!"

Yet U.S. Steel management did not feel constrained by the logic of its "blame imports" campaign. They went ahead at the same time with negotiations to buy steel abroad themselves and concluded a pact to import steel slabs from Pohang Iron & Steel of South Korea. The steel would be made at one of the world's largest and most modern mills. When U.S. Steel finally announced its pact (after months of trying to kill speculation that such a deal was brewing), it also announced the elimination of its steel production facilities in Provo, Utah. Because U.S. Steel's capacity to seek profits regardless of domestic impact is unconstrained, one cannot rule out the possibility that other such pacts in other countries will also be concluded.

Labor, as represented by United Steelworkers (USWA), has not been as successful at defending itself. It is far more constrained in its options than management, because labor is not as mobile as capital is; thus, accommodation with foreign producers is unlikely. It is also constrained by the fact that its leadership has, for the last several decades, seen its own best interests served by promoting a cooperative relationship with management. Management has been more cynical in its regard of such symbiosis. As a result, the major USWA strategy has been to push for a joint labor-management effort to increase restrictions on imported steel. Of the top six steel-making corporations in the United States, only the largest, U.S. Steel, refused to join in this effort. In return for cooperation on this lobbying effort, the USWA accepted further layoffs as well as significant wage and benefit cuts.

In June 1986 the union spent a considerable amount of time and resources on an event called "Save American Industry and Jobs Day." The day featured several hours of speeches, videos, and music broadcast live from Washington and other sites around the nation and screened via satellite in union gatherings across the land. One was held at the Pittsburgh Hilton Hotel. Workers at the Pittsburgh meeting enjoyed the free beer and hotdogs but appeared unconvinced that anything of help to them would come of the day. They were right.

The USWA has had some limited success protecting the incomes of its members through striking. In July 1985, Wheeling-Pittsburgh Steel Corporation, the nation's seventh largest steel company, was struck by USWA workers who refused to accept the 28 percent average hourly pay reduction demanded by management. It was the first steel strike in twenty-five years. The strike of 1959 had idled more than half a million steelworkers for nearly four months. By the mid-1970s, labor and management agreed to a no-strike pledge that gave workers guaranteed raises of 3 percent a year on top of cost-of-living adjustments (COLAs). Management got labor to agree that only management had the right to manage the business. For a few years both sides were happy, but poor management and wage increases that regularly outstripped productivity gains contributed to the demise of steel in the 1980s. All previous agreements were off as both sides struggled for survival.

When the Wheeling-Pittsburgh strike ended ninety-eight days later, steelworker wages were cut only slightly, and Wheeling-Pittsburgh's CEO, Dennis Carney, was forced to retire while Paul Rusen, the Steelworkers' chief negotiator, was named to the board of directors. The success, or the limited losses, at Wheeling-Pitt set the stage for hard bargaining at LTV, Bethlehem, and National Steel in 1986, where agreements resulted in similar wage reductions in return for profit-sharing.

In the summer of 1986, U.S. Steel locked out its work force. The company wanted wage concessions like those the USWA had negotiated with failing firms. It also wanted more freedom to hire out much of the in-plant work to nonunion contractors. A long and bitter six months ensued before a settlement was reached that gave up little on contracting out, cut labor costs by $2.50 an hour (a compromise position), and guaranteed new investment, including a continuous caster at the Mon Valley Thomson Works.

These strikes were costly to both the union and the companies, and they established that, despite conditions that caused many to predict the union would concede rather than risk a strike, the union was able to resist caving in entirely.

Another major effort to respond to the decline of steel was an attempt to use community political structures to force a takeover of a mill abandoned by U.S. Steel. This effort was spearheaded by the Tri-State Conference on Steel and is discussed in more detail in Chapter 4. Here it is only important to point out that this effort, which eventually won the support of most of the area's communities, labor organizations, and political bodies, represented a response that differed greatly from that of either the USWA or U.S. Steel. It did not blame foreign competition, which it could do little about. Instead, it focused directly on the different incentives facing the USX megacorporation and those facing the residents of the Mon Valley. While it was not most advantageous for USX to continue making steel there, it was in the interest of the area's residents. They therefore asserted the right of a community to protect local productive resources over that of the increasingly distant corporation's right to eliminate them. They also asserted that demand for the steel did exist in the region and would be even greater if infrastructure spending were increased. The community effort did not succeed because it could not obtain sufficient capital to take control.

A variety of explanations for the steel's decline exist, as do a variety of suggestions about how to respond to them, and there are several choices about what to do, albeit within very real constraints. In order to consider fairly the challenges the groups in this study made to corporate decisions, it is essential to see that options other than those chosen did exist. Our challengers were not merely irrational opponents of progress, and progress is not a unique, preordained path that despite short-term difficulties works inexorably to the long-term benefit of all.

Different people see different realities, and the many-sided story makes it clear that the decision as to *who* will decide is tremendously important. Those with the power to decide whether to invest, to lay off, to strike, to seek protection, or to seek new markets must first choose how to define the problem. Depending on that choice, various remedies follow. There is debate, controversy, and no obvious objective way to decide which was the predominant cause of steel's decline. In the 1970s and 1980s, a variety of policy choices were available to deal with steel's problems. Each would have different results for different sectors of

Pittsburgh's population. The chapters that follow show that the course of progress in Pittsburgh was decided by an elite group of men (I use the word "men" advisedly) and that these decisions often damaged hundreds of thousands of area residents who were consciously excluded from the decision-making process.

The choices that matter the most for this study are those that led to the near elimination of the region's steel industry. Further choices have been made and are yet to be made about what to do with the wreckage left by the shutdown of steel. We now turn to some of the decisions that have led away from steel.

The Rise of Postindustrial Pittsburgh

The settlement of Pittsburgh began with the establishment of Fort Pitt at the point of land where the Allegheny and Monongahela rivers come together to give birth to the Ohio. The town grew as the jumping-off point and resupply center for the settlement of the Midwest. It was to the cider mills of Pittsburgh that Johnny Appleseed returned each year in search of new seeds. As the population of the Midwest grew, so did the iron and glass industries, as well as the many manufacturing firms that grew up to serve the region. The railroad age caused a mushrooming demand for steel, so new mills sprang up for miles along the Monongahela Valley, which reaches deep into coal-mining country. As the region grew, so did the clouds of coal smoke that hovered over it.

By the late 1940s, strong sentiment developed among Pittsburgh's corporate elite—bankers, publishers, industrialists, and merchants—that something could and should be done about the smoke that often left the skies as dark as twilight throughout the day. The cleanup was accomplished so that corporations already headquartered in Pittsburgh would not leave and others might be attracted.[32] Though there was a sense that giving priority to attracting corporate headquarters might hurt the steel industry, the region's leadership was now diverse enough and strong enough to be willing to challenge the dominance of coal and steel. It was also wise enough to avoid alarming or involving the general populace. Their public pronouncements spoke only of "smoke control," with no hint of the anticipated industrial decline. David Lawrence, then mayor of Pittsburgh, explained the significance of the campaign for smoke control

32. The story of smoke abatement is told by David Lawrence (then mayor) in Stephan Lorant, *Pittsburgh: The Story of an American City* (New York: Doubleday, 1964).

for Pittsburgh's elite: "It was Pittsburgh's breakthrough from the landing beaches; the other triumphs have come in a great accelerating rush."[33]

With smoke on the decline, businesses rushed to demolish the old, blighted Pittsburgh downtown and the surrounding low-rent but unattractive housing. The area near the site of old Fort Pitt is now known as the Golden Triangle, home of gleaming new corporate office buildings, the center of what is now the nation's third-largest corporate headquarters city. USX, Westinghouse, Rockwell, Alcoa, Pittsburgh Plate Glass, and H. J. Heinz are some of the better-known occupants of the Triangle.

Former Mayor Lawrence's account makes it clear that the Pittsburgh Renaissance, as that period is locally touted, was accomplished despite the heavy costs imposed on poor and working-class residents. He notes that in the midst of the smoke-abatement campaign he could not win the support of labor during the Democratic mayoral primary election. What carried him through was the strong support from the staunchly Republican Mellon family. He explained: "Without the joining hands of the city's Democratic administration with the Mellon economic power, the revival of Pittsburgh could not have taken place."[34] In the 1980s as well, Pittsburgh's nominally Democratic political apparatus has been a willing collaborator with most phases of the modernization pushed by Mellon Bank and other local corporate powers, despite the costs to its labor constituencies.

The area of industrial decline, rusting steel mills, and shuttered factories is to the southeast of the Golden Triangle, up the Monongahela Valley. Neither the corporate executives who live north of the city in Fox Chapel, nor the young professionals who serve them and live in Squirrel Hill to the east, need ever see the decay of the Valley. Their visions of the new Pittsburgh often sound as though the Valley did not exist. The geography of Pittsburgh helps facilitate the effort to keep the social discontent of the decaying steel towns from casting new clouds of gloom over the shining city of the future. In the 1980s, the challenge for Mon Valley residents was to find some way to intrude on the plans of this new, postindustrial elite.

In addition to the new corporate skyscrapers, Pittsburgh has developed a prominent high-tech component of its economy. In the period from 1982 to 1985, as steel lay dormant and nearly dead, high-tech firms in the region expanded employment by 25 percent. By the mid-1980s, high-tech firms employed more workers than steel.[35] Spurred by the

---

33. Quote from ibid., p. 402. Information on corporate finessing of public opinion is from an interview with Jack Robin, former executive director of the Allegheny Conference on Community Development, published in *Pittsburgh Magazine*, March 1983.

34. Lorant, *Pittsburgh*, pp. 403–6.

35. *Pittsburgh Post-Gazette*, December 11, 1985.

long tradition of close relationships between local leaders in academics and industry, as well as by the technical excellence of faculty and students at Carnegie-Mellon Institute, Pittsburgh was named to be the home of one of the nation's very few "supercomputers." It also won out against fierce national competition to gain the Software Engineering Institute, a new $20 million a year research institute associated with the Department of Defense. The spinoffs from both these projects were expected to be enormous.

In another area of high technology, the University of Pittsburgh's Presbyterian Hospital became the world's leading organ transplant center. This growth sector was not without its own share of controversy. Area residents became upset by the hospital's practice of giving priority to wealthy foreigners over U.S. citizens and then charging them four times as much for the scarce, life-saving organs.[36] Clearly, the high-tech revolution did not benefit all classes equally.

In a revealing 1985 article, the president of Carnegie-Mellon, Richard Cyert, predicted that computer-operated manufacturing techniques would allow elimination of the majority of manufacturing jobs. He predicted that the share of U.S. jobs in manufacturing would continue to fall from the 22 percent share it had in 1980 to about 10 percent early in the next century. Cyert felt such a move would be necessary if the United States is to compete with countries where labor costs are low. He described in glowing terms a factory system developed to produce machine tools. Using conventional technology, the plant would employ 120 skilled and semiskilled workers per shift. With the new computer-driven robotic plant, only four workers are needed on each of two shifts, and no workers are needed on the third. Such a system could eliminate (or save, depending on one's perspective) 352 jobs, or 92 percent of such a company's work force. Employment in middle-management would also decline and, added Cyert, "top management will be much closer to the people on the factory floor."[37] One can easily imagine that Cyert was also envisioning the elimination of unions along with the elimination of jobs.

Not surprisingly, Carnegie-Mellon hosts a Robotics Institute. Engineering professor William Whittaker led the development of the institute's "Terragator," a robot-controlled vehicle. In singing its praises, he unwittingly revealed the institute's cavalier disregard for the social con-

36. *New York Times*, September 16, 1985, p. A-10.
37. Richard M. Cyert, "The Plight of Manufacturing: What Can Be Done?" *Issues in Science and Technology* (Washington, D.C.: National Academy of Sciences, 1985), pp. 87–100; quote from p. 97.

sequences of its work: "Why not have the ore stripped from an open-pit copper mine carried by a Terragator rather than by a dump truck run by a totally unnecessary man?"[38]

Cyert knew that most of these "totally unnecessary" people would end up in low-paying service-sector jobs if and when they found new jobs. As a member of the Pittsburgh elite, Cyert was well aware that "unnecessary" people, such as those of the Mon Valley, present a challenge for social management:

> Not only do we risk losing the middle class as workers are displaced to lower paying jobs in the service sector, but it is likely that the incomes of the owners of capital—namely, the owners of corporations—will increase. As a result the country could face political struggles over income redistribution.

His concern was not with issues of social justice. Rather, he worried: "Unless we anticipate and study this problem before it occurs . . . we may institute policies that redistribute income in a way that reduces the incentives for innovation, investment, and risk taking."[39]

Cyert was not only president of Carnegie-Mellon and a concerned intellectual, but also in the mid-1980s sat on the boards of several corporations, including American Standard, Koppers, H. J. Heinz, and First Boston Bank. He was one of those whose "incentives" (i.e., profits) should not be "reduced." His concern was with maintaining the legitimacy and stability of the profit-making system that enriches some while devastating others—the "unnecessary" ones. In Pittsburgh this was not merely a matter of speculation about the future. The problem of social management was enormous. As the Mon Valley collapsed when its wealth was deliberately transferred to other sectors, elites like Cyert had to be concerned about possible challenges to the legitimacy of their right to rule and to extract tribute.

Industrial employment in the Pittsburgh region dropped by 44 percent between 1980 and 1986, and employment in its much larger service sector rose by more than 25 percent (see Figure 2). Mellon Bank economists note: "Unfortunately, these jobs tend to be lower-skilled and thus lower-paid, so they do not fully replace higher-wage manufacturing jobs."[40] The use of the word "unfortunately" shows an awareness on the part of Mellon Bank economists that does not translate into a policy of

---

38. "Self-Propelled Robot Car Needs No Driver," New York Times News Service, *Pittsburgh Post-Gazette*, May 13, 1985, p. 28.
39. Cyert, "The Plight of Manufacturing," p. 99.
40. *Mellon Economic Update: Pittsburgh*, 4th quarter (Pittsburgh: Mellon Bank, 1987).

concern by bank management. In February 1986 the bank terminated the contract it had with National Cleaning Contractors to provide janitorial services at two of its downtown high-rise office complexes. With it they terminated the labor agreement National had had with the Service Employees International Union (SEIU). The contract was awarded to a new firm, Arcade Maintenance, which, according to the SEIU, was controlled by managers in Mellon Bank's realty division. Wages were cut from $7.75 an hour to between $4.00 and $5.25. Most workers were shifted from full-time to part-time status.[41] Part-time workers thus became ineligible for such benefits as health care.

The poor wages and working conditions of the service sector were not just analyzed by Mellon and other corporations. They were consciously created by them, not because the market forced them to do so (Mellon profits were consistently strong throughout the 1980s[42]), but because conditions in the region's labor market—conditions they have helped create—allowed them to do so.

As Pittsburgh grew from frontier village to industrial center, its population mushroomed. Most of its new residents were industrial workers. As the city entered the twentieth century, vast fortunes accumulated in the hands of its industrial and financial elites. Only in the late 1940s did the incomes of industrial workers begin to rise to a middle-class level. By that time, however, the corporate elite had already begun to move to eliminate smoke and steel and to move into a postindustrial future. The decline of the Mon Valley was the most obvious result of that decision; the problem of managing increasing economic inequality in the new high-tech service-sector economy was another. These were problems that concerned decision-makers at Mellon Bank, Carnegie-Mellon, and other corporate institutions—problems they would have preferred to handle as they had handled past problems: with as little outside interference as possible.

Yet Pittsburgh also has a history of resistance to elite control. It was in Pittsburgh that the country's first nationwide strike—the railroad strike of 1877—reached its most militant proportions. Pittsburgh's steel industry will always be remembered as the home of the bloody Homestead Steel strike of 1892 and the related attempt to assassinate steel magnate Henry Frick. It was also the home of the more successful, if less radical, Steelworkers Organizing Committee (SWOC), which began in 1936 and

41. "SEIU Protests Wage, Benefit Cut," *Pittsburgh Post-Gazette*, February 22, 1986, p. 29.
42. Based on 1975–85 earnings. *Corporations Review 1985* (Pittsburgh: Herbick & Held); *Pittsburgh Post-Gazette*, July 17, 1985.

eventually became the United Steelworkers of America. While workers in Pittsburgh, as in most cities, have a tradition of begrudging acceptance of the powers that be, they also have a history of militant resistance to the plans an economic elite and their political collaborators made for them.

In the 1980s, as elite decisions devastated their communities, some people added new chapters to Pittsburgh's history of working-class resistance. Despite lack of leadership from their political representatives and their union leadership, groups of Mon Valley residents struggled to find a way to force Pittsburgh's economic elites to pay heed to their needs. The next three chapters examine the efforts of three such groups and the responses of the elites.

2

THE "PROPHETIC MINISTRY" TAKES ON CORPORATE EVIL

In November 1984, people around the nation began to hear about the Rev. D. Douglas Roth, a Lutheran minister jailed when he disobeyed a court order to leave his parish. As unemployment had risen in Roth's town of Clairton and throughout the Monongahela Valley, Roth's ministry had changed with it. As a result of work he had done with a group of local clergy, he had come to see local unemployment not as the result of uncontrollable market forces but as the result of conscious decisions made by executives in corporations such as U.S. Steel and Mellon Bank. As he witnessed the rising tide of divorce, suicide, alcoholism, and general despair in the Valley, he felt compelled to condemn as "evil" the decisions that had led to this suffering. "If you are hurting someone but you don't know it, that's unfortunate, but if you know you are hurting someone and you continue to do it for your own selfish reasons, then that is evil," Roth explained.

Roth felt individual corporate decision-makers were quite aware of the impact of their actions and must be held accountable for those actions. His willingness to speak out against what he called "corporate evil" brought him the support of many parishioners and the "revival" of many workers who previously had no church affiliation. It also brought him the enmity of many corporate figures, troubles within his parish, and arrest for refusal to obey a court order obtained by his bishop to stop preaching about unemployment in the local steel mills and leave the

Clairton parish. As he was being physically removed and led to jail, Roth told reporters: "I have to obey God rather than man. I'll be willing to go to jail for the unemployed if that's what it takes."[1]

How and why would a man like Roth come to feel strongly enough to speak out against the local power elite, even when he knew it would lead to the destruction of his church career? And why would the church and the county government feel they had to arrest and imprison this man for ninety days? But Roth was only the most visible member of a whole group, an alliance of ministers and union members known as the Denominational Ministerial Strategy (DMS) and the Network to Save the Mon-Ohio Valley. Together they posed a fundamental challenge to the moral basis of capitalist investment decisions.

Conceptually, this group's challenge was the most radical of the three groups studied here. While one group (the Mon Valley Unemployed Committee) demanded better treatment for those unemployed by elite decisions, and another group (the Tri-State Conference on Steel) demanded that some of those decisions be reconsidered, this group—the Network/DMS—challenged the very basis of those decisions.

The threat posed by this small group of clergy and unionists was amplified by the potential that such coalitions might pose. As Roth was being arrested in Pittsburgh, the Catholic church was undergoing considerable ferment nationwide as the result of the work of Bishop James Malone. Malone's involvement with thousands of steelworkers victimized by the shutdown of steel mills in Youngstown, Ohio, had inspired him to join Milwaukee Bishop Rembert Weakland in pressing the Catholic Bishops Conference of the United States to draft a pastoral letter on the economy that voiced similar concerns about the heartless and often damaging nature of corporations' investment decisions.[2] How that challenge was diffused is another story. Suffice it to say that its existence amplified the danger to elite hegemony of a similar movement getting under way within Protestant denominations. Internationally, both the Vatican and the U.S. government were engaged in efforts to undermine another movement in the Catholic church that had become known as liberation theology.[3] It often had destabilizing and sometimes revolution-

---

1. *Ithaca Journal*, November 15, 1984.

2. U.S. Catholic Bishops, "Economic Justice for All: Catholic Social Teaching and the U.S. Economy," *National Catholic Reporter*, January 9, 1987, pp. 1–44. Its first three guiding principles were: (1) Every economic institution must be judged in the light of whether it protects or undermines the dignity of the human person. (2) Human dignity can be realized and protected only in community. (3) All people have a right to participate in the economic life of society. This draft was adopted in November 1986 but had been under discussion for at least three years.

3. Ana Ezcuria, *The Vatican and the Reagan Administration* (New York: CIRCUS Publications, 1986).

ary consequences for elites throughout Latin America. A church-rooted movement for economic justice was not to be taken lightly.

This chapter details the critique developed by Roth and the other clergy of the DMS and describes some of the tactics that group chose to publicize its critique. It also shows the many ways in which the power of the elite establishment was used against this group to minimize their threat.

Because the challenge posed by the DMS was the most fundamental of the three groups here studied—that is, the elite could not compromise with it without diminishing the basis of their own power—the defeat of the DMS was the most thorough. While the elite did not hesitate to use power in obvious ways, such as jailing group members, we shall see that the more subtle third dimension of power—the reservoir of attitudes that cause most members of society to recoil from any challenges to the status quo—would eventually be most effective in marginalizing this group.

As Roth became more involved with the group known as the Denominational Ministerial Strategy, his ministry began to change from what had been a fairly traditional parish ministry. The DMS was formed in 1980 by five Protestant denominations in the greater Pittsburgh area as a way to give clergy training in how to deal with issues affecting churches in urban areas. Of the five denominations—the Lutheran Church in America (LCA), the Episcopal church, the United Methodist church, the United Church of Christ (UCC), and the Presbyterian church—only the first two provided actual funding. The others gave at least quiet encouragement to participating clergy.

To increase the effectiveness of clergy involved in a variety of urban concerns, the group hired Charles Honeywell from the Industrial Areas Foundation, a community-organizing training center set up by Saul Alinsky. Building on Alinsky's methods of analyzing community power and figuring how to cause enough discomfort to win obtainable concessions,[4] and using the Christian faith he shared with members of the group, Honeywell worked overtime to transform the way the clergy perceived their work within the communities they served.

Gradually the group began to focus more and more of its attention on the issue of unemployment. Initial efforts were of the traditional type: providing food baskets and pastoral support for unemployed parishioners. They viewed the problem as temporary, and saw the appropriate response as one aimed at individual unemployed workers. But as time went on, the group came to realize that the problem was too big to deal with on an individual basis.

4. Saul Alinsky, *Reveille for Radicals* (New York: Random House, 1969).

As a result of his DMS training, Roth had begun doing research at the county courthouse. In the fall of 1982, when his town of Clairton declared bankruptcy, Roth became aware of legislation providing for state and federal help for disaster areas. This discovery became the catalyst that moved DMS from a study group to a group involved in directly challenging the power elite of Pittsburgh. Why not declare the Mon Valley a disaster area? he thought. The relief money could be used to rebuild jobs, just as it might be used to rebuild homes in the wake of a massive flood or tornado.

When the governor refused to provide any help, the group began to ask why the state was so unwilling to help local people when they were in such need. The group's trainer, Charles Honeywell, suggested that they look at who made contributions to state politicians, and when they did they found that many local corporations were major contributors. The group then approached local corporations, asking that they use their influence with the state legislature to secure disaster relief. "We were not very polite about the way we asked them," Episcopal clergyman James Von Dreele related. "They said they were sympathetic but that they had no influence at all with the state legislature. . . . This despite that fact that Mellon bank had $23 billion of assets at the time and had just gotten state laws changed to allow it to expand state-wide."[5]

A central feature of the training DMS clergy received was that the best way to understand how and why things happen is to look at the money involved. Explained Pastor John Yedlicka, "All one needed to do to find out who was making the decisions, pulling the strings, wielding the power, was to follow the money. That was consistent. You could make book on it."[6] DMS members learned to do basic research about who owned what in Pittsburgh, about who sat on what board of directors, and about what the investment policies of major corporations were.

In February 1983, Mellon Bank, acting with two other local banks, foreclosed on Mesta Machine, the largest domestic manufacturer of capital goods for the steel industry. The next day Mesta filed for Chapter 11 bankruptcy protection. Twelve hundred jobs were eliminated. The DMS eagerly jumped into the fray.

Research had shown that although local banks were unwilling to refinance Mesta's $19.6 million debt, Mellon had more than $100 million invested in Mesta's chief competitor, Japan's Sumitomo Industries. The DMS succeeded in making its research quite public and thus forced Mellon's CEO, David Barnes, to respond to the situation publicly. In a

5. James Von Dreele interview, June 18, 1985.
6. John Yedlicka interview, July 24, 1985.

television interview, Barnes stated that he saw nothing wrong with an investment policy that sacrificed local jobs for foreign jobs as long as it yielded a higher rate of return. This did not play well in Pittsburgh, where regional unemployment was over 15 percent.

To make matters worse, Mellon froze payments from Mesta's bank account, thus making it impossible for Mesta to give workers their final paychecks. The workers' union, the USWA, asked Mellon to release sufficient funds to allow payment, but Mellon refused, saying it could not do so without approval from the bankruptcy judge. Yet neither Mellon nor Mesta petitioned the judge to have funds released. As the months dragged on, frustration mounted. On May 27, USWA President Lloyd McBride sent letters urging nearly 200,000 union members and retirees to withdraw any funds they might have deposited in Mellon accounts. The DMS joined in urging all area residents to withdraw money on "D-Day," June 6. On June 6, protestors withdrew more than $200,000 from Mellon accounts, and the Pittsburgh City Council voted unanimously to withdraw its deposits from Mellon Bank if Mesta workers were not paid. (It is important to note that the mayor indicated he would block such a move. This may well reflect the difference between the popular constituencies of council members versus the elite constituency of the mayor.) As pressure mounted, Mesta asked the court to order payment of the workers, and Mellon urged "speedy action" on the request. The judge ordered payment on June 8.[7]

The involvement of DMS in these events was a major turning point for the group. They began to focus very publicly on what they identified as the immorality of Mellon Bank, and they did not stop when the Mesta workers got paid. In their analysis, Mellon was at the heart of the region's problems. According to Roth, Mellon had more than $6 billion invested abroad. "We're only suggesting they bring one of those billions home to Mon Valley. We suggest that they seek an 'optimum return' on investment rather than a maximum return."[8] He explains that an optimum return would trade off higher local employment against slightly lower profits.

The DMS concept of "optimum return" expresses both the reach and the limit of the DMS critique of corporate power. The critique insists that current investment practices are unacceptable because they do not take community interests into account. In this regard, it is quite radical. Yet DMS clergy do not follow up this attack by insisting that workers

7. This account is based on an article in *Business Week*, June 20, 1983, p. 27, and on an interview with James Von Dreele.
8. Roth interview, April 1, 1985.

and communities be granted a say in the investment process by changing the decision-making structures. Instead, they appeal to individual capitalists to repent, to renounce their selfishness, and to increase the altruism of their investment-consciousness. It seeks a corporate capitalism within which managers take on a pastoral responsibility for their communities. While most economists now believe that corporations do not follow strict profit-maximization, few have gone so far as to assert that what Kenneth Boulding has called an economics of altruism will anytime soon manifest itself as a solution for our economy's frequent injustices.[9]

The DMS belief that a secular elite could make wise decisions on behalf of society if it were guided by Christian principles as interpreted by the church's elite (in this case the self-appointed prophetic clergy of the DMS) recalls the most conservative European corporatism. Thus, the radical impulse of the DMS critique is blunted by its reactionary church-elite-dependent tendencies. Its radical potential was sufficient to inspire a firm corporate reaction. Its reactionary reliance on a *hierarchically* approved moral basis of action would lead to its undoing.

Counterattack by Pittsburgh Elites

The public attacks on Mellon Bank by the DMS apparently provoked the wrath of a number of powerful people. According to Von Dreele, "Right after D-Day they started working in the congregations to disrupt the ministries of DMS pastors." Pastor Yedlicka explains: "People began to rattle the cage by taking out or putting away their wallets and saying, 'Look, so-and-so, If you don't quit supporting DMS I'm going to quit giving my offerings.' "[10]

Von Dreele of St. Matthew's Episcopal Church in Homestead successfully beat back a serious challenge to his ministry after a hard fight. Von Dreele is convinced that the troubles in his parish were initiated by a member—a retired judge—with close political ties to both U.S. Steel and Mellon Bank. In an attempt to get rid of Von Dreele, he said, "some members subverted the stewardship drive by refusing to make calls for pledges. Some went from twenty dollars to one dollar in their weekly offerings. They squirreled away money so we couldn't pay our bills. It

9. Kenneth Boulding, "The Basis of Value Judgments in Economics," in S. Hook, ed., *Human Values and Economic Policy* (New York: New York University, 1967). See also R. H. Scott, "Avarice, Altruism, and Second Party Preferences," *Western Economic Journal*, 7, no. 3 (1969), 287ff.

10. Yedlicka interview, July 24, 1985.

took six months to discover $7,500 they had hidden . . . all to force us [St. Matthew's] toward bankruptcy."[11] Von Dreele eventually got the backing of his bishop and enough of his congregation to turn back the challenge. The struggle caused some members to leave and others to join. The result, in this case, was a more secure ministerial base and a refocused congregation.

At the regional level, pressure from major contributors took effect much more quickly. At this time, Episcopal church Bishop Hathaway got at least one letter threatening to withhold a $10,000 contribution if something were not done about the DMS. Shortly thereafter, the Episcopal church withdrew its sponsorship of the DMS. Less definitive evidence suggests that major contributors were putting pressure on the regional leaders of each of the five denominations to withdraw all support from DMS.

As the DMS mounted its campaign against Mellon's role in the Mesta shutdown, the Lutheran Church (LCA) moved to eliminate funding for DMS trainer, Charles Honeywell. The Rev. Paul Himmelman, director of urban ministries for the Western Pennsylvania–West Virginia Synod of the LCA and a major DMS backer, strongly defended Honeywell and the group. Consequently, he soon lost his job. Apparently to make sure that no replacement would take a similar approach to urban ministry, Himmelman's position was also eliminated. The Rev. Donald Anderson, executive secretary of the synod, freely admitted that Himmelman's firing was related to his support for the DMS, adding, "Some of the work he was involved in was not fully acceptable to many in the Pittsburgh area."[12]

Newspaper coverage of the Himmelman firing pointed out the apparent sins of DMS clergy. Under the frank headline "Anti-Mellon Minister Dismissed," the Pittsburgh Post-Gazette explained: "Ministers . . . used picketing and press conferences in recent months to urge people to withdraw their money from Mellon Bank." Reflecting on his abruptly terminated ministry, Himmelman explained his view: "The [Christian] word and sacrament is desecrated if it doesn't hit the streets and meet people in the community, and you can't do that without causing some trouble." What got him in trouble, he believed, was that the leadership of the church and the majority of laypeople as well had come to believe "that the church shouldn't make waves or rock the boat or lead to any kind of upheaval that will challenge the support for the church."[13]

11. Von Dreele interview, June 18, 1985.

12. Philip D. Long, *The Book on Pittsburgh: The Other Side of the Story* (Pittsburgh: DMS/East Liberty Lutheran Church, 1985), p. 53.

13. *Pittsburgh Post-Gazette*, October 6, 1983.

Himmelman had put his finger on a reservoir of power that Pittsburgh elites would use—eventually with great success—to eliminate the challenge posed by the DMS. In the terms developed in Chapter 1, this aversion to rocking the boat is part of the third dimension of power that works against any challenge to the status quo. When used effectively, this aspect of power turns attention away from the institutions being challenged and away from the reasons for that challenge. It then redirects that attention toward the behavior of the challenging group, making that appear to be the problem as a threat to the peace and civility of society.

All these attacks on the DMS occurred before it began using the more distinctive—some have said radical—tactics that led it to a still more controversial position within the Pittsburgh community. A look back at the DMS—the context in which it emerged, and its development from study group to challenger of the corporate structure of Pittsburgh—gives us a better appreciation of why the group provoked such a repressive response.

Pittsburgh is known for its numerous distinct neighborhoods, many of them with strong ethnic characteristics. Settlement of the city occurred mostly in successive waves by distinct ethnic groups, each group fitting into slots in the region's economic hierarchy. Most ethnic groups have been associated with distinct churches, and in turn each church has been somewhat influenced by the economic roles of its members. Over time, the tight association of denominations with unique ethnic groups has diminished, but if one wanted to predict the likelihood that any given denomination would play a role in challenging or in supporting Pittsburgh's economic elite, it would be helpful to look at that church's ethnic and economic background.

The backgrounds of the several Protestant denominations in the Pittsburgh region that started the DMS—the Lutheran, Episcopal, United Church of Christ, Methodist, and Presbyterian churches—do not lead one to expect they would lead a challenge to the local economic elite. Wealthy Scottish Presbyterians have long dominated the region's industrial and financial empires. Carnegie and Frick, the builders of Pittsburgh's steel industry, were Presbyterians, as were George Westinghouse and the Mellons. Richard B. Mellon left money to build the awesome East Liberty Presbyterian Church as a memorial to himself and his family. The family sepulcher is a prominent feature of the building.[14] The Shadyside and to a lesser extent the Fox Chapel Presbyterian churches provided the "spiritual homes" of many contemporary corporate executives, including Thomas Faught of Dravo Corporation and David Graham of U.S. Steel.

14. Some locals refer to the church as "the Mellons' fire escape."

Corporate executives were both major donors to these churches and highly respected figures in their congregations. Many early Protestant churches, in an effort to explain the different material fortune of God's children on earth, developed the doctrine of "the elect," which is that those with material wealth are those most favored by God and the most worthy of respect. While few contemporary Protestant churches officially proclaim this doctrine, they have not entirely shed their de facto adherence to it. Thus, to a certain extent, an attack on corporate leaders within the context of the church can be seen as an attack on the divine order represented in the hierarchy of the church's body.

The Episcopal church and the United Church of Christ (formerly the Congregational church) originally drew their membership from English backgrounds. In the history of Pittsburgh, this meant that they would have spent little or no time as laborers in the mills, but would have moved quickly into managerial and commercial positions as the region developed. The largely Germanic and Scandinavian Lutherans spent time in the mills but moved up, if not out, as the influx of Catholic and Orthodox immigrants from eastern and southern Europe arrived in the early decades of the twentieth century.

Although the political involvement of these churches is not necessarily determined by their ethnic and class backgrounds, it is clear that each church will have influential members who would oppose having their church involved in challenging the right of Pittsburgh's economic elites to conduct business as they see fit. Thus, it is not surprising that when the DMS began to challenge Mellon Bank openly, it was the Presbyterians, closely followed by the Episcopalians, who were first to sever ties (and thus financial resources) to DMS. Nor is it surprising that, of these groups, it is the Lutheran clergy who have formed the continuing core of the group. While the Catholic church, with its more direct ties to steelworkers, has never been officially involved with the DMS, it has been the mainstay of the Tri-State Conference on Steel, which tried most directly to save jobs in the mills.

To understand what sort of challenge the DMS posed to Pittsburgh's power elite, we must note that when the DMS moved from delivering food baskets to asking for state aid to condemning corporate practice, its degree of challenge changed radically. Delivering food baskets poses no challenge at all to elites. In fact, it strengthens them; it diverts people from looking at causes to looking at effects, and, to the extent that churches are seen as extensions of a society that includes corporate elites as major church donors, it creates an image of a compassionate society caring for its less fortunate members. This should further act to prevent people from challenging the legitimacy of society's decision-making process.

When DMS asked for state aid, it in effect asserted that society as a whole had a responsibility to care for the unemployed. The focus was still on the effects of unemployment rather than its cause, but at this level the DMS began to perceive connections between political and economic elites that soon led them to examine the cause.

In retrospect, one wonders why the state could not have found some way to placate or at least delay and defuse the DMS at this stage of the game. It is quite clear, though, that the corporate leaders the DMS asked to help pressure the legislature would have opposed any major relief efforts. As one executive said, "The worst thing about the DMS is that they give people faith that things will get better. People need to give up and either move out or accept lower paying jobs."[15] State intervention would have greatly complicated the transition the elite sought to bring about.

When DMS openly questioned the right of corporate elites to continue making decisions solely on the basis of profits, and when they used Christianity rather than Marxism as the basis of their critique, the elite were forced to respond. Most previous attacks on the legitimacy of capitalism have been eventually discredited as un-American, but there is nothing much more American than a Protestant church. Thus, the DMS attack had to be seen as a very dangerous challenge to the ideological hegemony of the corporate elite.

Because respect for the church and for Christian morality is probably much more deeply embedded in American society than respect for the sanctity of the corporate elite, a direct ideological response would have been foolhardy. Instead, the wealthy used their obvious strength. As major donors to the churches, they could quickly throw their weight around behind the scenes, and that is exactly what they did. Their efforts led to the withdrawal of denominational support for the DMS and to the beginning of agitation within various congregations for the removal of DMS clergy.

DMS Escalates

Research as a Strategy

The attacks on the DMS caused the group's members considerable difficulty and put them in a serious financial crunch, but it also strength-

---

15. Interview with Pittsburgh corporate management consultant who asked to remain anonymous, Fox Chapel, April 4, 1985.

ened their resolve. "The heat we were getting was just too intense for us not to know that we were hitting on something real."[16] The group began to talk more frequently about their work in terms of a "prophetic ministry." As a prophet is never well received in his or her own time, criticism was taken as confirmation of that "prophetic ministry." The DMS clarified the biblical foundations of its message, expanded its research efforts, and marched out to meet Goliath.

Research by the DMS on Mellon Bank confirmed what most Pittsburghers intuitively knew, that the bank was at the heart of nearly all major decisions in the region. Its directors sat on the boards of most Pittsburgh-based corporations, including hospitals and universities as well as more clearly commercial concerns. For example, Mellon owned outright or controlled as one of the top five shareholders Alcoa, Gulf Oil, Koppers, U.S. Steel, Westinghouse, Pittsburgh Plate Glass, LTV Corporation, Dresser Industries, Armco, Allegheny Ludlum, Textron, Heinz, Monsanto, and others. Through U.S. Steel it could also influence Bell & Howell, Midland-Ross, Marathon Oil, and Trane, among others.[17] Its loan portfolio gave it leverage far beyond its number of directors, and its law firm—Reed Smith Shaw & McClay—provided another apparent line of communication among the elites, including, as we shall see, the elite of the Lutheran church. These many-faceted connections allowed Mellon to be the major influence in such policy groups as the Allegheny Conference on Community Development and the Regional Industrial Development Corporation.[18]

Research included other banks, as well as corporations such as U.S. Steel and Dravo. It even dared to go as far as what the DMS asserted was a link between the powerful elites and the Pittsburgh mob. DMS members asserted that Edward De Bartolo—owner of a construction firm based in Youngstown, Ohio, as well as a horserace track near Cleveland, the Pittsburgh Penguins hockey club, and the Pittsburgh Spirit indoor soccer team—was actually at the heart of organized crime in the region. They substantiated their charges by citing incidents like the refusal of Chicago White Sox owners to sell him the team franchise because they felt he was too close to organized crime. The man clearly had tremendous influence with regional politicians. DMS members also believed there was a connection between the Park Corporation (the Mellon-backed scrap company that was buying out local industrial properties, such as Mesta or U.S. Steel's Homestead mill, when they shut down)

16. James Von Dreele, telephone interview, April 1, 1985.
17. From DMS research reported in the *Pittsburgh Town Crier*, October 1983, p. 6.
18. For more on the structure of elite power in Pittsburgh, see Chapter 5.

and organized crime. This would be consistent with the frequently observed ties between organized crime and disposal companies in many other cities. The DMS has used DeBartolo as a dramatic way to publicize much of their research on the region's power elite.

DMS members believe the elite are complicit in various crimes of economic violence against the people of the region. To emphasize this point, they masqueraded as overly-drawn mafiosi, complete with violin cases, and went to meet DeBartolo at the airport. This dramatic and embarrassing "photo opportunity" allowed the DMS instant access to the local press with some of their research. A DMS handout at this event included pictures of DeBartolo as well as other corporate executives and then Senator John Heinz. In a reversal of normal charges that banks launder money for criminal organizations, the largest printing on the flier claimed: "We're involved in laundering money for Mellon Bank."

One use of DMS anti-Mellon research appears to have been quite effective. A letter from Michael Horn of the New Jersey Department of Banking dated January 4, 1984, thanks Charles Honeywell and the DMS for sharing their research. He said information on Mellon Bank, "particularly the foreign lending involvement, . . . is in fact of interest and may be helpful in the efforts of the Department of Banking to prevent the acquisition." Mellon's effort to enter the New Jersey banking market was subsequently blocked.[19]

At this stage, the DMS strategy was threefold: (1) to continue research for the sake of understanding, (2) to use research and other tactics to embarrass corporate elites into making conciliatory changes, and (3) to seek a direct meeting with corporate elites to negotiate these changes. It is unclear how distinct or how sincere the third strategic point was, but it served a purpose, whether fulfilled or not. If the elite did respond by meeting with the DMS, they would in effect be agreeing that the DMS had some legitimacy and that the concerns DMS had raised needed to be incorporated within the decision-making structure. On the other hand, a refusal to meet with the DMS would, at least in the short term, also work to the DMS's advantage. It would confirm the charge that the elite were insensitive to community concerns.

The decision to use embarrassment, to "hold Pittsburgh's image hostage,"[20] had at least some effects. The Mon Valley Chamber of Commerce, set up to rejuvenate the Valley by luring new firms, says that when potential new firms heard of DMS they generally went somewhere else. That Pittsburgh was concerned about its image was as obvious

19. *Pittsburgh Post-Gazette,* November 28, 1984.
20. A frequent DMS phrase; Roth interview, April 1, 1985.

from the op-ed page of the major newspapers as it was from the millions and millions of dollars spent on the Renaissance II refurbishing of downtown.

Mellon Bank received much of the attention the DMS doled out in its image-bashing campaign. According to Von Dreele, "We've said to Mellon, we are in a war and we are going to dog you. We won't go away."[21] Another DMS activist, Jim Jones, claimed that the combination of research and confrontation is what made DMS distinct from other area groups, such as the Tri-State Conference on Steel or the Mon Valley Unemployed Committee. "They say if you talk long enough to Roderick [then U.S. Steel's CEO] he'll change his mind. We say if we research enough we can force the issue."[22]

Action at the Bank, the Churches, and U.S. Steel

DMS clergy and lay supporters frequently worked in close conjunction with a group of labor militants known as the Network to Save the Mon-Ohio Valley. The group included the presidents of three union locals as well as several labor activists from the area. It was created in 1982 to support the DMS's application for disaster relief. A DMS booklet explained the relationship between the two groups:

> While DMS aims to have corporations and churches repent, the Network aims to achieve a measure of justice—secular, civil justice. The tactics of the Network therefore are more a matter of secular power application. DMS helps the Network to understand how that power works and where to apply it most effectively. . . . The Network is the anti-deindustrialization Resistance Movement. DMS is its chaplain and counselor. . . .
> DMS urges, for example, that the Network avoid violent tactics which would harm individuals. In the final analysis, the Network makes its own plans after hearing the advice of DMS and devises the necessary tactics as a group.[23]

In effect, while DMS clergy provided the research and moral justification to carry out public actions aimed at putting pressure on Mellon Bank and other corporations, the unionists in the Network provided

21. Von Dreele interview, June 18, 1985.
22. Jim Jones interview, June 19, 1985.
23. Long, *Book on Pittsburgh*, p. 63.

most of the bodies and—with the exception of Roth—risked most of the arrests in these demonstrations. In addition to providing clergy with a certain amount of working-class legitimacy, members of the Network were the muscle behind the word—or, in union president Ron Weisen's intentionally inflammatory words, "We consider ourselves terrorists."

The muscle of Network activists and the wild-eyed glee with which they approached some of their activities did inspire a certain fear in the mind of the mid-level managers with which they sometimes tangled. Yet more frightening to Pittsburgh's elite must have been the vision embodied in Weisen's statement "The unions and the church—that's the most powerful coalition."[24] Such a coalition, with a militant vision, could have tremendous power in a community like Pittsburgh, where both union membership and church attendance were well above the national norm. Therefore, it is not surprising that corporate power on levels from overt to very subtle was used to marginalize these groups and eventually to dissolve their coalition. But this anticipates too much.

At this point, the two groups worked closely, with the initiative coming primarily from DMS clergy. For this reason, this study often uses the practice, common throughout Pittsburgh, of referring to either the combination "Network/DMS" or the DMS by itself as simply the DMS.

After the confrontation over Mesta Machine, the DMS decided to escalate its attack on Mellon Bank. They threatened to close the banks in response to plant closings. In October 1983, members of the DMS and Network activists staged their "penny action" at the Homestead branch of Mellon Bank. The tactic was simple. A person would go up to a teller and ask for five dollars in pennies. He or she would then proceed to count them before leaving the teller's window. Frequently the person counting pennies would lose track and have to start counting again. Counting could take especially long if the person counting happened to "accidently" bump some of the pennies off onto the floor.

This tactic, coupled with an informational picket in front of the bank, enraged the branch manager, who then called the police. Police attempting to "restore order" injured six activists. Area media covered this event, reporting both the statement of Network activists and the brutality of the police on behalf of the bank. The action succeeded in pressuring Mellon management both directly, by disrupting branch service, and indirectly, through the media.

From the penny action, the Network/DMS moved to dead fish and

24. Weisen, cited in Dave Davis and Tim Peek, "Pittsburgh Pastor Rallies Victims of Hi-Tech Visions," *In These Times*, December 19, 1984, p. 17.

skunks. Members rented safe-deposit boxes at various banks and proceeded to deposit frozen fish in them. As the fish (several per branch) ripened, the odor became strong enough to force branches to shut down for days while bank personnel sought out the hidden fish.

Many Network activists were also hunters and knew it was possible to buy skunk oil (used in minute quantities to disguise a hunter's scent) at hardware and sporting goods stores. They soon found out that when skunk oil was released within a bank lobby it took several days of attention from professional cleaners to remove the odor from the carpets and paneling. The slogan they used to explain these tactics was "Smellin' Mellon." To this day, skunk oil is the first thing many people think of when they think of the DMS. No one knows how many people think skunk when they think Mellon, but DMS hoped it would become a frequent association, at least for many of the region's unemployed.

Activists saw skunk tactics as a way to force attention to problems. Darrell Becker, head of Local 61 of the Industrial Union of Marine and Shipbuilding Workers of America, observed: "The labor movement needs new tactics. Strikes are not effective against a firm wanting to reduce its labor force. We have exhausted all normal channels. We don't like the tactics we use now, but we need them." [25] The DMS offered this official explanation for such unusual tactics:

> These tactical actions dramatize the evil in that particular institution in such a way that the media could not resist covering it, which in turn inflamed the indignation and arrogance of Mellon. We have no secular power to damage the financial base of such an institution. All we can do is damage the image which is in fact idolatrous by seeing that it becomes identified with a dead fish in the national media. [26]

Ray Smith, director of industrial marketing for People's Natural Gas and an opponent of DMS, was quite aware of the sort of training that DMS ministers were getting. He explained: "They are all trained in Alinsky methods. Alinsky says that most people have no power except by getting others to do something stupid. The best way to deal with DMS then is to ignore them. That's what U.S. Steel and Mellon Bank do." [27]

Refusing to meet with DMS and ignoring them as much as possible

25. Darrell Becker interview, April 2, 1985.
26. Long, *Book on Pittsburgh*, p. 61.
27. Ray Smith, telephone interview, June 5, 1985.

was one part of the strategy the elite used against DMS. This caused DMS to try other tactics to force a reaction.

"When David Graham (CEO of U.S. Steel) says we have to get down to x number of man-hours of labor in the Valley, it is a cold calculation. He does not think of people," explained Reverend Von Dreele. "People with complaints have no access to Graham at his office or at his club. . . . Where he is vulnerable to people is at his church. So we go to his church. Until executives feel the consequences of their actions personally, they will keep shutting down the mills."[28]

On several occasions, DMS and Network activists disrupted worship services at the churches that targeted corporate executives attended. The most frequently chosen church was the Shadyside Presbyterian Church, home congregation of top executives from U.S. Steel, Mellon Bank, and Dravo. At one early visit, Mike Bonn, then president of USWA Local 2227, a man who looked like a defensive tackle for the Pittsburgh Steelers, stood up from his place among the worshipers and delivered a sermon about the need to confront evil directly. The sermon featured extensive quotations from Dietrich Bonhoeffer, a German theologian who realized that his Christian faith compelled him to participate in a plot to kill Hitler. People screamed charges of heresy at Bonn and demanded he leave. Before he left, however, he told the congregation that the sermon had been written by a former Shadyside minister and delivered to that congregation six years earlier.[29]

On Easter in both 1984 and 1985, the DMS disrupted Shadyside services. In 1985 the DMS called unemployed workers from all over the city to bring pieces of rusty steel to lay on the altar as their offering to God. They arrived and hoisted signs that read "All We Have Left: Scraps of the Mills." Led by television actor David Soul, Roth, and union local presidents Mike Bonn and Darrell Becker, about twenty-five protestors advanced on the church carrying one large bar of iron. The four leaders were arrested before they could reach the church steps. Arthur Gilkes, a church deacon, remarked that DMS had "sensitized" the congregation to the plight of the unemployed. "We're always willing to talk to them," he said, "but not in the middle of an Easter service."[30]

Perhaps the most infamous DMS action was the disruption of Shadyside's Christmas party in 1984. While some of the DMS ministers were berating the crowd, three people with ski masks over their faces came in and threw water balloons laced with skunk oil around the room. This

28. Von Dreele interview, June 18, 1985.
29. Ibid.
30. "Scrap-Toting Activists Arrested," *Pittsburgh Post-Gazette*, April 8, 1985, p. 4.

quickly stopped the festivities. The action was condemned roundly in the press and throughout the community, especially because many children were upset by the attack. Three people were brought to trial for the incident. They were arraigned on charges that could have put them in jail for several years. This was communicated to the public as a deterrent. As a result of a plea-bargain arrangement, two were eventually sentenced to several months' probation—a fairly effective means of control.

Von Dreele admitted that the decision to skunk-oil the Christmas party may have been a tactical mistake, but, he explained, "pastors went there to confront the congregation about the grand Christmas party they were having while our people were suffering in the Valley. People need to compare this tactic with the tactics used daily against the people of Mon Valley, tactics like sheriff's sales of the homes of unemployed workers, malnutrition in families with no regular income, and pressures that force people to suicide and divorce."[31]

DMS tactics were meant to confront people directly, but they were also designed to have an effect through the media. Initially the DMS had considerable success at getting both national and local media to address issues they would have otherwise ignored. DMS was very conscious of using the press and planned many of their actions specifically to create images that the press would then present to a mass audience.

When three workers died as a result of an improperly relined steel furnace, Network/DMS activists delivered a large black box filled with fire bricks to U.S. Steel Headquarters. Ron Weisen, president of USWA Local 1320 of Homestead, explained to television cameras, "We are giving these bricks to Roderick because he says he can only afford a thin fireclay lining for furnaces that may not be running in the near future. His refusal to invest even that much in the Valley is killing people." To ensure an attentive press, the box was carried in a menacing fashion by several workers as though it had a bomb in it. For the benefit of the cameras, the box also contained a sufficient amount of dry ice to ensure that it would smoke profusely when opened.

In 1984 U.S. Steel stated that it would like to raze many of its mills in the valley. (In 1992 many of the mills were still in the process of being dismantled.) When it began dynamiting parts of the mill in McKeesport, DMS went to the Federal Building to request an explosives permit to allow them to blow up U.S. Steel Headquarters. When the Bureau of Tobacco and Firearms refused even to give them an application, activists went to the office of Senator John Heinz to ask his assistance. Heinz

31. Von Dreele interview, June 18, 1985.

responded with a vigorous denunciation, thus ensuring that the story would get printed.[32]

Despite much elite urging (as evidenced in letters to the editor, other opinion pieces, and corporate interviews) that the media stop giving DMS a forum by covering its actions, through 1985 and 1986 the group still managed to get a lot of press coverage. But the tone of the coverage was rarely favorable. For example, immediately before going to the Federal Building to ask for a blasting permit, DMS had held their second annual memorial Communion service on the large plaza in front of U.S. Steel headquarters in downtown Pittsburgh. The solemn service—to commemorate those who had died in recent accidents and those who had died from suicide or heart attacks related to unemployment, and to pray for repentance on the part of corporate executives and for success for workers attempting to take over the Duquesne mill—drew nearly one hundred communicants and many more interested onlookers from the lunchtime crowds. Yet press coverage of the day's events made virtually no mention of the worship service. Instead, it focused on blasting, painting the DMS as a group of possibly crazy publicity-seekers nearing the threshold of violence. An editorial cartoon focused on the threat of violence. It also used the fact that DMS referred to their target as the U.S. Steel Building (despite its recent sale to Rockwell International) to suggest that DMS was hopelessly out of touch with "important" information.[33]

Local columnists felt free to use DMS as the butt of derogatory jokes. In a column on the first Pittsburgh marathon ever, the planning for the whole Sunday morning event was labeled a DMS tactic because it disrupted church services throughout a large part of the city.[34]

National news was originally quite interested in the group, but a "60 Minutes" television segment devoted to the DMS signaled a change. It used footage of a small fire (used for warmth, not destruction) at a picket line DMS supported, and of carefully selected short statements by DMS clergy, to paint the group as a potentially dangerous cult of fanatical Christian deviates.

According to Von Dreele, the bad press presented no problem to the group. Without it they might have been seen as another group of do-gooder ministers who could have easily been ignored. "Three weeks of good press would destroy us," he says. "But we wouldn't let them get away with it."[35] Pastor John Yedlicka, a member of DMS until February

32. "DMS Says It Wants Bomb to Blow Up U.S. Steel Building," *Pittsburgh Post-Gazette*, June 5, 1985.
33. *News Messenger,* June 12, 1985.
34. Peter Leo, *Pittsburgh Post-Gazette,* April 22, 1985.
35. Von Dreele interview, June 18, 1985.

1985, disagrees. He feels the negative press coverage that DMS tactics so readily provoked allowed people to think of the group as "kookish," and thus discredited the serious message DMS was trying to get across.[36]

Yedlicka's perception may have been correct. The DMS strategy of using outrageous tactics to force media coverage that opponents of deindustrialization would not otherwise have received was a gamble. DMS hoped their message would get through despite the negativity heaped on them. Conversations with people throughout the Pittsburgh region, however, showed that most people were more familiar with the group's zany tactics than with their message. Yet these people often gave a mixed endorsement to the strategies' effectiveness. They often insisted that the DMS should have found better tactics to get across their important message. Thus, some of the importance of the message had gotten through.

The Purges

Actions against Roth culminated in his imprisonment and subsequent defrocking. They began apparently as a dispute within the 129-member Trinity Lutheran Church in Clairton. A dispute in the church emerged as early as Easter 1983, after Roth had called for disaster relief and shortly before the anti-Mellon D-Day campaign.

DMS members say the initial start of schism within the parish came from a wealthy woman, Nellie Miller, a former member of Trinity Lutheran who had transferred her membership to Nativity Lutheran. Miller was a friend of the Rev. Mont O. Bowser, the man the Lutheran synod chose to coordinate proceedings against Roth and his supporters at Trinity, including the arrests that would result from those proceedings. Throughout the proceedings, Bowser was closely advised by lawyers from Reed Smith Shaw & McClay, the law firm most patronized by Mellon Bank. DMS members recall that this advice led to one incident in which Bowser visited Trinity to talk to Roth and his supporters. Bowser was invited in to worship and appeared ready to enter when his lawyer whispered in his ear. Bowser then declined the invitation and left.

At the same time that proceedings were started against Roth, Pastor John Gropp of Christ Lutheran in Duquesne also came under attack. It is clear from the transcript of Roth's contempt trial that members of both parishes were in communication about how to proceed against their

36. Yedlicka interview, July 24, 1985.

pastors. A letter from Mrs. Mildred Luptak indicates that when she contacted Bishop May about the process he asked whether her group had the "stamina" necessary to see things through.[37]

Although the links between Nellie Miller, Mont Bowser, Bishop May, and the law firm of Reed Smith Shaw & McClay do not prove the DMS charge that divisions within parishes of DMS clergy were stirred up from the outside, they do establish connections that would have made such efforts feasible. This research has found evidence of a network that could certainly facilitate such a conspiracy, as well as evidence confirming specific instances of such decision-making. The evidence is sufficient to suggest that while some of the specific DMS charges of conspiracy may have been unfounded, it is likely that the use of such tactics by Pittsburgh's elites was more common, not less common, than the total of all specific DMS charges would indicate.

The motives of parish members seeking to oust DMS pastors were probably mixed. It is not uncommon for members of a church to tire of their minister and seek his replacement. In this case, Roth's personality may have played a part. Martin Krien, one of Roth's supporters, insisted that one could not ask for a pastor with a better character. "He worked on his own house, chopped wood, went out to cut the church Christmas tree. . . . He even waxed the church floors." But, Krien explained, if one were to rank personalities from one to three, Roth would get a "three." He felt that the reason Gropp survived the challenge in his parish was due largely to his very warm personality. Krien would give him a "one."[38] The testimony of one anti-Roth witness objected primarily to the "dictatorial tactics" of Roth that grew out of his "enthusiasm" for DMS.[39] Another Roth detractor complained, "He just doesn't have any social graces. He's from Nebraska."[40]

The issue of personality also came up in the subsequent ouster of Pastor Solberg. Ray Smith, president of the church council at Solberg's Nativity Lutheran Church, reported that, although Solberg was known for his warm personality, when he was confronted about his involvement with DMS "his personality changed; he became cultlike, adamant about his position."[41] However, in this case it is clear that Smith and others were upset even before the personality change, upset particularly about the activities of DMS.

According to Smith, Solberg had never discussed DMS from the pulpit

37. From documents in Long, *Book on Pittsburgh*.
38. Martin Krien interview, June 7, 1985.
39. Long, *Book on Pittsburgh*, p. 31.
40. Davis and Peek, "Pittsburgh Pastor Rallies."
41. Ray Smith, telephone interview, June 5, 1985.

or used anticorporate language until after some members saw him on television at a DMS activity. Members of the church demanded that Solberg sever all ties to the group. As Smith, also director of industrial marketing for People's Natural Gas, put it, "A simple denunciation of DMS would have been sufficient."[42] In all cases, but in this case even more clearly than in the others, it is quite apparent that association with the activities of the DMS was the primary cause of actions against the pastors and that other issues, such as personality, emerged from this central conflict.

In Roth's church, one of the major items of contention was that the church council included a donation to the work of DMS as one of its budget items. The fact that the amount would be given only if donations were earmarked specifically for DMS did not assuage critics. These members—some with possible elite ties, and others simply uncomfortable with any type of social activism—objected to any DMS moneys passing through their church. Martin Krien, a member of Trinity Lutheran for thirty years, suggested that such specific objections may have been merely tactical ways of phrasing more general sentiments. He explained: "They just didn't like DMS, and they didn't like him talking about DMS from the pulpit. They claimed it had nothing to do with religion, but it had all to do with religion. . . . It was profoundly Christian, as far as I'm concerned."[43]

The procedure used to remove Roth and Gropp, and subsequently to remove Pastors Daniel Solberg and William Rex, was found in the Constitution of the Lutheran Church in America. Specifically, sections pertaining to divisions within a congregation and obedience to authority were invoked. An LCA committee recommended that Roth and disaffected members of Trinity begin a process of reconciliation prescribed by Bishop May. Roth and his supporters, including a majority of the church council, were willing to accept the reconciliation process, but some members were not. In October 1984, May then ruled that Roth would have to leave Trinity and seek another parish. At this point Roth refused, saying he would stay and continue his ministry.

From that point on, when Roth conducted Sunday services several muscular members of the Network stood guard against efforts of the LCA to remove him. Bishop May asked Allegheny County Judge Emil Narrick to order Roth to obey his bishop's command to leave the church and allow a successor to replace him. Narrick complied, and when Roth refused to leave, the judge found him in contempt of court. On Tuesday

42. Ibid.
43. Martin Krien interview, June 7, 1985.

morning, November 11, 1984, deputies came and arrested Roth at the altar of the church for disobeying the court order. Roth was incarcerated for ninety days.

The arrest of Roth did not end the bishop's problems with the Clairton church. Bishop May appointed Pastor Bowser as interim minister, but when Bowser showed up to conduct Sunday services, he was turned away by Harry Dinkle, vice president of the church council.

Inside, supporters of Roth listened as Wayne Cochran, church council president, read Roth's "Second Sermon from Prison." The sermon deplored "the evil that puts people in the streets, that causes families to break up, convinces people there is no hope." The sermon charged: "Bishop May has not done what the Lord has commanded him, to fight the evil that is at hand. Be sure his sin will find him out."[44]

One of the major contentions of the DMS is that if a tactic hits home it is likely to produce an overreaction that will reveal the oppressive nature of one's target. These sermons evidently had such an effect, for when Roth managed to send out tape-recorded sermons the court ordered him to stop. When he persisted, the court sentenced him to an additional sixty days in jail.[45]

Because the church refused to accept Pastor Bowser, the Lutheran synod declared Trinity Church dissolved and ordered Bowser to claim the church property and its treasury. However, when he went to claim possession he found the doors chained shut and Roth supporters (including Wayne Cochran, president of the church council) inside. The baseball bats and gas masks he saw inside gave him the intended message that the church occupiers would not be easily dislodged.[46] Later that week, Roth's wife, Nadine, made it even clearer when she read a statement declaring that the church council members would go to jail before yielding to the bishop.[47]

On January 4, 1985 the state again acted to enforce the wishes of the bishop. Judge Narrick ruled that the council must turn church property over to the synod. He declared: "The guarantee of religious freedom has nothing to do with property."[48] Sheriff Eugene L. Coons led a contin-

---

44. This account is based largely on William Robbins, "Defiant Pastor Sends a Second Sermon from Jail," *New York Times,* November 26, 1984.

45. *New York Times,* January 5, 1985. The judge allowed the time to be served concurrently with Roth's ninety-day sentence. The purpose of such a sentence might have been to remind Roth of the court's displeasure and power without attracting the public attention a consecutive sentence would have provoked.

46. *New York Times,* December 4, 1985.

47. *New York Times,* December 10, 1984, p. A18.

48. *New York Times,* December 22, 1984, p. A8.

gent of forty-four riot-equipped police officers to oust Roth's backers. The officers broke down a wooden door at the back of the church and entered with weapons drawn. The occupiers put up no resistance and were immediately arrested.[49] Those arrested included Nadine Roth, the Rev. William Rex, unemployed shipbuilder Paul Brandt, union president Darrell Becker, sixty-five-year-old council vice-president Harry Dinkel, council member Rebecca Fosbrick, and Pamela Ramsey, who had been active in a strike at a Lutheran nursing home. Council President Wayne Cochran was arrested later that day when he appeared in Judge Narrick's courtroom. Narrick ordered the four church members each to pay $985 in compensatory costs and to serve sixty days at the Clearfield County Jail in a work-release program.[50]

Even this did not deter Roth's backers. The following Sunday, as sheriff's deputies watched from inside, about a hundred of Roth's supporters gathered to hold services on the church lawn. This time, actor David Soul read Roth's sermon, which declared: "Evil may win battles, but we are assured that in God's right time the final victory is his."[51] An angry Judge Narrick sentenced Roth to an additional thirty days (again to be served concurrently) for encouraging others to violate the law.[52]

On Sunday, March 10, after serving 112 days in jail, Roth himself preached the sermon on the Trinity Church lawn. In it he called Bishop May a pawn of moneyed interests. The next day, a disciplinary committee headed by May removed Roth from the ordained ministry of the Lutheran Church of America. The committee, which refused to discuss any of the content of Roth's ministry or his work with the DMS, found Roth guilty of "willful disregard and violation of the constitution."[53] Roth responded: "Now Mellon Bank and US Steel have defrocked their first pastor."[54]

Actions against Roth did not stop with his defrocking. In accord with the wishes of the bishop, the Clairton City Council barred Roth's supporters from gathering in groups of three or more on the sidewalk near Trinity Church.[55] The ruling was given teeth when Justice Sarah

---

49. Here again, by displaying signs that it might put up a struggle, the DMS provoked its opponents into a dramatic display of oppressive force. What remains unclear is whether those who watched riot police storm a church to arrest a sixty-five-year-old man and a minister's wife identified the event as oppressive or justified.
50. *New York Times,* January 5, 1985.
51. *New York Times,* January 7, 1985.
52. Ibid.
53. *New York Times,* March 13, 1985, p. A12.
54. Ibid.
55. *Pittsburgh Post-Gazette,* April 1, 1985, p. 5.

Fiore found seven people guilty of disorderly conduct for holding a sidewalk service on March 24 and fined each of them $300.[56] This effectively put an end to services at Trinity, except for the Palm Sunday Communion service that eight worshipers held on the four corners in front of the church, two to a corner.[57] DMS supporters were also barred from worshiping at many area Lutheran churches and were arrested when they tried to do so.[58] The church had little trouble getting the cooperation of civil authorities against the DMS.

Having apparently finished with Roth, the Lutheran synod moved to oust two more DMS pastors who had "created divisions" within their congregations. Pastor Daniel Solberg was removed from duty at Nativity Lutheran Church in Allison Park effective May 15. The Rev. William Rex was removed from his parishes: Rose Crest Lutheran in Monroeville, and St. Mark's Lutheran in Trafford, effective May 31, 1985.[59]

Solberg chose not to make his firing an easy affair. He locked himself inside the church on his last official night of duty, a Tuesday. Inside the church lobby, Solberg displayed a large sign charging seven Pittsburgh corporations with responsibility for his firing. Several members of the congregation joined him in his occupation.

The following Sunday, a synod-appointed interim pastor arrived to conduct services only to find the doors still locked. He held services on the church lawn for about fifty opponents of Solberg while about fifty Solberg supporters were admitted to worship inside with their pastor. In his sermon, Solberg charged that his opponents had "attacked the bold challenge of the gospel with lies."[60]

The bishop's investigation, which led to Solberg's dismissal, was (at least formally) concerned only with establishing whether there was "division" in the congregation. Thus, members were asked to testify without cross examination and without apparent concern for separating fact from allegation. For example, one member charged that Solberg was not open about his involvement with DMS, but another said he was very open. Without further investigation, the panel concluded that Solberg "for some time was unwilling to be open with his congregation about his deep involvement with the strategy of the Denominational Ministerial Strategy."[61]

56. *Pittsburgh Post-Gazette*, April 10, 1985, p. 4.
57. *Pittsburgh Post-Gazette*, April 1, 1985, p. 5.
58. Long, *Book on Pittsburgh*, pp. 23–27, contains documents that detail a number of these barrings and arrests.
59. *Pittsburgh Post-Gazette*, May 11, 1985, p. 1.
60. *Pittsburgh Post-Gazette*, May 20, 1985, p. 1.
61. "Report of the Investigating Committee for Nativity Lutheran Church," March 27, 1985; reprinted in Long, *Book on Pittsburgh*, p. 28.

One member charged that Solberg had chosen to attend a DMS meeting rather than a church council meeting; others said this was not true and they could prove it. The panel concluded: "The Rev. Mr. Solberg's heavy time commitment to the 'prophetic ministry' of the DMS seems to have been at the sacrifice of Nativity Lutheran Church and its members."[62]

The heart of the matter was found in a second finding: "The Rev. Mr. Solberg's insistence on continued involvement with DMS has seemed to be a disruptive force within the congregation for which there is no apparent solution."[63] On the surface, that charge seems true enough. Although Solberg had not pushed the issue within his congregation, once it was brought into the open he would have been satisfied only with the repentance of many of his opponents. They, in like manner, demanded his withdrawal from and denunciation of DMS as a valid part of his Christian ministry. DMS members, however, respond that Solberg's involvement with DMS would not have been an issue without the instigation of the church and the corporate elite (this time including the direct participation of an executive from the region's largest industrial supplier of natural gas) and that the dispute could have been resolved if people had been willing to turn to scriptures rather than the constitution of the Lutheran Church in America.

The LCA need not have clung so desperately to its constitution. In the 1960s and early 1970s, when some Lutheran pastors created "division" within their congregations by pushing the issue of racial integration, national leadership stood behind them. Addressing the press after Roth's defrocking, LCA Bishop Crumley explained: "The church was clear that there was one Christian position on this issue. It is not so clear on the matter of unemployment. There are many complicating factors."[64]

It was apparent from the work of the LCA's Commission on Economic Justice that the church would reach no "clear" position on unemployment. Set up in January 1985, supposedly to study the issue of unemployment, the commission's only accomplishment by July was a report denouncing the tactics of DMS.[65] Obviously, the disturbing presence of the DMS would not have been their main focus if they had been determined to find a scripturally justifiable position on the issue of unemployment. In the 1960s, church leaders found the issue of integration safe to deal with in religiously rooted terms. They preferred to avoid even discussing economic control in such terms.

62. Ibid.
63. Ibid.
64. Bishop Crumley press conference, June 7, 1985.
65. *Pittsburgh Press,* July 25, 1985, p. B1.

As a way of dramatizing their charge of corporate responsibility for Solberg's firing, some Solberg backers removed organ pipes from the church and mailed them to corporate officials. They included a note that read: "Since you're so anxious to get the church back, here's part of the vital organ."[66]

After eight days the occupation was ended. Solberg was arrested on May 21 and taken to the county jail. Justice Regis C. Welsh charged him with defiant trespass and criminal trespass and set bail at $5,000. Solberg refused to pay bail. Roth explained the new DMS policy on not paying bail or fines: "Never again will we pay one penny to go to church in America."[67]

Three days later, another judge offered to release Solberg on his own recognizance if he would agree to stay away from Nativity Church. Solberg refused to accept this restriction, claiming it was an infringement of his first amendment right to practice his religion freely. Solberg appealed his return to jail, but the appeal judge ruled that Solberg could sit and wait until his trial, scheduled for late September: "I think it is most commendable that your faith in Christ is steadfast and I would respectfully suggest to you that if you do not agree to the conditions of bail set by the magistrate and by Judge Strauss your only hope may be that He will do what He did for Saint Peter."[68]

DMS used this long imprisonment to keep the issue of their persecution alive in the press. They even held a special worship service outside the county jail on Father's Day.[69] Shortly after Solberg's arrest, his wife and other supporters attended a Sunday service at Nativity and, when it was time for the sermon, stood and read one Solberg had prepared. Two were arrested.[70] They had defied a letter sent to Charles Honeywell asking DMS to stay away. It read in part:

> The Congregation is emerging from a lengthy and intense struggle. A healing process has begun that we pray will restore Nativity to a vibrant Christ centered church. The presence of you and your associates will not contribute to the healing.[71]

66. *Pittsburgh Post-Gazette,* May 25, 1985, p. 4.

67. *Pittsburgh Post-Gazette,* May 22, 1985, p. 4.

68. Letter to Daniel Solberg from Judge Robert E. Dauer, Court of Common Pleas, Pittsburgh, July 22, 1985; reprinted in Long, *Book on Pittsburgh,* August 4, 1985, update, p. 2.

69. *Pittsburgh Post-Gazette,* June 17, 1985.

70. *Pittsburgh Post-Gazette,* June 3, 1985.

71. Letter from Raymond Smith and Thomas Beecher, May 23, 1985; reprinted in Long, *Book on Pittsburgh,* p. 27.

After the arrests, another letter was sent out to promote this "Christ centered . . . healing process." In short, it asked Nativity members who remained loyal to Solberg to leave the congregation:

> Following the May 26 worship service I asked all members present to be particularly sensitive to those of you close to Daniel Solberg. Members who are capable of reaching out and helping you return to the mainstream of our congregational life were urged to do so. . . .
>
> The time when division and conflict must be put behind us is rapidly approaching. I think each of you must soon decide whether Nativity will be able to satisfy your spiritual needs in the future, or whether it would be appropriate for you to seek another church home.[72]

A local professor who had shown up in the media as a supporter of Solberg was called in to his president's office and told that, due to the public attention drawn to his activities, he should not expect ever to get tenure at that institution. Because this represented a severe violation of academic freedom and policies on tenure and promotion, the professor was offered severance pay in return for a pledge not to make details of the case public.

Finally, after 126 days in jail, Solberg came to trial. Common Pleas Judge Robert E. Dauer dismissed the charges, saying that Solberg had not acted criminally by refusing to leave the church because he had never tried to hide the fact that he was in the building.

The following Sunday, Pastor Solberg, accompanied by his wife, his two-year-old son, and several supporters, returned to Nativity Church to worship. The new church council president, Milan Bucher, told Solberg that he had been warned not to return and that he could be arrested if he entered the church. Solberg replied that he had come to worship. He was not prevented from entering, and he stayed until his temporary replacement—whom one of his supporters referred to as a "scab preacher"—rose to deliver the sermon. On his way out, Solberg explained to reporters: "I went to church, a right for which I sat in jail 126 days. I will not give that right up. I simply exercised my privilege as a member and my right as an American to worship."[73]

The meaning of the stories of Roth's and Solberg's confrontations

---

72. Letter from Nativity Church council to Nativity / Daniel Solberg Support Group members, June 5, 1985; reprinted in Long, *Book on Pittsburgh*, p. 27.

73. *Pittsburgh Post-Gazette,* September 30, 1985, p. 4.

depends largely on one's moral judgment. DMS members were convinced that the Judeo-Christian position on Pittsburgh's deindustrialization was clear and that it demanded a confrontation with the powers-that-be, just as the clergy of the Rev. Martin Luther King's Southern Christian Leadership Conference felt called to confront the powers of the segregated South in the 1960s. For many who were unconvinced of the unique direction of the Christian message, the actions of the DMS seemed needlessly antagonistic. Some with vested interests threatened by the DMS had reason to encourage the latter perspective. DMS tactics and the responses to them seemed to convince adherents of the two camps of the rightness of their own positions. There is little evidence that they swayed people one way or another.

The DMS vs. the Ideological Hegemony of Corporate Capitalism

Contesting Hegemony Within the Church

The June 1985 annual convention of the Western Pennsylvania—West Virginia Synod of the Lutheran Church in America was dominated by its confrontation with the Rev. Douglas Roth. In addition to being a dramatic turning point in the history of the DMS, the convention provides us with a basis for understanding how the thought-forms of dominant members of society have embedded themselves as ideological constructs within nonelites.

Roth chose to appeal the decision of the executive board of the synod to defrock him. The board of appeal was the convention of the synod, a gathering of some 500 ministers and laypeople from throughout the area. The synod did not receive Roth warmly. When the measure to defrock Roth was introduced, both Reverend Gropp and Charles Honeywell rose to defend Roth. They asked the synod to consider that which had not yet been considered: whether Roth's "ministry" with the DMS was entirely compatible with the scriptures, the basis of the Lutheran church.

The convention responded by moving to close debate. The measure carried by 392 to 143. The vote on defrocking immediately followed, with 499 in favor and 33 opposed.

In light of this overwhelming vote, the *Pittsburgh Post-Gazette* editorialized: "If Mr. Roth and his friends would only pause to think for a moment, they might realize that the whole Lutheran Synod can't be in the clutches of 'Corporate evil.' "[74] Let us pause for a moment to think how the whole synod might have been in the grips of what we shall here call an "ideological hegemony" that benefited the interests of corporate elites. If one believes, as DMS did, that corporate elites were involved in evil works, then this amounts to nearly the same thing. Having been at the convention and having interviewed a wide variety of delegates, this author has come to believe that most of them were in the clutches of something.

Ideological or cultural hegemony has been described as:

> . . . the permeation throughout civil society . . . of an entire system of values, attitudes, beliefs, morality, etc. that is in one way or another supportive of the established order and the class interests that dominate it. Hegemony in this sense might be defined as an "organizing principle" or world-view that is diffused by agencies of ideological control and socialization into every area of daily life. To the extent that this prevailing view is internalized by the broad masses, it becomes part of "common sense."[75]

Many delegates interviewed after the vote said they had formed their opinions about Roth primarily from what they had seen in the media. So one possible link in the mechanism of hegemony emerges.

One way elites perpetuate their hegemony is through the mass media. Though their control is sometimes exercised by overt use of financial muscle, as in (non)advertising or control of management through ownership, elites also benefit from the fact that many media professionals have previously internalized many of the values that support the status quo, and thus control themselves accordingly. In the language of the above quotation, their notions of "common sense" both assume and help to perpetuate the power of elites. Most members of the media are thus more likely to incline their messages favorably toward established leaders than toward unorthodox challengers.

Therefore, it is possible that "corporate evil" acted to inform the synod vote—not directly, but through the internalized impulses of the media—and that the *Post-Gazette*'s follow-up editorial is a further reinforcement of a hegemony that would sooner paint its challengers as "unthinking" or "misguided" than have itself decried as "evil."

The ability of a corporate elite to shape public opinion overtly is part

74. "Misguided Minister," *Pittsburgh Post-Gazette,* June 10, 1985, p. 8.
75. Carl Boggs, *Gramsci's Marxism* (London: Pluto Press, 1976), p. 39.

of the first dimension of power. Included in this category also is the use of major (non)contributions to the church to influence the activities of its leadership as well as that leadership's use of the courts to remove Roth physically from his church and imprison him.

Yet in this case the power that was probably most significant was the more invisible third-dimensional power—that reservoir of unquestioned attitudes and beliefs that accumulate over decades as a result of living in an environment shaped by power used in a variety of ways, some of them much more overt. Chief among these beliefs is the notion that the way things are is the way things should be. A correlate of this belief is that those who question existing institutions are at best misguided and, in this case, deplorably wrong.

The Rev. Dr. Richard Solberg, Daniel Solberg's father, suggested how this subconscious loyalty to existing arrangements worked to prevent those voting on Roth's appeal from even considering the possibility that Roth's position might be valid. Dr. Solberg, who was also former academic dean at Thiel College, where the synod met, and the director of higher education for the national Lutheran Church in America, lamented that as a Lutheran he was "ashamed" of the proceedings that had so hastily defrocked Roth. Dr. Solberg charged that the delegates suffer from a "doctrinal heresy" that confuses "one holy catholic church" with the LCA. Whereas the LCA is merely an institutional arrangement—which in this case benefits from this subconscious defense mechanism—the "holy catholic church" is the spiritual reason for the LCA's existence. This heresy, he explained, allowed them to defrock Roth for violating the constitution of the LCA while taking no notice of the spiritual validity or invalidity of the ministry they were seeking to end.

Another set of ingrained norms that works to the advantage of any status quo includes not only respect for authority but also respect for civility, decorum, "gentlemanly behavior," and the like. In their bank actions, and even more in their church disruptions, the DMS had repeatedly violated these norms—and not only that, but they had violated those norms at the previous year's synod gathering and were threatening to violate them at the current gathering as well.

If anything, these norms are held more strongly by Lutherans than by other groups. Their cultural heritage derives from the experience of largely German and Scandinavian immigrants who, as soon as they learned a new language and "proper" behavior, were elevated by their Episcopalian and Presbyterian betters to a status above that of rank-and-file industrial workers. Their success was predicated on propriety within a hierarchical society.

As discussion proceeded and votes were cast, it was apparent from the faces and comments of those in attendance that they were deeply offended by the DMS. Comments such as "No one should behave that way" or "they don't even show respect for the bishop" were common.[76] It is entirely consistent with this collective desire to restore civility that delegates voted to prevent discussion of the substance of Roth's crimes or his defense. They knew how they felt.

Dr. Solberg further explained that one result of the fact that the church exists in what he saw as an extremely secular and materialistic society is that those who are most respected in each congregation are those that have achieved success in their business and professional lives. Thus, although members of the synod could pass resolutions that urged corporations in general to act differently in South Africa, they could not deal with the issue of unemployment in Pittsburgh. That is, they might charitably help individuals who had been affected by unemployment, but they could not address the causes of unemployment. To do so might require chastising the most respected members of their churches. Thus, the desire to prevent conflict, division, and lack of civility worked again to protect Pittsburgh's corporate hierarchy. Solberg also charged: "Church members are blinded by the belief that property is sacred; that corporations must serve the stockholders' interests above all else. But individuals make corporate decisions, and they must be held morally accountable for the effects of those decisions."[77]

Delegates to the convention showed no willingness to consider the morality of holding specific executives individually accountable for corporate decisions, but they were willing to hold Roth individually accountable for his actions and for those of all disruptive DMS and Network activists. The vote for his defrocking was cast with determination.

It was followed by indignation and despair when, in the wake of the vote, Roth seized the podium and insisted that he would not leave until the synod showed itself willing to examine corporate evil. To further heighten the conflict, some of Roth's supporters cried out "Crucify him! Crucify him!" The mood of the convention returned to one of apprehensive relief when, within the hour, Roth was arrested on trespassing charges and led away by a dozen police.[78]

76. Interviews conducted at Thiel College, June 7, 1985.
77. Interview with the Rev. Dr. Richard Solberg, LCA Synod convention, June 7, 1985.
78. The LCA handled the arrest astutely. The convention had attracted a good deal of local and national press, so to avoid dramatic video and photographic press coverage of the arrest, a press conference with Bishop Crumley, national head of th LCA, was called. Only when the press had been safely shepherded away did the police move in for the arrest.

After Roth's arrest at Thiel College, the work of the DMS centered more on the politics of the Lutheran church than on the politics of industrial employment. DMS activists would disagree with this judgment, arguing that they were pursuing the same issue—the arrogance and immorality of the economic elite—whether within the Lutheran church, Mellon Bank, or U.S. Steel. However, it probably did not look that way to most workers in Pittsburgh.

A major exception to this trend toward intrachurch struggles was a series of demonstrations held in the town of Ambridge in the wake of the October 1985 closing of the Armco Steel plant. Focusing on the role of Mellon Bank in the closing, demonstrators distributed leaflets, held a fairly well attended rally, pressured local businesses to support their efforts, and "stuck up" a local branch of Mellon bank by dumping diluted honey and bags of popcorn on the sidewalk in front of the main entrance.[79]

However, as key DMS actors like Roth, Solberg, Honeywell, and Long focused more on the church, Ambridge seemed more like a sideshow than the heart of the struggle. The Ambridge effort had drawn eager support from many Network activists and showed potential for greater mobilization. Yet when DMS ministers decided to travel to Milwaukee, Wisconsin, or Columbus, Ohio, to risk arrest at conventions addressing the merger of the LCA with other segments of the Lutheran church, their actions tended to demobilize rather than mobilize working-class supporters. After Network founder Ron Weisen stopped working with the DMS, he explained: "It became a church battle, that's what happened."[80] Court cases and church politics effectively diverted most of the DMS energies away from activities that spoke to working people or that threatened corporate power.

Some of the DMS ministers were still getting together in the early 1990s. They were a dramatic presence at the 100th Anniversary of the bloody Homestead steel strike. The occasion marking the armed resistance by the town of steelworkers to Carnegie's efforts to break their union was a fine occasion to distribute another leaflet of resistance to modern-day class conflict.

Douglas Roth, however, moved with his family to Kansas. At this writing, he is an active lay member of his local Missouri Synod Lutheran church. He still feels he is involved in ministry, but his work is largely as a vocational rehabilitation counselor finding jobs for disabled people. Pittsburgh had become a toxic environment for him, he says, and had

79. *Pittsburgh Post-Gazette*, March 16, 1986, p. 5.
80. *New York Times*, April 7, 1988, p. A25.

few opportunities for him. His wife, he believed, was unable to find adequate employment because of blacklisting by people who had ties to Mellon Bank or U.S. Steel. His children faced frequent taunting at school because of his notoriety. It showed once more, he said, that "when you challenge evil it tries to make you pay too." Roth does not regret what he did. "It needed to be done. It was good to call attention to the wholesale destruction of working people." Asked about the charge that few workers understood or appreciated what the DMS had been doing, he said that most working people caught on, "But few could take the personal step to say 'me too.' They could see the cost. They had their jobs and didn't want to rock the boat. Many felt uncomfortable about the issues we raised. And what most people want is to live a comfortable life. Comfort was not what our ministry was about."[81]

Contesting Hegemony in the Unions

Just as the clergy in the DMS were attacked, so were the Network leaders. In the spring elections of 1985, the USWA International provided funds for candidates willing to challenge the reelection campaigns of Ron Weisen, president of Local 1397 at the U.S. Steel Homestead mill, and Mike Bonn, president of Local 2227 at the U.S. Steel Irvin mill.

DMS activities became the major issue at a time when neither the International nor U.S. Steel wanted close attention paid to their strategies for future (un)employment. Mike Bonn did manage to introduce another issue. He insisted that the local should ban overtime work at the mill for three years, or as long as there was a glut of members needing any work at all. This position was a bold one, as it was clear that the only mill in the Valley to maintain a respectable level of employment was the Edgar Thomson mill. Local leadership at Thomson was distinguished by its willingness to cooperate with work-rule changes and extensive overtime, at the expense of other workers in the Valley. Bonn was defeated 983 to 395.[82]

The local media were quick to interpret Mike Bonn's defeat as a sign that the Network and the DMS were out of touch with the working class. Members of rival organizations like the Mon Valley Unemployed Committee were called on to attest to the fact. One explained that the DMS "did things that not only startled corporate America but also offended working-class America."[83] He was probably right. The DMS

81. *Pittsburgh Post-Gazette,* April 18, 1985, p. 1.
82. Larry Evans in *Pittsburgh Post-Gazette,* April 18, 1985, p. 1.
83. *Pittsburgh Post-Gazette,* April 25, 1985, p. 16.

had managed to offend not only the corporate elite and LCA delegates, but ordinary workers as well. They were unable to supplant the cultural hegemony that sustained corporate Pittsburgh.

One week later, however, Weisen was reelected by a vote of 925 to 590.[84] He asked all workers to come together in their fight against U.S. Steel. Although employment in his local had dropped to only one-tenth of its former height, Weisen was glad some members were still working. In defense of some of his Network-related activities, he commented: "I think the bad press U.S. Steel Corp. is getting nationwide is the only reason these plants are still open." Four years earlier, Weisen had predicted that mills in the Valley would be phased out. After his reelection he added, "I still expect that to happen. We've slowed the process."[85] Within two years, Homestead was entirely closed.

Another union activist, Darrell Becker, president of Local 61 of the Industrial Union of Marine Shipbuilding Workers of America (IUMSWA), also ran into trouble in his bid for reelection. Empowered by DMS research methods as well as support for direct confrontation, Becker had decided to take on Dravo Corporation for its decision to shut down their local barge-building operation. When his research convinced him that the national union had been cooperating with plant shutdowns and layoffs around the nation, he decided to take on the union leadership as well. Becker took his message about the need to research, stand up, and challenge to workers all over the country. He spoke to farmers and butchers as well as to shipbuilders.

An entrenched national leadership was not pleased by his efforts. IUMSWA leadership used a variety of maneuvers to try to eliminate Becker. They ruled him ineligible for office (he had lost his factory job and was working only part-time as president of his local) despite overwhelming support for him in his local.

When the National Labor Relations Board (NLRB) ruled that Becker was eligible based on employment by his union, the IUMSWA moved to revoke Local 61's charter. Becker resolutely responded by running for president of the International. The International blocked his election at its October 1986 convention, but the U.S. Department of Labor found numerous improprieties and ordered a new election. Since that time, IUMSWA leadership moved precipitously to be taken over by the Machinists. In the summer of 1988, while Becker was serving ninety days in jail for demonstrating on the sidewalk outside Shadyside Church on Easter in 1985, a representative of the International, Ted Kalas, was

84. *Pittsburgh Post-Gazette,* April 26, 1985.
85. Ron Weisen interview, July 18, 1986.

caught breaking into Local 61's union hall. Clearly IUMSWA leadership was clumsy and inept, and Becker exposed much of their corruption, but the move to be taken over by the much larger Machinists union eventually caused Becker to become discouraged about his chances. He said, "As part of the Machinists, it would have taken a lifetime to reform the Shipbuilders, and I didn't have it to give for that."[86] The Machinists did adopt some of the reforms Becker had campaigned for, but with his local eliminated and no job in the industry, Becker was now clearly ineligible for further activity in the union. Becker worked briefly as a part-time organizer with the United Electrical Workers, one of the most militant unions in the country. He decided to find other work when his superiors canceled an organizing drive he had started, and in a way that made him worry about the futures of people who had taken risks at that plant to organize. In 1992 he was working as a bar manager in Uniontown, Pennsylvania, "becoming reconstituted into an unhappy restauranteur."

It is useful to compare Becker's experience with that of other union leaders associated with the Network. While Becker's union activities were complicated by his having to serve time in jail for his Network/ DMS activities, he gained greatly by the support and training offered him through that group.

Mike Bonn, also arrested with Becker, dropped out of Network activities after they cost him his union position. Bonn's renunciation of DMS saved him from doing jail time when Shadyside Church, recognizing his "repentance," dropped charges against him.[87]

Ron Weisen was reelected president of his local, but he faced ostracism not only by the media and the USWA International, but also by the Tri-State Conference on Steel and the Mon Valley Unemployed Committee as well—two groups he had helped found. As DMS clergy got more involved with internal church politics, he chose to work less with the DMS. The Network to Save the Mon-Ohio Valley ceased to function.

Conclusions

This case and the subsequent case studies will be evaluated in terms of the concepts addressed in the introductory chapter. We need to ask the

86. Darrell Becker interview, July 6, 1992.
87. "Charges Dropped Against Local Man," *McKeesport Daily News*, July 16, 1986, p. 13.

extent to which the history of the DMS shows that elites used their power to manage Pittsburgh's economic transition, and the extent to which they worked deliberately to discourage nonelites from influencing the process. Specifically, we will be concerned with these four questions:

1. What demands did the group make of elites?
2. How did elites respond to the group?
3. Were groups able to stay mobilized?
4. Were groups able to achieve their goals?

Answers to these questions should allow us to determine which of the four cells described in Chapter 1—pluralist democracy, nondecisions or repression, bureaucracy, or elite hegemony—best characterizes the outcome of this case.

It is obvious that the DMS saw itself in a confrontation with a coherent and hostile elite. Their work and their experiences have done a fair amount to reinforce in the minds of Pittsburgh residents the idea that an elite does exist and does make most important political and economic decisions in the region.

Decisions leading to massive unemployment were made by a small group of corporate executives. DMS research has shown the links through which centralized decision-making can be coordinated. The repressive responses that DMS activities provoked demonstrate active links between the elite of corporations and churches as well as the willing complicity of the local police and judicial systems. DMS was also squelched by elite-favoring, don't-rock-the-boat attitudes held by the general public. Because these attitudes systematically favor elite outcomes over popular challenges, we shall regard those attitudes of the general public as expressions of elite power. The pervasive acceptance of the exclusivity of corporate decision-making was especially in evidence at the defrocking convention of the LCA.

The demands the Network to Save the Mon-Ohio Valley and the DMS made of the region's elite were that key corporate leaders change their investment practices. They demanded that corporate leaders include local employment protection as one of their investment criteria even if it meant a slight decline in profits, and that this be seen as a moral obligation. They therefore insisted that individual corporate leaders be held morally accountable to the community, not merely economically accountable to their investors. Furthermore, the Network/DMS demanded that corporate leaders not only recognize the validity of their moral demands, but also recognize the validity of their group by meeting with them to negotiate compliance with their demands.

These demands struck at the heart of the elite-controlled decision-making process. Following the principle that elite response to challengers will be proportional to the degree of threat posed by their challenge, the elite resisted completely. Resistance took a variety of forms.

The first and ultimately most effective form of resistance was to attack the jobs held by the clergy, labor leaders, and their supporters. Some were removed easily, some after a lengthy struggle, and some managed to resist the attacks. Although these attacks did not immediately deter further challenges, they did cause the attention of the challengers to be at least partially diverted from their original challenge. It must be said to the credit of these activists that they tried hard and often creatively to turn the defense of their positions into yet another avenue to challenge and expose the elite decision-making process. Unfortunately, in the case of the clergy, their responses involved them so deeply in church politics that their efforts no longer had meaning for more than the inner circle of industrial workers associated with the Network. Eventually, most of these were also discouraged by what they saw as an obsession with church politics.

Arrests, jail, fines, and attorney's fees had a wearing effect on even the most dedicated. As the costs of the challenge increased, workers who saw no likelihood of success in the near future sought other ways to solve their problems. In the very visible case of Union President Mike Bonn, the decision to disassociate from Network/DMS activities had immediate payoffs. He did not have to go to jail, and other, less threatening opportunities to help workers began to open up for him.

It is common for people to suggest that all the repressive responses the DMS has had to suffer were the direct result of socially if not legally unacceptable activities. But a chronological review of the history shows that this is not the case. The first and perhaps most decisive attacks on DMS occurred in response to fully legal and reasonably orthodox attempts by the DMS to expose the corporate plan to deindustrialize Pittsburgh. Their campaign for Mesta D-Day withdrawals provoked the withdrawal of denominational support for their group, long before the "Smellin' Mellon" tactics emerged. It was early on that people moved to create divisions within the parishes of DMS ministers. It was because of strong criticism of national leadership that unions decided to attempt to get rid of Weisen, Bonn, and Becker. The fact that the substance of proceedings against Network/DMS activists often focused on later tactics does not explain away the motivations for them.

The most decisive repressive response used against the Network/DMS was partially deliberate—on the part of the elite and intermediate actors—and partly the result of habitual responses of a well-conditioned society. It consisted of the decision of the media, of church laypeople,

and eventually of workers throughout the region to regard DMS participants as some sort of lunatics. Media emphasis on the outlandish tactics
of the DMS, while downplaying the DMS message, further alienated the
general public. This left the DMS isolated and unthreatening and made
it impossible for their important message to be heard.

But we have to give the DMS some of the blame for their own demise.
Their self-identification as prophets made it easy for them to retreat into
self-righteousness and to lose touch with those they had been trying to
reach, for as prophetic witnesses they were immune to criticism. Support
was taken to be enlightened, and opposition was taken to be support as
well, for (in their view) opposition proved that their attacks were hitting
home. Looking back on the events of the 1980s, Darrell Becker reflected:

> It was strange that common people being most affected by
> shutdowns couldn't see the connections between those who were
> killing their jobs and those who were after the ministers. They
> should have been able to see the banks as enemies. Unions should
> have been able to see that. I guess the news kept us discredited
> better than we could explain. Then when we got manipulated
> into fighting a bishop it was way too far out for people to see the
> connection.[88]

The response of the *Pittsburgh Press* to one of the innovative and
potentially valuable ideas of the DMS made this point quite clearly. In
July 1985, DMS proposed legislating a minimum wage of $7.50 for all
workers in the industrial parks U.S. Steel wanted to build after tearing
down steel mills. DMS strategists proposed the idea because they anticipated that it would be quickly rejected by politicians and that corporate
leaders would expose the elite's belief that even $15,000 a year was
considered too much income for Pittsburgh workers.

Initial response was somewhat surprising. The *Pittsburgh Press* high-
lighted the proposal in a lead editorial, but the thrust of the editor's
message was that such an idea would get nowhere if DMS supported it.
The editor asserted that it "may be too late" for the DMS to change
tactics. He suggested instead that a "more acceptable organization," such
as the Mon Valley Unemployed Committee, should take up the cause.[89]
A year after that editorial appeared, Pittsburgh's other paper carried
another lead editorial on the DMS called "An Obituary for the DMS."
It blamed what they hoped was the group's unlamented demise on
strategies that caused them "to strangle in its own unreasonableness."[90]

88. Darrell Becker interview, July 6, 1992.
89. "The DMS Focus Shift," *Pittsburgh Press,* July 20, 1985.
90. *Pittsburgh Post-Gazette,* June 1986.

Pastor John Yedlicka, a former member of DMS who claimed he still supported the group's goals, recommended that the group change names, change tactics, and change trainers (i.e., fire Honeywell). Only if they did this, he felt, could they regain any credibility for their important message.[91] The sad fact is that without at least the credible threat that their ideas might spread more widely, the immediate power of the DMS was reduced to near zero. To use biblical terms, its role became like that of the prophet crying in the wilderness.

The cumulative result of responses by various elites was the marginalization of what remained of the DMS and the gradual disintegration of the Network. The potential of the DMS to spread as a church-based movement was contained. The threat to Pittsburgh's elites from this organization was virtually eliminated. In terms of Figure 1, we can conclude with no doubt that elites took a decidedly nonfacilitative approach to this group. By the end of 1986, though the group had not entirely disappeared (in terms of its ability to offer a challenge to elites on behalf of working people) we would have to categorize it as more demobilized than mobilized. As ministers, the members of the DMS had the advantage of beginning at point *A* (see Figure 4). As respected members of their own small communities, they could expect to have their voices heard.

Although in its early activities, such as the D-Day action to help force Mellon Bank to pay Mesta workers, the group resided awhile in conditions that resembled pluralist democracy (point *B* in Figure 4), they soon moved to the arena of confrontation, nondecisions, and repression (point *C*). In the end, their de facto demobilization left them, their supporters, and sympathetic onlookers in conditions best described as elite hegemony (point *D*).

Conversations with a variety of workers in Pittsburgh—anecdotal evidence at best—suggest that there was a certain sympathy and respect for Network/DMS activists based on their goals and the strength of their commitment, but few endorsed their tactics. Anyone who cared to look could see the message the media so frequently urged them to see: that the group had accomplished little or nothing and that they had had to suffer for their efforts. Over and over again the media reinforced the third-dimensional power of the elite with the message "Challenging us is a waste of time."

It remains to ask what the struggles of the Network/DMS have accomplished. Opponents charge that DMS never got even one job for an unemployed worker. That is true. Job gains directly creditable to

91. John Yedlicka interview, July 24, 1985.

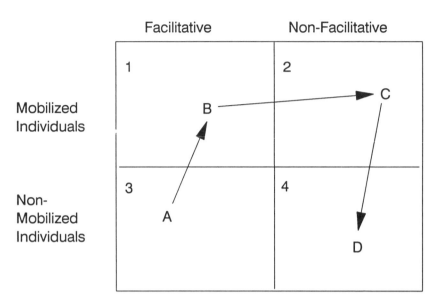

Fig. 4. DMS-Elite Interaction Matrix

DMS are nonexistent. In fact, DMS efforts cost some people their jobs. However, it is likely that successes of both the Mon Valley Unemployed Committee and the Tri-State Conference on Steel have been built, at least in part, on the noisy, confrontational work of the DMS. Some supporters of these groups have admitted as much. What all agree is that the DMS—more than any other group—succeeded in focusing attention, both locally and nationally, on the plight of the unemployed. The training of ministers and industrial workers accomplished by the DMS, as well as some of their more effectively educational media splashes, may have long-term effects that prove even more significant.

In the end, it is fair to judge DMS on its own grounds, which are theological. Pastor Long articulates the DMS position: "We are under no illusions that we can rid the world of evil. We don't seek to perfect the world. Our job is only to expose the problems and to denounce evil where we see it. We don't propose solutions. We only call people to repent."[92]

DMS succeeded in denunciation. Its voice was heard throughout the

92. Philip Long interview, June 19, 1985.

country. Those called to repent did not repent, but that is not surprising. They chose instead to try to silence the "prophetic ministry" of DMS. That is not surprising either. Persecution is the usual fate of prophets and, as this work argues, of anyone who seriously challenges the power of the economic elite.

3

GRASS-ROOTS POLITICS VS. CAPITAL
The Tri-State Conference on Steel

From 1977 through 1979, the people of Youngstown, Ohio, watched the shutdown of three major steel mills. Workers, clergy, and other community leaders joined together to form the Ecumenical Coalition for the Mahoning Valley and advocated the formation of a locally controlled Community Steel Corporation to be financed, in part, by the federal government. Broad community support was mobilized. Local, state, and federal government officials were assiduously lobbied. Federal courts were asked to intervene. The effort was lost. Ten thousand jobs were lost.[1]

But something was gained. In the words of Staughton Lynd, the Youngstown-based historian and lawyer who became a key collaborator in the formation of the Tri-State Conference on Steel, "The struggle in Pittsburgh differs from that in Youngstown precisely because Youngstown happened."[2] Tri-State grew out of Youngstown's Ecumenical Coalition. It was in place before U.S. Steel began its Pittsburgh shutdowns. Its determination to resist shutdowns was made clear in the goals adopted at its first general membership meeting on January 24, 1981:

1. For the story of Youngstown's closings, see Staughton Lynd, *The Fight Against Shutdowns: Youngstown's Steel Mill Closings* (San Pedro, Calif.: Singlejack Books, 1983), and Thomas Fuechtmann, *Steeples and Stacks: Religion and Steel Crisis in Youngstown, Ohio* (Cambridge: Cambridge University Press, 1989).
2. Lynd, *The Fight Against Shutdowns*, p. 192.

1. That U.S. Steel, J&L and other giant corporations be forced to make *binding* commitments to reinvest some of the wealth they have accumulated off Mon Valley workers over the years back into the existing mills and mill communities, and reverse the current trend of disinvestment and abandonment.

2. That no mill, plant or portion of a plant (10% or more) be shut down without direct consultation with the affected unions and communities, and all possible alternatives explored for keeping the mill open.

3. That in the event of an unpreventable shutdown, the company must pay the social and human costs of their actions, i.e., that the unemployed workers and affected communities be adequately compensated.

Our motto is simple: generations of Mon Valley steelworkers have made the big steel corporations rich over the years and they aren't just getting up and walking away![3]

From the beginning, the group challenged the corporations' legal right to disinvest and, through grass-roots community pressure and political organizing, sought to create alternative structures that would allow communities to take over plants that corporations chose not to use.

In abstract terms, this challenge is fundamental in that it asserts that some rights—in this case "community rights"—may outweigh the rights of capital to control the decision-making process. What is remarkable about the Tri-State experience is that the group's principles and goals have met surprisingly little direct opposition. Rather, problems have centered around the lack of sufficient means to meet those goals. Ironically, the group has always chosen to challenge the prerogatives of capital by raising enough capital to buy out the mills they have sought to revitalize. In doing so, they affirm the commonly accepted capitalist premise that the possession of capital—not community integrity or the creative power of labor used as rationales in their statement of goals—gives one the right to determine the decisions of investment or disinvestment, employment or unemployment, which make or break communities. However, they were not able to raise sufficient capital to buy their way into the corporate decision-making game. As we shall see, this led to a series of frustrations.

Tri-State, as its name implies, grew out of concerns that reach beyond Pittsburgh. The Tri-State Conference on the Impact of Steel was originally formed by labor, church, and community activists in steel com-

3. *Tri-State Conference on Steel Newsletter* 1, no. 1 (March 1981).

munities of Pittsburgh and Youngstown who opposed U.S. Steel's plans to build a new supermill at Conneaut, Ohio, on the shores of Lake Erie. When the mill was proposed in the late 1970s, it soon became clear to those who formed Tri-State that the new mill's opening would mean the end of steel production in older mills scattered throughout Ohio, Pennsylvania, and West Virginia. The workers argued it would be more efficient to modernize the mills in communities where workers already lived rather than building not only the new mill in Conneaut but also the community of workers it would require to operate it.

In the early 1980s, U.S. Steel decided not to undertake major modernization anywhere, and Pittsburgh members of Tri-State soon had their hands full with local concerns. Many Tri-State workers were active in the early stages of the Mon Valley Unemployed Committee and/or the Network to Save the Mon-Ohio Valley, discussed in Chapters 2 and 4. As time progressed, the strategies of the three groups became quite distinct, and the overlaps of personnel disappeared.

The early efforts of Tri-State were in two main areas: education/ organization and planning. As a leaflet later explained, "The original objectives of Tri-State were to spread the alarm throughout the Mon Valley about its soon expected abandonment by United States Steel Corporation and to develop a plan to save steel jobs and reindustrialize the region."[4]

Early work on organization and education was well conceived but had little effect. A demonstration was called for May 4, 1981, at the annual meeting of U.S. Steel stockholders. Nearly 200 demonstrators came. Ron Weisen, president of USWA Local 1397 in Homestead, rose and asked board chairman David Roderick if he planned to modernize the facilities at Homestead's mill. Roderick answered no. He also suggested that he was considering canceling previously announced plans to install a continuous caster at the Edgar Thomson Works in Braddock.

Tri-State sought to communicate its message—"The Threat Is Real From U.S. Steel!"—to combat what they saw as U.S. Steel's diversionary efforts to focus community anger on low-cost foreign steel. Tri-State pointed out that foreign steel was not to blame for what workers took to be severe but temporary layoffs in the early 1980s. Rather, it was management's decisions to invest profits from the mills into other more profitable lines of business that was leading to layoffs. From the Youngstown experience, they had learned that decisions not to modernize meant that decisions to abandon would not be long in coming. Yet the steelworkers of Pittsburgh, used to temporary downturns and conditioned

4. Tri-State Conference on Steel, "Who Is Tri-State?" 1984.

by their long dependence on U.S. Steel as the main motive force in their communities, did not respond easily to suggestions that challenged the legitimacy of a system that had lifted them from poverty to the comforts of middle-class America. And urban planners in Pittsburgh were more concerned with planning for a future built primarily on high-tech and service-sector employment in their gleaming new city of the future, than with making a serious effort to save existing steel mills.

U.S. Steel continued to promise future investment. In 1979, as part of a consent decree negotiated with the Environmental Protection Agency, U.S. Steel's Roderick had pledged: "U.S. Steel is committed to remaining in the steel business in the Monongahela Valley. . . . U.S. Steel can now act aggressively to revitalize our Pittsburgh-area operations."[5] In 1981 the corporation lobbied Congress for changes in both the Clean Air Act and federal tax law to free up the billions of dollars they said were needed to carry out modernization plans. The region's congressional representatives supported both changes. Then, in November 1981, U.S. Steel announced it would spend $6 billion—on the acquisition of Marathon Oil, not on modernizing steel mills. Mon Valley residents were outraged.

Tri-State's analysis immediately gained credibility. Its leaders began to be quoted in the media. As Ron Weisen told the Associated Press, "six billion dollars would modernize and update every U.S. Steel facility in the country."[6]

Until this point, Tri-State had been unable to make much headway in either mass education or grass-roots organization. Yet they were able to move ahead in their second area of concern, the development of strategies for taking over the plants they could already see U.S. Steel was planning to abandon.

Using the Power of Eminent Domain

As early as 1981, Tri-State began proposing the use of eminent domain to take over idled plants. Eminent domain is the power of government bodies to force the sale of private property to a public entity when that property is needed "for the common good." The state, a local govern-

5. U.S. Environmental Protection Agency, *Environmental News*, May 22, 1979.
6. Cited in Staughton Lynd, "The Genesis of the Idea of a Community Right to Industrial Property in Youngstown and Pittsburgh, 1977–1987," *Journal of American History* 74, no. 3 (December 1987).

ment body, or a newly created public authority could exercise that power to seize steel mills and get them running again.

To go into effect such a plan would require three steps: (1) Tri-State would have to demonstrate that such plant takeovers would be "in the public interest." (2) A government body willing to exercise its power of eminent domain would have to be found or created. (3) Funds would have to be raised to purchase the properties at "fair market value" and to put them into operation again.

The Public Interest

Tri-State became quite adept at making a compelling case for the right of the community to take over abandoned mills. They supported their contention that "unfair foreign competition" had not made steel production impossible by exposing the figures behind U.S. Steel's logic.

The steel industry in the United States had never been competitive. U.S. Steel was created in 1901 in a deal financed by J. P. Morgan that merged several steel, coal, iron-ore, and shipping companies in order to eliminate most competition and to manage the rest. Until the 1960s, U.S. Steel and other steel corporations managed the setting of prices and market shares to ensure profits that were higher than the average profits earned by other manufacturing industries. Yet since 1960, profits in steel surpassed other industrial profits in only one year, 1974.[7] Investment in the steel sector slowed, and in the early 1970s Japan surpassed the United States in labor productivity, a measure that largely reflects capital investment per worker. In 1982 David Roderick announced that U.S. Steel would undertake no new investments that could not return at least a 20 percent profit. In the period 1969–77, profits from the steel industry in the United States had averaged only 6.7 percent.[8] Thus, it was clear why U.S. Steel, a profit-seeking institution, was choosing to invest in business lines other than steel.

Tri-State noted, however, that the 6.7 percent rate of profit was higher than that earned by steel sectors in any other country on earth. And investment in steel was expanding in other countries while it was declining in the United States. Obviously other countries had believed that investing in steel was important enough to the health of the rest of

7. Federal Trade Commission (FTC) figures reported in Leff, "U.S. Steel Corp. and the SVA" (see Chapter 1, n.2), p. 25, exhibit 4.

8. The Roderick statement and figures from the FTC and the Office of Technology Assessment appear in "Steel Valley Authority: A Community Plan to Save Pittsburgh's Steel Industry" (Pamphlet, Tri-State Conference on Steel, 1984), p. 4.

their economies that they had found mechanisms to guarantee adequate investment in spite of the signals given in private investment markets.

The Pittsburgh region, Tri-State argued, should follow a similar logic in preserving and modernizing its steel industry in spite of the understandable but narrowly focused decisions made by steel corporations. Saving the region's steel industry would not only preserve the jobs and tax base that had supported local communities, but also provide a product that could be used to rebuild crumbling bridges, highways, locks, dams, water systems, sewer systems, and railroads throughout the Northeast. Rebuilding the region's infrastructure would initiate a cycle of expansion built on its own initial employment as well as on improvements in other sectors of the region's economy that would be aided by the improved infrastructure.

Tri-State's analysis led them to conclude that the corporate decision-making system was not serving the public interest and that new mechanisms must be created to take its place. In their words:

> Private enterprise has not been able to provide productive jobs for this area to replace the many thousands lost to deindustrialization of the steel industry. We are convinced that it never will. . . . The people of the Tri-State region, not a handful of bankers and multinational corporate leaders, must control the means of producing the jobs needed for our economic survival.[9]

The power of eminent domain was what "the people" could use to wrest control of investment from corporate officials who were unable or unwilling to serve the region's long-term needs.

Finding a Willing Government Body

Tri-State's first actual attempt to convince a government body to use eminent domain occurred in 1982. Colt Industries announced that it would close its Crucible Steel Company in Midland, Pennsylvania, about twenty miles northwest of Pittsburgh. Evidently, Cyclops Steel was interested in buying the mill, but Crucible refused to sell.

Tri-State board member Monsignor Charles Owen Rice, a priest and champion of labor struggles since the 1930s, arranged a public meeting at a Midland parish hall to discuss the possibility of Midland's borough council invoking eminent domain. Tri-State lobbied members of the

9. Ibid., pp. 9, 11.

borough council, the local union, and other community members, but the council voted not to seize the mill in order to force the sale. LTV Corporation, which had bought out Jones & Laughlin Steel (J&L), eventually bought the mill and converted it to production of stainless steel, but it reopened with only 400 of the original 5,000 jobs.

Disappointed members of Tri-State felt that their lack of success must be attributable to their status as outsiders suggesting a frighteningly new strategy. They would have more success confronting shutdowns, which would strike even closer to home.[10]

In October 1982 Nabisco announced that it would close its Pittsburgh baking plant early the next year. Tri-State joined with nearly thirty other local organizations to form the Save Nabisco Action Coalition (SNAC). A variety of pressure tactics were used to convince Nabisco to keep the plant and its 650 workers in operation. A national boycott of Nabisco brands was threatened, stockholders were lobbied, 1,500 residents pledged to withdraw their funds from Pittsburgh-based Equibank, which had close ties to Nabisco, and Pittsburgh Mayor Caliguiri publicly supported a bill introduced in the Pittsburgh City Council to have the Urban Development Authority take over the plant with the power of eminent domain.

The pressure was sufficient to convince Nabisco to keep the profitable plant open. It is uncertain whether the city council would have approved the use of eminent domain. Yet the case had been made that such a tool could be used to save jobs in Pittsburgh, and the mayor had publicly endorsed it.[11]

In February 1983, Mellon Bank, Pittsburgh National Bank, and Union National Bank foreclosed on West Homestead's Mesta Machine, the world's largest producer of steel mill equipment for the previous fifty years. Tri-State joined in the efforts to save Mesta (as did the DMS and the MVUC), suggesting the use of eminent domain. The president of the union's local, a member of the West Homestead borough council, succeeded in getting the council to pass a resolution to create the West Homestead Municipal Authority, which would have the power to take the mill. However, West Homestead Mayor John J. Dindak vetoed the council's action, and the council lacked sufficient votes to override.

Picking up on research done by the DMS, Tri-State noted that the mayor and some of the council members who supported him had

---

10. This account of Tri-State efforts in Midland is based on reports in Leff, "U.S. Steel Corp. and the SVA," and Lynd, "Genesis of the Idea."

11. See Cynthia Deitch, "Grass-Roots Community Mobilization," University of Pittsburgh, 1983; also Leff, "U.S. Steel Corp. and the SVA," and Lynd, "Genesis."

apparent links to Mellon Bank, Mesta's main creditor. Tri-State's news-letter observed that many of the area's politicians were likely to continue honoring their ties to the powerful bank rather than their ties to the community unless there was sufficient mass mobilization to force them to do otherwise.[12]

These three efforts had come on fast and furiously. They provided no clear successes for the use of eminent domain, but they gave the group experience and exposure and demonstrated that politicians in the region were at least willing to seriously consider using their power to take over plants in order to save jobs. The next effort would lead to the successful creation of the Steel Valley Authority, a result of Tri-State's efforts for the sole purpose of being able to use eminent domain to gain control over the region's fast-disappearing industrial base. It grew out of the struggle to save a blast furnace named Dorothy.

The Struggle to Save Dorothy

In March 1980 there were more than 22,500 United Steelworkers mem-bers working in eight mills in the Monongahela Valley, but five years later, there were barely 5,000 working in the mills. Many of the jobs were lost in the "temporary layoffs" of 1982. In December 1983, U.S. Steel got more honest about its plans and announced further permanent cuts as part of its "rationalization plan." The cuts included nearly 4,000 additional jobs in the Mon Valley. On the list of permanent shutdowns was the largest blast furnace in the Valley, Dorothy Six,[13] located at the Duquesne mill, about fifteen miles upriver from Pittsburgh.

The mill was abandoned in the spring of 1984. In September, Tri-State activists found out that U.S. Steel was planning to dynamite the facility by November to make way for an industrial park. As discussed above, U.S. Steel had sound financial reasons for wanting to decrease its investment in steel. In 1984 barely 30 percent of its assets were in steel. Yet Tri-State and many others in the region saw a very different and equally reasonable future for the Valley's steel industry—one that in-cluded restoring many of the region's facilities to active production. Dorothy was crucial to their plan.

The Dorothy Six blast furnace, built in 1960, was not as efficient as

12. See Leff, "U.S. Steel Corp. and the SVA," and Lynd, "Genesis." For a discussion of other aspects of the campaign to save Mesta, see Chapter 2.

13. In the patriarchal culture of U.S. Steel, furnaces were named after supervisors' wives.

the smaller, newer facilities at the Edgar Thomson mill across the river in Braddock. But it was not decaying. In late 1983 it won the U.S. Steel Ironmaster Award for turning out a record-breaking 5,000 tons of raw steel a day. If the Tri-State scenario for rebuilding the region's infrastructure were played out, this steel would be needed by Homestead's plate and structural rolling facilities and by McKeesport's National Works pipe mill. Dorothy's blast furnace was much more efficient than the antiquated open-hearth furnaces at these two mills.

Yet even without this new demand for Dorothy's steel, there existed a growing market for steel slabs precisely because making such slabs was the least profitable part of the steel industry. Since 1979 the number of blast furnaces in operation in the country had dropped by 70 percent.[14] The U.S. had become the only industrialized nation that could not meet its own steel needs. Even as U.S. Steel was urging its workers to write Congress to protest against imported steel, it was negotiating to bring in steel slabs from Korea. Anyone interested in preserving a domestic steel industry could see that there might well be an important need for Dorothy's steel.

By this time, Tri-State had gained at least some respect from the United Steelworkers. The union was also facing a crisis of declining membership. Though union leadership had refused to cooperate with efforts to preserve Youngstown's steel mills, they now joined with Tri-State to try to save Dorothy as the keystone of a strategy to reverse the rapid destruction of the steel industry. In December 1984, Steelworkers President Lynn Williams joined with borough councils, clergy groups, congressional representatives, state representatives, the mayor of Pittsburgh, the county commissioners, and labor activists in demanding that U.S. Steel postpone the planned demolition of Dorothy to allow time to conduct a study of the feasibility of saving the furnace.

The union, Allegheny County, and the City of Pittsburgh each contributed $50,000 to fund an initial feasibility study by Locker/ Arbrecht Associates. The study would evaluate the possibility of acquiring the Dorothy furnace as well as Duquesne's basic oxygen shop and the primary mill that would be used to roll hot steel ingots into semifinished slabs ready to be shipped to other mills for finishing. It was anticipated that the reopened mill might be run, at least to some extent, as a worker-owned facility.

U.S. Steel resented having their judgment questioned by production workers, clergy, lawyers, and politicians, but they grudgingly agreed to cooperate with the study. They allowed analyst Mike Locker to tour the Duquesne mill, accompanied by union and county officials.

14. David Morse, "Surrender Dorothy," *In These Times*, February 19, 1986, p. 8.

Postponing demolition and allowing the inspection tour by themselves could have been a classic "nondecision" if workers had not acted to prevent catastrophe. Blast furnaces work under conditions of intense heat. Much like a standard automotive engine, part of the furnace must be cooled with water that circulates in pipes. If the furnace had been left idle all winter with no attention, the water pipes would have burst, thus raising the cost of restarting operations prohibitively. This was one way U.S. Steel could have scuttled rescue efforts without any overtly hostile decision.

Members of USWA Local 1256 who had run the blast furnace volunteered to contribute their own labor to winterize it. They also raised the money needed for the project. Dorothy required $4,000 worth of antifreeze and other materials, and U.S. Steel required $16,000 for insurance. The project provided an interesting contrast to the stereotypical image of union workers as those who, through their own greed, had bled the companies to death. In this case, skilled workers gave their own time and money and even paid the company for the right to preserve its facilities.

The struggle to save Dorothy took on a symbolic importance far greater than that of the 500 to 600 jobs that would initially be involved if the mill were reopened. It became a symbol of hope for the entire region's industrial work force, a sort of last stand against the tide of deindustrialization. News of this Mon Valley struggle spread to workers all over the nation, and in mid-January the Rev. Jesse Jackson came to Duquesne. Addressing 500 people in a snowstorm at the plant gates, he called for "a reindustrialization . . . a fundamental change in how the steel industry is run."[15]

Results of the Locker/Arbrecht study were announced on a cold night, January 28, 1985. Six hundred people jammed the basement of Sts. Peter and Paul Church in Duquesne to hear the report. The conclusions were overwhelmingly positive. There was a market for the slabs Dorothy could produce, and production costs could compete with foreign slabs being shipped into the region. Estimated costs of restarting the furnace were $90 million. If a continuous caster were added to produce higher-quality slabs more efficiently, the cost jumped to $240 million. It was estimated that within three years the plant would net $35 million in profits.[16]

The announcement sent a surge of hope through a valley that had received little other than bad news for the last five years. The sense of determination and hope was well expressed in an opinion piece written by one of the Mon Valley's state representatives, Tom Michlovic:

15. "What Steelmaking Means to Pittsburgh," *Steelabor*, February 1985.
16. Figures cited in Leff, "U.S. Steel Corp. and the SVA," p. 23, exhibit 2.

. . . We do not intend to drift into oblivion because some corporate balance sheet dictates it.

. . . We must change some of our long-held beliefs. The first of these is an unquestioned reliance on company decisions as good ones. In times past, when a company decided to pursue a particular course, no one questioned its expertise or commitment to the common good.

Well that's how we got into this mess. As more and more of those decisions were made with a global strategy in mind, a company no longer felt compelled to be loyal to its workers, its home community, or for that matter, to its country.

The second belief that we must change is that pervasive sense of hopelessness that confronts any community which is ravaged by unemployment.

In my years as a public official, I have never realized how potent a force hope can be. That hope is everywhere apparent in overflowing meeting halls and in thousands upon thousands of homes throughout the Valley. It is a hope based on the economic reality that there is an alternative to closed factories and bankrupt communities.[17]

The positive study touched off a flurry of activities, one of the first of which was an effort by U.S. Steel to debunk the report. The company concluded that startup and three years of operation would require nearly half a billion dollars rather than the $90 million anticipated by Locker and Arbrecht. Furthermore, U.S. Steel suggested that the market described in the study did not exist, that costs would be higher than those assumed, and that the facility would lose $110 million in the first three years. U.S. Steel released its own study to this effect in mid-April.[18]

However, as State Representative Michlovic had made clear, people were no longer willing to accept the decisions of U.S. Steel. The USWA announced it would commission an in-depth study of both marketing and financing that would, if positive, be used to recruit the investors needed—public and/or private—to get the furnace cooking again. It hired both Pittsburgh-based Russell, Rea & Zappala Inc. and Lazard Freres & Company of New York to make what they would regard as the conclusive determination of Dorothy's viability.

In the meantime, members of Local 1256 worked on two fronts. First

17. Tom Michlovic, "Mon Valley's Determined to Manufacture Steel Again," *Pittsburgh Press*, April 3, 1985.
18. Ibid.

they parked a small house trailer in the corner of a shopping center parking lot across the street from the Duquesne mill's main entrance, christening it "Fort Duquesne." Two hundred laid-off steelworkers signed up for four-hour shifts to establish a round-the-clock vigil. They established a phone tree to alert some 500 steelworkers and residents who had vowed to blockade the plant gates if demolition crews attempted to enter the facility.

Asked about the vigil, U.S. Steel public affairs representative David Higie stated: "We have agreed to delay demolition . . . and we will hold to our word. If we take anything in or out of the mill, the union will be notified." Steelworker Ron Rudberg replied: "We couldn't trust U.S. Steel when we were working there. We can't trust them now. . . . If it takes six months, we'll be here. There is no tomorrow."[19]

As tensions heightened at one point during the summer, George Lakey, a pacifist who had worked with peace and environmental activists around the country, was invited to attend a regular membership meeting at the local union hall. The local's president, Mike Bilcsik, was doubtful about how well his members would receive Lakey's unannounced workshop in techniques of nonviolent civil disobedience. To his surprise, many of the members, both young and old, joined in the training session actively. Participating in role-play scenarios of how they would stop work crews from demolishing equipment, they addressed the issues they confronted—the moral and class differences between demolition workers and policy-making company executives, the efficacy of nonviolence versus violence, and how to deal with their anger—with a sincerity and sophistication that I had never observed at training sessions of several more likely groups of civil disobedients.

A week after the vigil was established in February, Tri-State got word, secondhand, that U.S. Steel was planning to remove a major part of equipment from the Dorothy furnace to use in a mill in Gary, Indiana. The phone tree was activated. Legislators were contacted, and lawyers prepared to file injunctions to halt the removal. Four hours later, when workers got information they felt they could understand and trust, they called off the alert. The part to be moved was not attached to the furnace and had a replacement cost of a mere $500,000 as opposed to the $2 million axial air-wheel they had feared U.S. Steel would try to move.[20]

There were no more major confrontations at the plant gate, but Mike Bilcsik observed: "That trailer is doing a lot more than just helping us

19. "Vigil: Workers Watch Mill from Trailer Outpost," *Pittsburgh Press*, February 14, 1985.
20. "Dorothy 6 Workers React to USS Plan," *Pittsburgh Press*, February 22, 1985.

watch the mill. It's making people aware that we are serious about this thing."[21] As such, it functioned as another part of Tri-State's efforts to change not only the decisions of U.S. Steel executives but also the thinking of Valley residents as well.

A different sort of mass action occurred at "Fort Duquesne" in mid-May. Nearly 500 workers and their supporters held a "Save Dorothy" parade and rally. The mile-long parade included marching bands, drum and bugle corps, fire engines, and ambulances, from towns throughout the Valley, and contingents of workers from different union groups, including one group from the shut-down mills of Youngstown, Ohio. Tri-State organizer Mike Stout expressed the crowd's sense of urgency when he told them, "If we don't save Duquesne, we don't save the Mon Valley."[22]

A loose coalition of Tri-State people, members of Local 1256 (Jim Benn, a key Tri-State leader, was also a member of 1256), and other concerned community members began serious consideration of various types of worker-buyout options for the mill. Workers were willing to go along with nearly any arrangement that would restore their jobs. Despite organizers' suspicions that union members would have trouble adopting ideas that were new to them and against the grain of accepted business practice, it required very little from Tri-State and other members of the ad hoc 1256 coalition[23] to convince them it would be advantageous to build as many worker-control provisions as possible into any new mill organization plan. If workers had more control, they would be able to put the needs of preserving employment above those of maximizing profits. Reemployment was the top priority, but reemployment with security through worker control was the goal. At moments like these, the hegemony of capitalist ideas built up through decades of conditioning seemed quite fragile.

The obvious obstacle to any worker-buyout plan was that there was no way workers could come up with $90 million or $240 million or $500 million to restart the furnace. Their only hope was that they could offer to help finance part of the cost of the project through an employee stock ownership plan (ESOP). Such a plan would allow the workers to take out a large loan, which the company would pay off over time while accruing very favorable tax advantages in the process. In return for obtaining the loan, the workers would receive shares of stock in the company.

21. "Vigil."

22. "Rally Cheers Future of Dorothy Six Plant," *Pittsburgh Post-Gazette*, May 19, 1985.

23. In the summer of 1985, Hathaway served as an ad hoc member of this ad hoc group, especially providing more information on aspects of worker ownership and control.

While Local 1256 was discussing such options, the USWA International staff was talking to the financial and marketing consultants they had hired, and to U.S. Steel, about what arrangements might be made at a reopened Duquesne mill. The Duquesne coalition believed it essential that they be able to influence any business plans being drawn up. Otherwise, they felt, they might be put in a take-it-or-leave-it situation when the consultants emerged with a buyer and a new business plan. When the Duquesne coalition asked USWA District 15 Representative Lefty Palm to arrange a meeting with the consultants to communicate the workers' ideas about arranging some control through an ESOP, Palm replied, "I'll get some input to them when you need it." Coalition members took this to mean "No. Just leave the driving to us." Their emotional response to this is summarized by a comment of Mike Bilcsik: "When it comes down to either the International or this project, to hell with the International."[24]

Within weeks the International had put Local 1256 into trusteeship—that is, they took control of the hall, all resources, and Mike Bilcsik was no longer president. Coalition meetings tapered off while everyone waited—and waited—for the results of the conclusive study.

The Steel Valley Authority Is Created

Underlying Tri-State's involvement in the various aspects of the struggles to save Dorothy was an ongoing effort to establish the Steel Valley Authority (SVA). Tri-State's early experiences convinced it that, rather than trying to convince a string of local government bodies to perform the extraordinary act of invoking eminent domain to save a specific facility, it would be preferable to create a regional authority charged specifically with preserving and revitalizing industries and clearly empowered to use eminent domain.

The idea of creating a distinct public authority emerged from a unique gathering of local workers and church and community leaders, as well as concerned academics and labor activists from around the nation, which Tri-State organized in October 1983. By the summer of 1984, they had published a fourteen-page booklet entitled *Steel Valley Authority: A Community Plan to Save Pittsburgh's Steel Industry*. Thus, when the effort to save Dorothy took off in the fall of that year, Tri-State was well prepared to lead a crusade for the creation of the Steel Valley Authority.

Tri-State proposed that local municipalities use Pennsylvania's Munic-

24. From meetings at Local 1256, June 9 and 16, 1985.

ipal Authorities Act of 1945 to form the Steel Valley Authority. The statute clearly allowed the creation of an authority with the right to take industrial properties through the power of eminent domain, so long as the action was "for the public good" and the authority paid "fair market value" for the property.

Tri-State initially asked municipal governments to pass resolutions in support of undertaking the initial Dorothy Six feasibility study. Twenty-five municipal governments took this nonbinding, no-cost step. Tri-State then returned to these bodies and asked them to take the more substantive step of calling for the creation of the SVA. Even before the January 28 meeting, at which the glowing results of the first study were announced, the Munhall borough council (part of the Homestead mill was in Munhall) voted to establish the SVA. They also called for other governments to join them.

After the good news of January 28, several towns decided to hold hearings on joining the effort. Tri-State reached beyond the steel-mill communities of the Monongahela Valley to include adjoining Turtle Creek Valley as well. Turtle Creek hosted a variety of hard-hit industries, including a Westinghouse factory that had jettisoned a thousand workers within the last year. Well aware that the authority's first focus would be in Duquesne, Joseph Pantalone, representing the Turtle Creek Council of Governments, said, "Maybe they will hit the Turtle Creek Valley later." Swissvale Mayor Charles Martoni, a member of Tri-State, felt that "with a little more time we'll have every community up and down the Valley involved."[25]

Public hearings held in the different towns often drew hundreds of people. The crowds expressed a fervent desire to do something to save jobs, and they saw the Tri-State proposal as the first substantial "something" to come along. Few were convinced that it would definitely work, but as McKeesport Mayor Louis Washowich and so many others said, "At least trying is better than not doing anything at all."[26] Several speakers at hearings offered to support the authority with the reservation expressed by Rankin councilmember Charles Belavic: "As long as there is no financial obligation to us, we are willing to give them all the moral support we can, but we can't go into bankruptcy for them. We are on the brink already."[27]

In June, the City of Pittsburgh voted to join in establishing the

25. "Towns Favor Tri-State Plan for Industry," *Pittsburgh Press*, January 31, 1985, p. E1.
26. "Steel Authority Held 'Only Way to Go,'" *McKeesport Daily News*, March 26, 1985, p. 1.
27. *Pittsburgh Press*, January 31, 1985.

authority. It also offered to contribute $50,000 in much-needed seed money to get things moving. By July, a draft of the intermunicipal agreement that defined the structure of the SVA was being circulated for ratification. That fall, the boroughs of Homestead, Munhall, Rankin, East Pittsburgh, Turtle Creek, Swissvale, Glassport, McKeesport, and the City of Pittsburgh petitioned the Commonwealth of Pennsylvania for incorporation of the Steel Valley Authority. In January 1986 the SVA came into being. Tri-State member, attorney, and chronicler Staughton Lynd, called it "the crowning achievement of Tri-State's more than five years of agitation."[28]

The structure of the SVA reflects both the goals of Tri-State and the economic limitations of the Mon Valley communities. The board of directors includes three members from each municipality, many of them Tri-State supporters. Frank O'Brien, a former USWA local president and state legislator and an early advocate of using eminent domain to save jobs, became the SVA's first chairperson. Tri-State activists, including steelworker Mike Stout and Chuck McCollester, chief steward for the United Electrical Workers (UE) at Westinghouse, were also named to the board. Reflecting the union background of Tri-State, the SVA charter requires the SVA to respect "to the fullest extent possible" prior labor agreements in any facility it would take over.

The SVA also began with a number of constraints. To protect the financial interests of Mon Valley governments, the charter states that:

. . . None of the municipalities can be encumbered with the financial liabilities of the Authority.

. . . The Authority shall not have the power to levy any tax, charge assessment or other servitude. . . .

. . . All property acquired and held by the Authority shall not be tax-exempt.

The only way the Authority could raise money was through grants, through the sale of bonds (which may be tax-exempt), and through fees charged for the sale or use of any properties it might acquire.

The Authority is constrained politically by the requirement that it "not exercise the power of eminent domain over any property located in any municipality . . . without the approval . . . of such municipalities" as well as all nine of the chartering municipalities.[29] Given this provision,

28. Lynd, "Genesis," p. 952.
29. Intermunicipal Agreement, draft copy, n.d. (in Hathaway's possession).

it is uncertain whether the SVA could ever have taken over the Duquesne mill, since Duquesne Mayor Charles Zabelski was strongly opposed to Tri-State efforts from the beginning. Purchasers would have had to ask the county to use its authority to take over the plant.

With the SVA's incorporation, Tri-State had accomplished two of the three objectives needed to bring its plan into effect. It had convinced a major portion of the public that using eminent domain to take over an industrial facility could well be "in the public interest." It had also found several government bodies willing to create for it the public body it needed to exercise the power of eminent domain. What remained was the third step, finding funds to purchase a facility at "fair market value" and to put it into operation.

The Failure to Fund

Tri-State did not find the funds to reopen the Dorothy Six blast furnace in Duquesne. On January 8, 1986, Lazard Freres announced the results of its long-overdue study. There would be no buyer. U.S. Steel had been right, they said. The mill would definitely require the added expense of a continuous caster. Material costs in the first study had been too optimistic. The mill would lose at least $28 per ton of steel produced. "Under the current circumstances," the report concluded, "financing for the rehabilitation of Dorothy Six will not be forthcoming from the private capital markets." The phrase "current circumstances" bears some investigation.

The Lazard Freres study did confirm that a growing market for semifinished slabs did exist. As domestic slab production declined, it was being replaced with imported steel. Beyond that point, the study differed from the early Locker/Arbrecht study on almost every point. U.S. Steel had refused to cooperate with Mike Locker, who conducted the first study.

In lieu of information, Locker chose to make assumptions that turned out to be wrong. Most important, he made the Econ-101 assumption that U.S. Steel would respond primarily to prices in the relevant steel markets. He ignored the more likely possibility that U.S. Steel would use its vast market power to control prices and production levels in those markets rather than respond to them.

That first simple assumption led to a series of other incorrect assumptions. If apparent prices and markets were what mattered, U.S. Steel might be willing to enter into a cooperative relationship with the Duquesne mill that would involve selling goods and services from U.S.

Steel's underutilized ore mines, ore ships and trains, coke ovens, and so on, to the Duquesne mill in return for slabs that could be finished profitably at U.S. Steel's Homestead mill. Other slabs would be sold to other consumers in the area.

What the later study soon revealed, however, was that U.S. Steel would not only refuse to cooperate with the reopened mill, but also, said Locker, "given their overall strategy, . . . they told us in no uncertain terms that if the facility went they would throw everything they had at it to compete with it." According to Tri-State organizer Jim Benn, U.S. Steel had targeted potential customers—mostly much smaller steel companies—for harassment or death through raising prices for U.S. Steel–controlled inputs and lowering prices on competing products. Furthermore, Benn charged, if Dorothy opened with a new caster, U.S. Steel would install a caster at the Edgar Thomson mill to compete head-to-head.[30] What the marketing study conducted for Lazard Freres by Rosa Torres-Tumazos showed was that the market for slabs that Dorothy would face would be demanding enough to require a caster capable of producing a wide variety of slab sizes to serve a variety of shifting customer needs. This, along with the higher prices for supplies and transportation, doomed the project.

If the private-capital market was not interested in getting involved in a market U.S. Steel had chosen to abandon, neither was the federal government. Though many in the Mon Valley had asserted the federal government's responsibility to preserve the nation's basic steel capacity, few had been foolish enough to suggest that the Reagan administration was likely to provide any aid. This did not prevent the press from noting the oft-repeated story of how the federal government had modernized most of the region's steel-making facilities during World War II and then sold the improved facilities to the steel companies for 10 percent of the cost.[31]

Lessons from Dorothy

Responses to the study were varied. Some of the local media expressed relief that, now that the anachronistic struggle to save Dorothy was out of the way, the region could get on with its task of building a high-tech

30. Mike Locker quoted in Morse, "Surrender Dorothy," p. 9; Jim Benn interview, July 24, 1985.

31. Even the *New York Times*, January 9, 1986, p. A12, carried this history in its story on the final study results.

future. One paper recognized that the movement had lifted the pall of gloom and apathy that had hung over the Valley for too long and that it had spurred public officials into "a more creative and active role." They were urged to continue in that vein by working with both U.S. Steel and the United Steelworkers to ensure that some modernization would take place in the Valley. Lefty Palm of the Steelworkers asserted the union would insist that U.S. Steel install a caster at the Edgar Thomson Works, a demand the union won as part of the settlement of its long strike begun later that year.[32]

The struggle to save Dorothy galvanized the community and in the process proved a number of important points. It proved that communities could and would challenge corporate decisions. One U.S. Steel executive said, "No longer are people willing to say, 'O.K. U.S. Steel, that's the right decision. Let's go with what you want to do. People are questioning."[33] It proved that, as part of the challenging process, workers could commission feasibility studies and delay plant demolitions, that communities could find both the will and the political structures to allow them to use eminent domain to take over industrial properties, and that a well-mobilized coalition of labor, church, academic, and political figures could make their voices heard. The SVA had been created, and it would continue to exist. Tri-State vowed that its efforts to revitalize industrial employment opportunities would not stop.

On the less optimistic side, the failure at Dorothy also proved that, regardless of the widespread support Tri-State had built through a remarkably successful and complex organizing campaign, without control of massive amounts of capital—either public or private—little could be done. Decisions made in U.S. Steel's boardroom based on management's preferred investment policy, not on market necessity, would not be overruled by community will.

Tri-State After Dorothy

While proceeding with the formation of the Steel Valley Authority and waiting for the final word on Dorothy, Tri-State began consulting with members of the United Electrical Workers who were trying to prevent the elimination of 2,000 jobs producing railroad equipment. American Standard had announced it would close its two Pittsburgh-area plants, Union Switch & Signal and Westinghouse Air Brake Company

32. Morse, "Surrender Dorothy."
33. Cited in Leff, "U.S. Steel Corp. and the SVA," p. B3.

(WABCO). WABCO would reopen with nonunion labor in a new plant in South Carolina.

With the Dorothy Six project out of the way only days after the SVA came into existence, the SVA filed an injunction to stop American Standard from removing equipment or otherwise dismantling the plants. The SVA argued that the plants appeared profitable and that it would like to take them over to preserve local jobs.

In February, members of the United Electrical Workers local sponsored a public meeting at which the president of a UE local in New Bedford, Massachusetts, described the way his community had used the threat of invoking eminent domain to force Gulf & Western to sell rather than close its Morse Tools facility there. Workers hoped the same would happen for them.

That summer, Judge Baron McCune called the SVA's bluff. While acknowledging the Authority's right to use eminent domain to seize the properties for the public good, he denied the SVA's efforts to further delay the plants' closings. His reason: the SVA had neither buyers nor money.

Tri-State's newsletter called the court decision a partial victory.[34] They also began to work on their fundamental problem, lack of capital. In 1987 they succeeded in getting the state to create the Pennsylvania Industrial Development Finance Corporation, which was charged with providing capital to local public authorities—such as the SVA—that had been unable to attract sufficient private capital to finance industrial ventures in "blighted areas."

The corporation was funded by the state, but Tri-State hoped it would also attract investment capital from pension funds and socially responsible investment groups. By the summer of 1988, its funding level was still inadequate as a sole source of support for the types of massive industrial projects Tri-State had thus far pursued. The value of its $10 million initial capitalization was further limited by the legal prohibition on investing more than 20 percent of its resources through any one authority.

While pursuing funding assistance from the state, Tri-State was also busy finding another place to spend the funds. In February 1988, Allegheny County released a study that would "guide public investment in support of private efforts to retain those portions of the local steel industry that can be competitive in the foreseeable future." The study confirmed once again what had been discovered in the Dorothy studies—

34. "Some Good News in Court," NewsBulletin, Tri-State Conference on Steel, July 23, 1986.

that a large and growing market did exist for semifinished slabs. After surveying four potential local plants, the study concluded:

> The only facility which represents a realistic, potentially viable, stand-alone business opportunity is the LTV South Works Electric Furnace steelmaking shop. This facility, with the installation of a new continuous slab caster, appears to have the possibility of becoming a viable supplier of semi-finished steel slabs.

While the study was pessimistic about restoring any other steel facilities in the area, it was optimistic about the likely profitability of the relatively modern electric furnaces at the South Works. It estimated that with an investment of $220 million for installation of a caster and modernization, the mill would be able to produce 1.6 million tons a year while employing 410 people in secure jobs.[35]

Tri-State proposed an innovative financing plan that offered the potential to meet two goals. It hoped to attract sufficient capital to make a go of the operation. The plan would also provide both workers and the community with enough control to make stable employment a major criterion of the new firm. The plan was predicated on the SVA purchasing the facility and leasing it to a new company that would agree to certain provisions, such as advanced notice of major layoffs. Ideally, the new company would be owned by a combination of private investors, local investors who would control a block of stock reserved for them, and the company's workers, probably through an ESOP.

After years of working on the project and spending more than half a million dollars, Tri-State and the SVA had to give up on the plan. The funds, contributed largely by a regional development program backed by the Public Utilities Commission but also contributed by Allegheny County and the United Steelworkers, had allowed the hiring of an experienced steel executive and the development of an impressive business plan. This had led to support from a three-part consortium including a group of high-powered corporate investors from the United States, a private Brazilian steel group known as EMESA, and the German industrial conglomerate MAN, which specialized in steel technology.

In July 1991 the deal fell through. A variety of factors were responsible, including a tightening of industrial credit after the savings and loan disaster, a decline in steel prices in 1991, the opening of investment opportunities in eastern Germany, and, probably most important, LTV's

35. Department of Planning, County of Allegheny, *Steel Retention Study—Executive Summary*, February 1988.

refusal to sell its property for less than $35 million despite market appraisals of $8 million. The SVA's Bob Anderson said he believed that LTV really did not want to encourage any more competition in the steel industry by allowing the facility to restart. He also observed that the huge investments coupled with great uncertainty meant that only strong transnational corporations could now make major investments in steel.[36] In the fall of 1991, LTV began demolition of the South Works plant, selling the mill for scrap.

The plan for what would have been South Side Steel sought to involve private investors, workers, and community groups in ownership of the mill in a way that directly addressed the need to make capital accountable to communities. However, when one remembers the 30,000 steel jobs lost in the Mon Valley since 1979,[37] the conclusion of Allegheny County's study that there is little hope of reviving other steel jobs—and the cost of at least $750,000 of public and private capital for each of the jobs saved—regret for the project's demise is somewhat tempered.

Tri-State reached out to involve itself on other fronts as well. It succeeded in inserting itself into plans being made to redevelop the old Homestead Works. A machine shop may be reopened. A small plot of land was sold to a credit union. Tri-State said its main concern was pressing for development geared at providing stable employment at good wages. Redevelopment of the Homestead site would probably take at least ten years due to low demand and the problem of toxic-waste cleanup.[38]

Building on this work done in Homestead, Tri-State and the SVA went on to other municipalities engaged in trying to redevelop abandoned industrial properties. In what may be one of their more significant political legacies, they helped create community task forces with heavy labor representation to try to insert concerns about stable employment at decent wages into this early planning process. Only time will tell how successful these efforts at establishing community input into economic decision-making will be.

Tri-State also branched out further into the tri-state region. It has a group in Wheeling, West Virginia, and longtime Tri-State organizer Jim

36. Bob Anderson, interview at Steel Valley Authority, Homestead, March 16, 1992.
37. Leff, "U.S. Steel Corp. and the SVA," pp. 7–8, reports 28,000 jobs lost in the Valley between 1979 and 1985; Hoerr, *And the Wolf Finally Came*, p. 11, reports 31,000 lost between 1981 and 1987. Mellon Bank, reporting on the five-county Pittsburgh region, cites 60,000 primary metal jobs and an additional 50,000 manufacturing jobs lost between 1979 and 1985.
38. "End Near for First 2 Mon Blast Furnaces," *Pittsburgh Post-Gazette*, July 22, 1988, p. 4.

Benn moved to Cleveland to establish a full-time presence working with steel and other industries in that area. Organizer Jay Weinberg reached into the future by exploring the possibility of making Pittsburgh a center for producing high-speed rail transport equipment using new magnetic-levitation technology. Mag-lev production would be a perfect blend of Pittsburgh's high-tech and industrial sectors. Weinberg hoped it could lead to a modest revival of industrial employment.

In 1988, commenting on the evolution of Tri-State, Jay Weinberg noted that it had changed from an organization responding to a series of crises to one able to pursue a more long-term plan of action. He felt they had become less naive, less dependent on outside sources for information and understanding. They had acquired more money and more expertise. He recalled, "It's always been a matter of discussion whether Tri-State should be a mass movement or a think tank." That discussion was eventually resolved in a de facto way in favor of the think-tank model.

The pressure from thousands of steelworkers to help save or restore jobs faded, as all had to find a way to adapt to the disappearance of steel as an accomplished fact. Tri-State settled in for long-term planning that might benefit workers in general but would neither save nor create any specific jobs in the near future. Many of the hopes that drove Tri-State in the early 1980s had become obsolete by the end of the decade.

Weinberg noted that they were in fact surprised by the large turnout at public meetings organized about the South Works project. Most of those attending had become involved with Tri-State when it had helped organize protests to ensure that former steelworkers would not lose their pensions when that corporation filed for bankruptcy. That effort had drawn 400 to a Pittsburgh City Council hearing and about 3,000 to a march on headquarters in Cleveland. The fact that South Side had been run by LTV rather than Tri-State's deliberate efforts explained the major turnout at initial South Side meetings. People wanted a forum to voice their specific concerns, and they responded in large numbers when Tri-State organized one for them.

In the days of the save-Dorothy struggle, meetings had grappled with the question of why most residents were watching during the march through Duquesne rather than marching. In one meeting, organizers split over whether to devote time and resources to a plan to survey Duquesne residents. Jim Benn argued that it was a necessary first step toward organizing the people to push Mayor Zabelski and others into supporting the efforts to join the SVA and save the mill. Mike Stout noted that they had strong support "at the ivory-tower level" and were weak at the base, but that "only the base will be at the plant gate if we need them." Weinberg argued that the survey would only provide the press with more data to use against them. The survey was never done, and grass-roots support remained quite sporadic, if it was present at all.[39]

Support at what Stout had called "the ivory-tower level"—academics, politicians, Catholic church leaders—remained strong and grew. In the spring of 1988, Tri-State, the USWA, and Carnegie Mellon University sponsored a debate between Presidential candidates Michael Dukakis and Jesse Jackson. Before the debate, Tri-State briefed the staffs of both candidates on local economic conditions and their plan for regional industrial redevelopment. During the debate, both Jackson and Dukakis endorsed a federal commitment to providing capital for industrial redevelopment and to making investments in rebuilding the nation's crumbling infrastructure a major priority. Both Tri-State's Jay Weinberg and the USWA's Lefty Palm attended the 1988 Democratic Convention as Dukakis supporters. At that time, confident that their man would win in November, they planned to try to hold him to his word. A supportive federal government could make a major difference in the possibilities of realizing some of Tri-State's dreams.

By the late 1980s, Tri-State had moved into new, spacious quarters in what had been a Catholic school. Their funding was stable at around $130,000 a year, coming from a variety of churches and foundations. Tri-State's offspring, the Steel Valley Authority, was well established, with a staff of three plus a solicitor and an operating budget of $200,000. It stood ready for its first major industrial takeover. Clearly focused on ensuring at least some degree of community control in whatever projects it undertook, the SVA was determined to remain distinct from the Regional Industrial Development Corporation (RIDC) and other quasi-public planning agencies (see Chapter 5).

Yet by the early 1990s, Tri-State's sense of purpose and its funding had both faded. Its two main organizers—Mike Stout and Jay Weinberg—left. Stout, using knowledge and contacts he had developed at Tri-State, went on to start a small printing firm, Steel Valley Printers, which employed primarily former steelworkers. When funding ran dry at Tri-State, Weinberg moved over to work at the SVA. The SVA continued to expand its influence, and in the early 1990s, as successor to Tri-State, went on to win the greatest victory of this chapter.

Success with City Pride: Jobs and a Voice for Workers

The story of City Pride Bakery shows both the limits and the potential of what the Steel Valley Authority could do to help workers have a voice

39. Hathaway's notes from the Duquesne coalition meeting, June 16, 1985.

in the economic destinies of their communities. Originally set up to help retain industrial production in the steel valley, the SVA gradually took on a variety of roles. Most major industries that were going to close had already done so. Redevelopment of the Valley was probably still years in the future. The SVA became a major resource for small municipalities that could not afford to hire their own planners. The SVA did studies and filed applications on a number of projects. It encouraged communities to be sure that future developments met community needs.

In March 1989, Pittsburgh's major source of bread, the Braun Bakery, announced it would close down. Some 250 jobs would be eliminated. After nearly a hundred years of baking, Braun had been taken over by Continental Baking Company, which was then gobbled up by Ralston-Purina. Ralston decided to "consolidate" operations by moving production to Philadelphia. Pittsburgh would be supplied by Continental Bakeries in Philadelphia, Akron, or Columbus.

The SVA coordinated a coalition to fight the closing. Working closely with the Bakery Workers Local 12 and with neighborhood organizations that together had used various tactics to block shutdowns of Nabisco and Clark Candy plants, the group started by going to the streets. They collected tens of thousands of signatures on petitions to Braun management and to local government to keep the bakery open. The city offered financial incentives, but management declined. The SVA filed an eminent-domain type of injunction to block the destruction of the Braun facility or the dismantling of equipment, but when close inspection revealed how decrepit the facilities and how obsolete the equipment were, this effort was dropped. From that point on, the SVA served as entrepreneur to start a new company, owned largely by workers through an Employee Stock Ownership Plan (ESOP), which would produce bread and provide jobs in a new building and with new equipment. Most ESOPs result from takeovers of existing firms. Since Braun was now gone, this would be the largest ESOP start-up in the country. It would be called the City Pride Bakery.

Workers again collected signatures from thousands, this time on pledges to buy City Pride bread as soon as the business could be opened. The group used this support to bolster a request for development funds of $90,000 drawn from state, county, and city governments. Heavy snows in the winter of 1989, which blocked the streams of trucks now bringing bread long distances to Pittsburgh, led to real shortages in the stores. This supported both the sense of urgency and the likelihood of success for a new bakery. In February 1990, Giant Eagle, the largest supermarket chain in the Pittsburgh area, signed a letter of intent to buy bread from City Pride. This letter would be worth at least $12 million of sales in the first year. Mayor Sophie Masloff of Pittsburgh, an acquaintance of the family that had started Giant Eagle as well as its current CEO, made several phone calls that helped move the deal ahead. With this letter of intent, the SVA was able to round up the $8 million needed to get the project off the ground. Mayor Masloff, local congressional representatives, and other politicians lobbied Mellon Bank to support the project. Mellon, along with Pittsburgh National, Integra, and Equibank, provided $2.8 million in loans. Some $2.1 million in equity capital was provided by venture-capital firms. State and local governments provided another $1.8 million in loans and grants. Socially motivated backers, including the national Co-op Bank Development Corporation, the national Episcopal church, three religious orders, and the Industrial Co-op Bank Revolving Loan Fund, provided another $600,000. And three neighborhood organizations invested $600,000 from funds they had obtained from a foundation and from the federal Department of Health and Human Services (HHS).

The list of financial backers tells us a number of things. It speaks to the ability of the SVA to muster support from a wide variety of backers. To do this it used a variety of means of persuasion, including putting together an enticing business plan, making moral appeals to church-based organizations, and drawing on a broad base of political resources. This meant using local Republican politicians to approach HHS in Washington; using union networks to communicate to state and local politicians; and using people like Mayor Masloff and other influential politicians to pressure private actors, such as Mellon Bank and Giant Eagle, to cooperate with what might otherwise look to be a proposal from the great unwashed.

The bakery began deliveries of fresh bread to area stores in mid-September 1992. The 150 initial workers include approximately sixty former Braun employees. Other workers are drawn primarily from a population of long-term unemployed, many of whom were receiving welfare. Extra funds were spent for training these new workers. This aspect of the project—getting able-bodied people off welfare rolls—may explain some of the support the project received, especially from Republicans, as welfare reform became a hot political item nationwide.

This story makes it clear that in different cases different actors are the relevant elites, able to make effective decisions. There are also different levels of elites. In this case, the SVA worked with politicians who had had little influence in reshaping decisions about employment in steel. The SVA effectively used its elite allies as emissaries to other elites. Its elite allies were presumably motivated by the desire to win favor with local voting constituencies and were willing to subvert the business plans of corporate actors who had largely withdrawn from the Pittsburgh region. This begins to look suspiciously like grass-roots democracy at work.

Another factor that grows out of the list of funders is the ownership structure of the new enterprise. Majority ownership initially resides with the venture-capital group. The four lending banks also exercise a degree of supervision based on their substantial loans. Neighborhood groups have nearly 20 percent ownership of equity, and a seat on the board of directors. Workers initially have 10 percent ownership, which will grow to 30 percent by the end of the fourth year. Workers are represented by their union and have votes on the board of directors. Optimistic plans call for the steady growth of the bakery and its work force, with workers eventually buying out the venture capitalists.

This tripartite ownership and control plan proposed in an unsuccessful effort to buy out steel mills in Youngstown, and later as the basis for Tri-State's South Side Steel plan, has become reality at City Pride. Private capital is necessary because private interests control most available capital in the United States. Giving ownership and control to workers and the community should solve some of the problems that have led to plant shutdowns around the nation. Both workers and community groups will be sufficiently interested in financial success to be concerned with economic efficiency. They will also be deeply concerned with maintaining employment, good incomes, and good working conditions in ways that anonymously owned, profit-maximizing corporations are not. This is likely to have positive effects on their investment patterns.

Over time, it is possible that community groups will want to sell out their shares in order to use their resources in other projects. This would be regrettable because ownership by these groups works to ensure that the bakery remains accountable to community concerns. Worker interests and community interests are not necessarily the same. Workers will be concerned about jobs and income levels, but although communities share those concerns, they are also concerned about pollution, safety, noise, and long-term economic stability. On a board of directors, a community group might express these concerns with a greater intensity than workers. Community directors might also be able to help resolve what economists have called the extinction problem, which many worker-owned firms face eventually. Such firms are often threatened with extinction or loss of worker control when a large group of employees reaches retirement age and wants to cash out on the value of stocks they have accumulated through years of working. They do this most commonly by selling their shares to private investors. A bloc of community-owned shares could help maintain an interest in the firm's survival as a locally controlled and accountable enterprise long after large numbers of individual workers have withdrawn from it. It may also make it easier for new generations of workers to become part-owners of the firm.[40]

The initial structure of City Pride is distinctive in a number of additional ways. Of the initial 150 employees, approximately half are former Braun workers. Others hired are primarily long-term unemployed residents of the neighborhoods surrounding the bakery, many of them drawn from welfare rolls. Initial funding for the bakery includes significant amounts to be spent on job training. Even though workers are actually working now, they will continue to have on-site educational opportunities. All will get training in the skills necessary to be successful worker-owners. Those without high school diplomas will get on-site classes leading to high school equivalency exams. There is also on-site child care for workers with young children. Initial wages average about $10 an hour—somewhat below union scale—but plans call for full union wages after the first three years. Much of the enthusiasm of local politicians was generated because of these provisions designed to help employ the long-term unemployed.

The name, City Pride, is indicative of something important. It not only expresses the broad-based support that went into putting the bakery together, but also speaks to a bit of community triumph over the cold calculations of a huge corporation. Ralston-Purina's decision to maximize its profits through consolidation had a certain internal logic to it. It also arrogantly ignored workers and their community while assuming no other corporate rival would challenge its plan to have Pittsburgh pay higher prices for stale bread. As a community, Pittsburgh was able to come together to create its own corporation and rebuff Ralston's logic.

In the 1990s, Tri-State's offspring—the Steel Valley Authority—was able to accomplish, on a very limited scale, what Tri-State had been unable to do in the 1980s—reverse a plant shutdown and create a new basis for worker control of their jobs and their communities.

Conclusions

Goals

Evaluation of Tri-State's experience is best begun by looking back at the group's original goals. If one condenses the three goals quoted at the beginning of this chapter they become:

40. For a discussion of the importance of community participation as a counter to the extinction problem, see, for example, Christopher Gunn, *Workers' Self-Management in the United States* (Ithaca, N.Y.: Cornell University Press, 1986); or Jaroslav Vanek, *The Labor-Managed Economy* (Ithaca, N.Y.: Cornell University Press, 1977).

1. Force U.S. Steel and Jones & Laughlin Steel to reinvest rather than disinvest
2. Force advance notification of plant shutdowns
3. Force corporations to pay the social costs of any unpreventable shutdowns

Furthermore, these goals were to be realized from the acknowledgment that the labor of generations of steelworkers had created community rights to industrial properties that could outweigh the rights of private ownership.

Of the three goals, one was to a limited extent accomplished through federal legislation—the provision to require advance notice of plant closings. In the summer of 1988, in the context of the Presidential election, Congress passed legislation requiring sixty days advance notification before most shutdowns. The multifaceted protests of Pittsburgh groups, including Tri-State, helped spur this action. This legislation was firmly resisted by management throughout the United States as an infringement on their right to manage their businesses without interference from workers or government. The rhetorical context of national elections meant that the Reagan administration withdrew its veto threat after it had sufficiently weakened the bill. Supporters of the bill hoped it would allow workers in some communities time to organize to prevent a shutdown, or at least time to plan a move to new employment. Yet this legislation did nothing to prevent firms from closing down plants when it suited their internally calculated corporate interests. In most cases it will only soften that process marginally, and as such it is an important but very limited gain. The SVA's involvement with firms closing in the Pittsburgh region since the bill's passage has shown that many corporations are ignoring its provisions and that, even when they comply, sixty days is insufficient time for workers to organize alternatives to plant closure. It barely gives them time to scramble for new jobs.

Tri-State's other goals required corporate commitments to reinvest capital in the mill communities. Attempting to change society's definition of corporate responsibility to such a dramatic extent is a major challenge to the elite decision-making process. So is asserting that the labor of workers creates rights that can compete with those of property owners to control industrial property. These were fundamental challenges. Our analysis would predict that such fundamental challenges would be resisted.

The resistance that confronted Tri-State was indirect but very powerful. After Tri-State formulated its original goals, its engagement with the practicalities of attempting to change the established system of power in Pittsburgh convinced it to alter its approach. Rather than fail completely at changing the system, it decided to try to accomplish at least something. Abandoning the part of their goals that overtly sought to change the community's definition of corporate responsibility allowed Tri-State to become more fully involved in the process of politics—the art of the possible, as it has sometimes been called. They discovered new doors opening and abandoned the struggle for what appeared futile. Tri-State's hopes for a potentially more favorable Washington administration were dashed with the defeat of Dukakis. It is unlikely that the new avenues opened by creation of the SVA will serve the community of former steelworkers from which Tri-State's organizers emerged. Yet they may establish a basis so that the efforts of other workers can meet with success.

Elite Response

The response of Pittsburgh's elites to Tri-State was somewhat mixed. In terms of the major challenges to corporate responsibility, the response of Pittsburgh's corporate elite was to ignore them. Given the inability of Tri-State to use the power of eminent domain, the decisions of the elites to ignore these challenges were sufficient to defeat those challenges. Their nondecisions were a reflection of what we have called the second dimension of their power.

But this way of thinking about power is not without controversy. One might object that Tri-State's failure to reopen U.S. Steel's Dorothy Six or South Side's electric furnaces was not so much an expression of elite resistance as it was the expression of economic reality. For good reasons, no one wanted to invest hundreds of millions of dollars in either of these plans. Given the economic conditions, their potential for success was questionable at best. This analysis suggests that the will of the elites had nothing to do with what, in the end, proved to be hard but realistic economic decisions.

Yet economic conditions are not merely given; they are created over time. In this case, they were created by elite investment decisions, some of which had no regard for the economic health of the Pittsburgh region. By the 1980s it may have been too late to intervene in this process. The South Side furnaces looked more promising than Dorothy did, but in each case the new venture would have had to face huge and hostile corporations that were willing and able to use their market power to prevent the emergence of unwanted competition. If workers had gained input into investment decisions in the 1950s and 1960s, the 1980s might have been different. But in the 1950s and 1960s the USWA was trading a willingness to concede management's right to manage in exchange for a policy of steady wage increases. The ability of corporate elites to prevent workers from reopening Dorothy or South Side was an expression of decades of corporate control. That control was reconfirmed when both U.S. Steel and LTV managed to block the emergence of new rival steel producers—in this case worker-owned firms—when their economic plans called for reducing the nation's overall capacity to produce steel.

Local politicians did respond to Tri-State by moving to help delay the demolition of Dorothy, by helping create and fund the Steel Valley Authority, by joining in the call for national plant-closing legislation, by helping establish the City Pride Bakery, and by offering various types of rhetorical support. Politically it would have been difficult to say no to Tri-State's requests for these actions. In addition to responding to the concerns of corporate actors, politicians do occasionally have to face voters. Because supporting Tri-State in these important but limited ways posed little or no threat to the region's economic elite, they also posed little or no risk to the politicians. This calculation of costs and benefits to politicians does not mean that some of those politicians did not sincerely support the goals of Tri-State. Some of them clearly did. Yet in terms of major decisions, these supportive politicians cannot be considered part of Pittsburgh's elite. Their rhetorical, legal, and limited financial support was relatively impotent in terms of actually affecting the overall direction of the region's future.

The City Pride Bakery story allows us to begin to draw certain lessons about the potential for democratic influence on matters of economic change. If we look only at City Pride, we can draw rosy conclusions about the functioning of pluralist democracy interacting with the free-enterprise system. Local workers sensing injustice appealed to the SVA and other public agencies for help in resisting the heartless actions of a transnational corporation. Local politicians responded to their constituents by supporting a plan that made good economic sense. Success followed.

Yet when we compare this with the cases of Dorothy and South Side, we see there is much more room to intervene when the amount of capital involved is considerably smaller. The steel projects called for nearly half a million dollars to be invested for each job created, while the bakery project promised to provide ten times as many jobs for the same capital commitment. Risks were smaller and success was more likely. Mellon Bank could be persuaded to invest when the amount required of it was a mere $700,000, a trivial amount compared with the loans it had made to foreign steel companies.

We can conclude that City Pride was a better investment, and it probably was. We can also conclude that there is more room for democracy to be involved when the capital-labor ratio is small. If we look at which decisions have more impact on the shape of a community like Pittsburgh, we may be less comforted in reserving democratic influence only for decisions involving relatively small sums of money. When local coalitions like that which created City Pride are able to influence decisions that shape economic possibilities for hundreds of thousands, not just for 200, we will know that something significant has changed. Until then, the small-scale democracy evidenced by the City Pride story remains just that—small-scale—in a time of massive transformation.

The story of Tri-State shows us that the elites in control of U.S. Steel, LTV, Mellon Bank, and so on, managed to transform the Monongahela Valley. The apparent solidity of their power caused Tri-State to reduce the scale of its goals—from asserting the rights of labor to have a major voice in any economic restructuring of their valley, to more-limited but politically achievable goals. Elites successfully blocked the reopening of steel mills, but they were willing to concede the creation of the SVA and City Pride.

Mobilization

Steelworkers, intellectuals, and church people mobilized in the early 1980s to form the Tri-State Conference on Steel in order to resist the disinvestment in steel that subsequently took place. The height of their mobilization occurred during their efforts to save Duquesne's Dorothy Six blast furnace. More than 1,000 workers, their local governments, and other community members were all mobilized in a common effort to reverse a decision by U.S. Steel. Several of these workers claimed to be willing to risk jail, injury, or even death in the process. After the failure of this effort, most of the rank-and-file supporters returned to individual efforts to address their futures. The mass base was demobilized. Steelworkers Local 1256 in Duquesne ceased to exist.

A core of leaders continued to function. In 1987, almost to their surprise, they briefly mobilized several hundred workers on issues related to LTV's South Works. Different from the campaign to save Dorothy, this effort did not have the same air of challenging a corporation's decision. Rather, it seemed they might be able to work with government agencies to buy out an abandoned corporate facility that LTV, facing bankruptcy proceedings, might have been willing to sell. The LTV mill had already been closed for some time. The South Side mobilization was one of interest and support, not challenge and confrontation.

In the late 1980s, Tri-State existed primarily as an organization of the original leaders who continued to address the problems of deindustrialization in Pittsburgh, but on a far different basis than in the early and mid-1980s. In the early 1990s, Tri-State faded to barely existing. Two of its former activists—Jay Weinberg and Bob Erickson—took jobs with the SVA, which carried on Tri-State's legacy. As Erickson put it, "There are no more massive plant closings with a need to rally workers. It is no longer Tri-State's time."[41]

Tri-State joined the SVA in supporting the City Pride effort, but Bakery Workers Local 12 did most of the mobilizing. Tri-State and the SVA labored on behalf of workers, but it no longer mobilized them.

Accomplishments

In judging Tri-State, it is essential to look at both its tangible and intangible accomplishments. In terms of preventing the shutdown of steel mills—their original goal—they were a complete failure. Aside from creating jobs for a few organizers, the only significant job-saving successes they had were in joining the Save Nabisco Action Coalition, which saved 650 jobs at the cookie and cracker plant and—ten years after their beginning—helping create 200 jobs at City Pride. Though they prevented the demolition of Dorothy Six, their efforts were too late to reopen it. It was left to rust, along with many other abandoned hulks lining the banks of the Monongahela.

Tri-State rallied communities and politicians up and down the Valley to establish the Steel Valley Authority, but until the early 1990s it did not have the funds it needed to take action. Tri-State was able to influence decisions to delay, to study, and to create commissions, but not decisions to employ, to invest, or to rebuild the Mon Valley. For steelworkers, the interesting but limited success in helping to create City Pride came far too late. In this regard, Tri-State's experience has reinforced the disempowering belief held by so many workers that it is wiser to stay at home and look out for "number one" than it is to waste time protesting the decisions of the powerful corporate elite.

On the other hand, Tri-State has helped make some further cracks in the ideological hegemony of the corporate elites. Even U.S. Steel executives admitted that local residents no longer respected their judgments.

41. Bob Erickson, telephone interview, June 15, 1992.

Though the word "socialism" could not be used overtly by supporters of the SVA, tremendous strides were made in gaining acceptance of ideas that challenge the suitability of the capitalist-dominated decision-making process.

While Tri-State sometimes joined with the DMS in railing against the immorality of corporate decisions that devastated the communities that produced much of the offending corporations' wealth, they also went a step further: They proposed creating new ownership structures. Rather than hoping for more-moral executives, they wanted to embed the interests of workers and communities within the decision-making structures of new firms like City Pride.

In creating the SVA, Tri-State gained at least the illusion of being able to force change in directions that they desired. Yet as Judge McCune ruled, their power of eminent domain was irrelevant if they did not also control vast amounts of capital. Tri-State and the SVA worked at getting state and local government to commit capital. At the Dukakis-Jackson debate they obtained at least rhetorical commitment from two would-be Presidents to the provision of federal capital. Yet Tri-State and the SVA would at best be able to compete to influence the expenditure of capital from these sources. City Pride showed that at least limited amounts of capital could be attracted. Without major transformation of the fundamental principles of our political-economic order, however, only those who control capital will have the ability to act decisively. Without capital, Tri-State was condemned to remain on the outside of the decision-making process.

Tri-State was unable to use the SVA to reopen steel mills, but if City Pride proves successful it will show that a popularly created government agency—in this case the SVA—can act as entrepreneur to create employment opportunities, to train the unemployed, to produce needed goods, and to empower workers and their communities. When creation of a worker-community-owned South Side Steel seemed possible, the attorney for Tri-State, Staughton Lynd, said it might be "the closest thing to socialism we are likely to get in the United States." New institutions with economic power will be controlled to a greater extent by labor and community representatives.

The example of a successful City Pride Bakery will be more modest than that of a reopened steel mill, but it may demonstrate a path for other efforts at reclaiming economic development from those who are guided only by narrowly defined, bottom-line considerations. Rather than relying on the unlikely moral transformation of a corporate elite, the new ownership structure of City Pride would lead the company to place a higher priority on providing stable local employment than on pursuing the abstract goal of maximizing profits by shuffling assets in a global market.[42]

By focusing on how decisions could be made differently if local concerns were put ahead of those of a global corporation, Tri-State and the SVA have encouraged people to consider new investment priorities. Proposals to rebuild the nation's infrastructure make a great deal of sense, both in terms of area employment and in terms of the region's long-term economic development. If people would begin thinking in this light, the jump to developing a new high-speed rail industry would not seem so farfetched.

Such thinking is clearly out of the capitalist mode of thought, in which production is motivated entirely by the pursuit of profits for an individual firm, not by the desire to feed, clothe, or house a community's people. Though it is still culturally unacceptable to use such words in Pittsburgh, it is fair to say that Tri-State's proposals were socialistic—in the best sense of that word—in their assertions that communities have rights that must be respected and that decisions about investment and production should be guided directly by a desire to meet people's actual needs rather than by an abstract pursuit of profits. Tri-State's ability to get people to consider new and empowering ideas was impressive.

As the result of Tri-State's efforts and a genuine ground-swell of public support, the Steel Valley Authority actually came into existence. It would be reasonable to guess that its creation would have faced more concerted opposition from Pittsburgh's corporate elites if they had feared it would really have the power to threaten their hegemony. Local political elites have shown they can coexist with the SVA and maybe even profit by it. Major banks have also shown a degree of cooperation. Yet if the SVA were to seriously threaten the interests of corporate elites, they would probably try to pull its plug.

If the SVA actually sees a successful City Pride Bakery and successfully undertakes other such projects, it will serve as a prototype for other regions as well. Early in 1992, workers attempting to save their jobs at a

42. The notion of worker ownership giving actual control is quite different from the experience of many ESOPs promoted to provide new financing, raise worker productivity, and/or prevent hostile takeovers, but not to give workers real control. For an excellent discussion of the problems and potentials of ESOPs, see Deborah G. Olson, "Union Experiences with Worker Ownership: Legal and Practical Issues Raised by ESOPs, TRASOPs, Stock Purchases, and Cooperatives," *Wisconsin Law Review* 54 (September–October 1982), pp. 729–823. For recent trends, see James Miller, "Some Workers Set Up LBO's of Their Own," *Wall Street Journal*, December 12, 1989, p. 1, and Richard Wentworth, "ESOP Gains as Anti-Takeover Defense," *Christian Science Monitor*, January 18, 1989, p. 9.

closing Stroehman's Bakery in New York City seized on news of City Pride. They attracted support from their mayor and state government and called in the SVA for help. The City Pride model's value as a prototype might well be more important than the few hundred jobs that would be created initially. Just as the Tennessee Valley Authority (TVA) inspired many European governments to undertake government-spon-sored regional development projects, so too a successful SVA could inspire other communities to take on more ambitious community-based development projects. Tom Croft, executive director of the SVA, is well aware of parallels with the TVA. He notes that the TVA was created with substantial funding from the federal government, and then writes:

> Under a responsible federal government, an SVA would have federal investment clout to effectively intervene in problems with footloose companies, corporate restructuring and hostile take-overs. Until the *i*-word [industrial policy] is addressed, however, impetus for projects like City Pride will not come from the top.[43]

Worker-Elite Interaction

In terms of worker-elite interaction (Figure 5), where we put Tri-State's experience depends on our standard for evaluation. We can judge Tri-State as seeking fundamental change or marginal improvements, or as radical or reformist. Here both evaluations are offered. The final chapter addresses the consequences of the different approaches.

We know that individual steelworkers not being listened to by either the steel corporations or their union chose to move out of cell 4 (see Figure 5), where they were not mobilized and where they confronted a hostile elite (*A*). When they mobilized to stop shutdowns and to force corporate accountability to community needs, they moved to cell 2 (*B*).

If one judges them as a mass-mobilizing organization devoted to their original goals, they remain in cell 2—the state of confrontation and non-decisions—through the summer of 1985. By January 1986, when the final study giving thumbs-down to saving the Dorothy Six blast furnace was released, most of the real base of the movement had been demobilized. Local 1256 in Duquesne had been dissolved by the USWA International, and rank-and-file workers were left to wait while financial experts and corporate executives decided what to tell top union leaders, Tri-State

---

43. Tom Croft, "The City Pride Bakery Story: A Work in Progress," draft copy, Spring 1992.

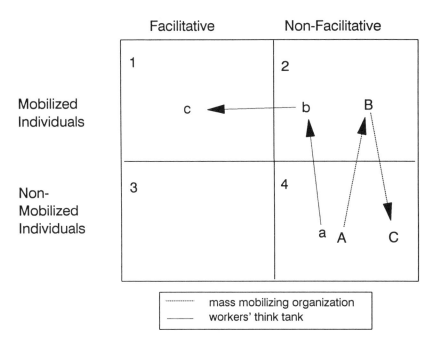

Fig. 5.   Tri-State–Elite Interaction Matrix

organizers, and eventually the workers as part of the general public. By January 1986, most rank-and-file Tri-State supporters were already back to cell 4. The negative announcement ensured that they would stay there (*C*). Whether one calls this the result of hostile elite power or merely economic reality (if we can separate the two), the lessons taught workers are the same. By this interpretation, we see Tri-State's experience largely reinforcing corporate hegemony and worker quiescence.

But one can also describe a rather different journey through the matrix of worker-elite interaction, if one does not judge Tri-State as a mass-mobilizing organization and if one judges them in terms of goals that emerged along the way. One can judge them in the terms Jay Weinberg suggested: as a think tank devoted to devising structures devoted to maintaining and/or restoring a degree of stable industrial employment in the Pittsburgh region. From this perspective, one can argue that workers who became Tri-State organizers and later SVA staff moved from cell 4 (*a*) into a period of confrontation (*b*) in which they successfully manipulated government officials at a variety of levels to obtain concessions and to move to position in the idealized cell 1 by early 1987 (*c*). In this light, one could include both the current Tri-State organization and the Steel Valley Authority as two parts of the same movement, with most resources and some personnel shifting to the SVA. The programmatic work—developing organizational frameworks and laying important ideological groundwork for struggles yet to come—continued.

Before comparing the two perspectives, it is important to emphasize some of their fundamental differences. Not only do they require different definitions of who the challengers are—a mass organization of industrial workers with some intellectual allies, or a group of intellectuals, some of whom were industrial workers—they also require a different definition of who the elite being challenged were—the corporate heads of disinvesting steel corporations, or the leaders of various government bodies. Unless and until the political elite develop both the will and the ability to challenge the corporate elite on major economic priorities, the latter focus is largely a distraction from the initial challenge. Such a distraction reinforces corporate power by hiding it.

Both these analytical approaches are important and, in their own terms, substantially justifiable. In terms of our effort to explain worker quiescence, the first description offers a portrait of our predicted pattern confirming elite hegemony and encouraging worker quiescence. Whether the innovations of Tri-State and the SVA will accomplish anything of lasting importance is yet to be seen. Even if the SVA succeeds in its goal of establishing a successful City Pride Bakery, only the future can tell whether the effects of Tri-State's successes will outweigh those of the elite who have resecured the silence of the vast majority of Mon Valley workers.

In terms of saving the Dorothy Six blast furnace, Tri-State was an unmitigated failure. Trying to revive Dorothy in 1985 may have been like beating a dead horse. However, this was not immediately obvious at the time. In hindsight it looks as if elites—in this case U.S. Steel and the financiers approached for investment capital—were right. But we must also recall that the effort to save the furnace came after years of accepting the (non)investment decisions and the vast market power of USX as parts of normal reality rather than as departures from healthy policy.

We can see now that a chain of decisions by the management of U.S. Steel led to Dorothy's death, a death that could not be postponed by last-minute tinkering. In this regard, the experience of Tri-State once again demonstrates an environment in which elite power—reflected through general acceptance of elite control over investment decisions— was sufficiently strong to convince workers that quiescence was their most rational option. In terms of reducing the future quiescence of workers, the models of worker/community ownership being implemented at City Pride, and the community task forces being created to attempt to influence future development projects, may prove to be important. Tri-State and the SVA will be a success only if they lay the foundation for organized workers—in Pittsburgh and other communities—to gain sufficient control within their own communities to allow them to redirect their economic transformations successfully.

The successes and failures of Tri-State and the SVA tell us something about the larger possibilities for workers to have a voice in influencing the economic transformation of their communities. All the mobilization Tri-State managed to achieve during the struggle to save Dorothy Six did nothing to stop the tide of destruction sweeping away steelworkers' jobs. Community mobilization allowed no entrée into a decision-making process that required that all actors be able to command hundreds of millions of dollars. Corporate executives had already sealed the Valley's fate. They were not about to allow democracy to get in the way. Besides, their theory of democracy—if they have one at all—is probably one that has little faith in common people's ability to understand complex issues.

But community mobilization guided by remarkably astute political strategy was able to force local governments to create the SVA. I believe this was possible not only because local politicians are dependent, to some extent, on keeping local voters happy, or because they may sincerely care about their communities, but also because economic elites sensed that the SVA would never command enough capital to interfere in projects of importance to them. The City Pride Bakery success shows that jobs can be saved, capital can be mobilized, new structures can be created—on a limited scale. Evidently workers and community action do have some room to work; they can use the democratic process. But so far only on a small scale. When global forces are driving change, one must ask, Is that enough?

4

FROM STREET RAGE TO RELIEF BROKER
The Mon Valley Unemployed Committee

> "We are a membership organization of unemployed
> people working together to help each other survive
> this economic crisis. We have organized to change
> government and company policies to recognize that
> everyone has a right to work and survival income
> between their jobs."
> —MVUC recruiting brochure, 1983

"There's always been a sense that you couldn't fight the system. We
began to fight it and win." So said Ray Ganczak, an active volunteer
worker at the office of the Mon Valley Unemployed Committee in
decaying McKeesport. He had been working at the J&L Southside plant
before he lost his job and nearly lost his house. He recalled seeing a
public-service announcement on television that mentioned the Mon
Valley Unemployed Committee's hotline. By putting pressure on Ganczak's bank and helping him refinance through the Veterans Administration, the committee helped save his house. They also gained his loyalty.

The Mon Valley Unemployed Committee (MVUC) is the organization
that made the most tangible gains of the three groups studied in this
book. Ray Ganczak's story is only one of a multitude that demonstrate
the gains from MVUC efforts. The committee's history is one of
remarkable innovation, persistence, and success, but also a story of co-
optation and failure. For its successes, the MVUC had to abandon most
of its original stated goals. In this light, the MVUC's success is paralleled
by the success of Pittsburgh's deindustrializing elite.

By 1988 the MVUC had established itself in the eyes of many workers,
politicians, business executives, and church leaders as a force to be
reckoned with and sometimes admired. Their well-equipped though still
humble office was a busy center coordinating bus trips to lobby both
Washington and Harrisburg and providing legal efforts on behalf of

workers seeking retraining, information on a variety of government and community services, and a hotline to help workers in crisis. The office was also the center of the recently expanded and securely funded Southwestern Pennsylvania Unemployed Council.

Beginnings

The Mon Valley Unemployed Committee traces its roots back to 1980, when a major layoff in steel led to layoffs of nearly 50 percent of the steelworkers along the Monongahela River valley stretching southeast from Pittsburgh. A handful of workers in three of U.S. Steel's mills—Homestead, Duquesne, and Irvin Works—urged their union locals to start "unemployed committees." The function of the committees was to keep workers in touch with an organization that had advocated their economic rights as workers and that would now need to advocate their rights as nonworkers.

The unemployed, or layoff, committees were inspired by a core group of activists. Some of them had served on the United Steelworkers District 15 Civil Rights Committee, which addressed issues of racial and sexual equality. All of them shared what Rob Toy of the Duquesne mill called "progressive politics." And all of them had a history of involvement with union politics and/or some college education. Out of this group of fifteen, there emerged leaders not only for the MVUC but also for the Tri-State Conference on Steel and the Network to Save the Mon-Ohio Valley.

Though their initial efforts were carried out in different union locals, this group began meeting together to talk strategy. Steel had always been an industry of ups and downs. Layoffs—though painful—were not uncommon. Most workers saw the layoffs of 1980 as just another downturn that would be followed by an upturn and a call to return to work. Some of the members of the unemployed committees began to suspect this one was different. Employment in steel had been flat or declining for several years. Modernization had not taken place. Youngstown, Ohio, had already been shut down as a steel town. To some it looked as though the end might be at hand.

During a period of layoff, workers were generally able to subsist on a combination of personal savings and unemployment compensation benefits. Unemployment benefits were available for up to twenty-six weeks. Because some believed workers would not be called back within half a year, they decided to seek an extension of the period in which laid-off workers could collect benefits. Those with a longer view also suggested that the federal Trade Readjustment Act (TRA) should apply to the steel industry. It would provide income as well as retraining for workers displaced by foreign competition.

In the summer of 1980, unemployed workers began to collect signatures on postcards demanding both extended unemployment compensation benefits and TRA benefits. Signatures were collected at plant gates, at shopping malls, and even in downtown Pittsburgh. By late September, 10,000 cards had been signed, and sixty workers went by bus to Washington to present the cards to government officials—the first of many lobbying trips.

Although the international leadership of the United Steelworkers of America was willing to rent a bus for the trip, they did not trust the group. According to Rob Toy, they suspected the activists were trying to undermine established leadership and support the candidacy of militant Ron Weisen of Homestead to take over District 15. Thus, when the group arrived in Washington they found that instead of the press conference they expected to hold they walked into a bureaucratic briefing on what programs were presently available and what programs were being considered. Unwilling to be undermined by the International's diversionary tactics, workers walked out of the briefing and arranged their own effective press conference and rally. Shortly after this trip, Congress voted to extend unemployment benefits for ten weeks.

Early in 1981, U.S. Steel called back most of the workers it had laid off the previous year, but the unemployed committees continued to meet on an informal basis. Late that year and early in 1982, U.S. Steel again laid off nearly half its area work force. It was now the beginning of the end.

The local unemployed committees joined together to meet the need. In February they opened a regional hotline that was available four nights a week. In March the group opened a food bank to serve laid-off workers from eight union locals. At one local, still-employed workers voted to deduct a small amount from each paycheck to help support the program. President Reagan heard of this and called the union local's president, Pete Eritrano, to congratulate him on their spirit of "voluntarism." Eritrano responded pointedly: "We want jobs."[1]

In May the committee called unemployed steelworkers to a march in downtown Pittsburgh. In pre-march publicity, organizers said they would demand unemployment compensation until workers were em-

---

1. Barney Ousler, "Unemployed Committees Organize to Protect Laid-Off Steelworkers," *Labor Notes*, 43, August 26, 1982.

ployed again, a freeze on all rents, and an end to utility terminations and mortgage foreclosures "until steel recovers."[2] Writing in the newsletter of one of the affected USWA locals, organizer Barney Ousler asserted: "It is the responsibility of the government and the companies to get this economy that they control back in shape."[3]

U.S. Steel responded with some publicity of its own. On the day of the march, they announced they would be calling back workers at the Edgar Thomson mill. This effort to divert and divide steelworkers got the headlines, but the fine print also mentioned that the open hearths at the Homestead mill would be closing "temporarily."[4]

In a response that clearly exceeded the expectations of march organizers, nearly 10 percent of all laid-off steelworkers in the Pittsburgh area came—2,500 of them—loud and angry in the streets. At the rally, the organizers' main goal was to unite workers around the issue of increasing the length of time the state would allow them to collect unemployment benefits from twenty-six weeks to sixty-five weeks. Yet workers insisted on voicing other concerns as well. Some had already lost their homes or cars because of inability to make their payments. Others had had their utilities shut off or were facing eviction from their apartments.

The members of the various committees who had organized the demonstration saw both a need and a potential to organize these workers into an effective force. They announced that they would merge their efforts and become the Mon Valley Unemployed Steelworkers Committee. They continued with the food bank and the hotline. They began to raise funds jointly, and in late July they managed to get both Senator John Heinz and Senator Patrick Moynihan of the Senate Finance Committee to come to the region to hear testimony about the need for extended unemployment benefits.

The union hall where the hearing was held was packed with 500 angry steelworkers eager to tell of their hardships. Outraged workers expressed their intuitive class anger, complaining both about local conditions and about the direction in which corporate and government leaders were taking the nation as a whole. One complained that programs to help the jobless were disappearing as fast as jobs. He complained particularly about the Reagan administration's move to drastically curtail Neighborhood Legal Services at a time when jobless workers needed help dealing with mortgage foreclosures, bureaucratic intransigence, and bankruptcy. Lefty Palm, director of USWA District 15, complained that the depres-

2. *Pittsburgh Press*, April 25, 1982.
3. *Local 2227 News*, May 1982.
4. *McKeesport Daily News*, May 12, 1982.

sion of the 1980s was not like the one of 1929. Now there are no rich people jumping out of buildings. He charged, "Reagan is taking care of them . . . at our expense!"[5]

It became clear from the calls to the hotline that steelworkers were not the only ones in trouble. It was also clear that there was a demand to address more than the issue of unemployment compensation benefits. In October, the activists of the Mon Valley Unemployed Steelworkers Committee decided to drop the word "Steelworkers" from its name and become the more broad-based "Mon Valley Unemployed Committee."

Paul Lodico, who was to become one of the committee's key organizers, had been an organizer for the United Electrical Workers since the 1960s. He had recently lost a job in Ohio and was in Pittsburgh preparing to co-author an oral history of an ongoing strike at Westinghouse Air Brake Company (WABCO). When he was asked to join the group in August, he decided "Why write about it when you can do it?" He recalls that at the time they had no paid staff, no office, and no funds. Over time he helped change that.

In October, workers again turned out en mass. Some 1,500 came to McKeesport for a rally. Organizers claim there would have been twice as many if they had been able to find more sponsors to pay for buses to get workers to the rally site, some twenty miles upriver from Pittsburgh. This time, workers were also joined by steel-town business and municipal leaders who feared for the economic viability of their operations because of the scope of layoffs. By then, nearly half of the area's 50,000 steelworkers had lost their jobs, and others were working reduced hours and afraid for their future. The mayor of McKeesport announced "We are with you." He made the municipal building available as a food-bank collection site and admitted that his administration was taking a "go easy" policy with overdue bills.

One worker attending the rally expressed the belief that the group's efforts would be in vain: "I don't feel this will do any good. Reagan and the other politicians won't listen. They do as they please." Others felt willing to support the group.[6] At the rally, the MVUC started a membership drive and signed up 450 new members. Unemployed members pay annual dues of one dollar; employed members pay five dollars. Within a year, membership had grown to 1,600.

That fall it became obvious to the committee that things were only going to get worse for steelworkers. They had succeeded in getting benefits extended to a full year, and they would eventually attain their

5. Frank Matthews, *Pittsburgh Post-Gazette*, August 2, 1982.
6. *Pittsburgh Press*, October 7, 1982.

goal of sixty-five weeks of full unemployment benefits. Yet for many who had already been laid off for nearly a year, that began to look like cold comfort. While efforts to extend benefit coverage continued, it became obvious that something would have to be done for people who were losing their utilities and their homes as winter came on.

To increase their leverage on public-policy-makers, organizers gladly spoke to the press at any opportunity—not only about people's problems but also about angry steelworkers who would soon be driven to fighting for what they needed to survive. And they studied—they read about the 1930s,[7] and spoke to older workers who could remember the techniques used in that decade as workers struggled with unemployment and with the creation of labor unions. "It seems a shame to have to say it, but it looks like we're going to have to fight all over again for the same social legislation that another generation battled for in the 1930s."[8]

Focusing Anger and Saving Homes

In August 1982 the MVUC announced the results of a survey conducted at their McKeesport food bank. More than half of those who held mortgages felt they would have serious trouble making payments by fall. Rob Toy, speaking for the committee, suggested that banks that refused to cooperate with unemployed steelworkers might be targeted for picketing. "It's really not a threat, but it's to make them aware that we will be monitoring them to see if they have legitimate reasons for turning people down."[9]

Members of the committee traveled to Philadelphia to talk with the Philadelphia Unemployment Project (PUP), a group that had helped organize against mortgage foreclosures. In October the MVUC began putting pressure on Vanguard Federal Savings & Loan to stop the sale of the home of Ron and Marie Richards. Ron, a former electrical worker, had been employed only three of the last fourteen months and had fallen behind in payments. When negotiations broke down, workers picketed the bank's office, asking customers to take their business somewhere besides the "Scrooge Loan Company."[10]

In November, December, and January, the committee organized pro-

7. Piven and Cloward's *Poor People's Movements* (1977) was mentioned specifically by both Bob Anderson and Paul Lodico.

8. Barney Ousler, as quoted in the *Pittsburgh Post-Gazette*, July 31, 1982.

9. United Press International (UPI) national wire, August 25, 1982.

10. *Pittsburgh Post-Gazette*, December 3, 1982.

tests of from fifty to one hundred unemployed workers at the monthly Allegheny County sheriff's sales. Protests were also staged at the Veterans Administration, the Federal Housing Administration, and several area banks and mortgage companies.

At the December sale, protestors released two "dirty dozen" lists of lending institutions and lawyers it charged were the worst offenders at seizing the homes of unemployed workers. For the benefit of attending television and newspaper cameras, they also held cardboard vultures over the heads of those bidding on properties. Organizers hoped that the media attention would put pressure on the "vultures" and help inform threatened homeowners that there are ways to delay the forced sales of their homes, many of them quite simple and effective.

Borrowing from the tactics of the 1930s "penny auctions," the committee tried to use their intimidating presence to repurchase the homes for the unemployed worker. Their low bids did not hold, however, and more than one hundred properties were sold to the highest bidder at what the *Post-Gazette* called "a small percentage of their worth."[11]

In language that perhaps shows members of the MVUC were also participating in meetings with the DMS clergy (see Chapter 3), MVUC organizer Rob Toy declared that the issue of stopping mortgage foreclosures had no legal basis but that it was a *moral* issue. He asserted: "It is evil to sell the home of a person who is long-term unemployed or who is sick. It's no fault of their own."

On the day of the December protest, the Pittsburgh City Council unanimously passed a nonbinding resolution urging all mortgageholders in the county to place a moratorium on foreclosures of unemployed workers' homes "until the economy begins to recover."[12] At the January sale, the MVUC announced to the press that their pressure had forced the removal of fifty-six properties from the day's sale list. Sheriff Eugene L. Coon then announced that he had removed another forty-two homes from the list. In a prepared statement, Coon said that the number of foreclosures in the county had doubled since 1979 and that this "crisis situation" had prompted him to survey those whose homes were on January's list to be sold. He explained: "Of those surveyed, a full 50 percent are currently unemployed and unable to find work; 35 percent are self-employed and are experiencing hardship due to the stagnant economy . . . ; 20 percent have fallen behind due to lengthy illness or injuries which prevent them from working at this time."[13] Then Coon

11. *Pittsburgh Post-Gazette*, December 7, 1982.
12. Ibid.
13. UPI Pittsburgh, January 3, 1983.

remarked: "I expect I'll be hearing from some banks. There are lawyers running around here screaming their heads off. They get a piece of the action, you know. They're on a percentage basis."[14] Attorney Bernard Markovitz, who earned top spot on the MVUC "vulture forecloser" list by acting as buyer in ninety-three cases in the previous year, responded: "I don't think Sheriff Coon has the authority to do it."[15]

That night the national evening news led off with a story on farm foreclosures in Iowa and Coon's action in Pittsburgh. Planning to run for one of the three county commissioner spots in the spring primary, Coon had evidently discussed the idea in general terms with Common Pleas Court Judge Nicholas P. Papadakos, but acted while the judge was away at a swearing-in ceremony in Erie, Pennsylvania. Two days later, on January 5, 1983, Papadakos, who was up for reelection in the spring announced a "temporary moratorium" on the sheriff's sale of any owner-occupied home in the county.[16] Of the decision he had reached with Coon, Papadakos said: "We agreed that the pressure grew to such an extent that action had to be taken."[17]

Editors of the *Pittsburgh Post-Gazette* wished that the judge and sheriff had not given in to the pressure—at least not the way they did. Their lead editorial admonished:

> . . . A moratorium on sheriff's sales could have a disturbing effect on a system that needs this admittedly harsh medicine to keep its mechanisms moving.
> In short, remove the incentive to pay debts—for any reason— and you risk undermining the system. It is harsh, it is cruel, but it is unfortunately true.

Commenting on the MVUC's use of cardboard vultures, the unapologetic editorial reminded the readers that "vultures too have their place in the scheme of things." Addressing the issues that had been voiced by many at the sheriff's sale—that moral and legal issues were in conflict— the editorial concluded:

> What is disturbing is the sight of judges and law enforcement officials using the law in what appears to be an intuitive "it feels right" way. Their job is to go by the book and leave the good

14. *Buffalo News*, January 4, 1983.
15. Ibid.
16. *Pittsburgh Press*, January 5, 1983.
17. Associated Press (AP) national wire, January 5, 1983.

works to those who bear that responsibility. It is not just a quibble; the law must work in the interests of the rich and the poor alike or else everyone is lost.[18]

The editorial did not say who would bear the responsibility for good works. Workers in the Mon Valley were not worried that the law would suddenly start favoring the poor over the rich. The editorial may have reminded some of the workers of the saying that equality under the law guarantees both rich and poor equal freedom to sleep under a bridge. The editorial's theoretical principles offered little comfort to workers on the verge of losing their homes. They were aimed, rather, at shoring up the legitimacy of a system of inequality that was under serious attack.

The moratorium on sheriff's sales provided only a temporary reprieve. Homeowners were still legally obligated to make monthly payments, though lenders were urged to be flexible about arranging new payment schedules. A nonprofit Pittsburgh group, Action-Housing Inc., raised a well-publicized but pitifully small $200,000 to assist homeowners who had taken steps to renegotiate payments. Action-Housing estimated that in the four-county Pittsburgh region 37,500 mortgage-holders, or 15 percent of all area mortgage-holders, were either delinquent by more than thirty days or on the verge of being delinquent because their unemployment benefits would soon expire.[19]

Republican Senator Arlen Specter met with 400 angry residents of the blue-collar community of White Oak and reported his fears in a letter to President Reagan: "I have a sense that we are sitting on a volcano which is about to erupt unless immediate, positive and forceful steps are taken through your leadership in cooperation with Congress."[20] Specter urged Reagan to push for a jobs program tailored to meet the needs of displaced steelworkers as well as for federal mortgage assistance for unemployed homeowners.

In March, 3,000 unemployed workers gathered in Washington to give Reagan a "pink slip," to hold a mock sheriff's sale of the White House, and to urge Congress to help them. While the largest group of workers came from Pittsburgh, others came from additional cities with chapters of the newly organized National Unemployed Network. The House did take up a mortgage-relief bill, but the White House opposed it as an unnecessary expense at a time when—in the President's eyes—the recession was ending.[21]

18. "A Questionable Reprieve," *Pittsburgh Post-Gazette*, January 7, 1983.
19. *Pittsburgh Post-Gazette*, January 20, 1983.
20. "Specter Fears Violence by Area Jobless," *Pittsburgh Press*, January 22, 1983.
21. *Pittsburgh Press*, March 11, 1983.

When President Reagan traveled to Pittsburgh the next month to address a conference on plant shutdowns and dislocated workers, more than 4,000 angry people showed up to let him know that—for them—the recession was not yet over. The MVUC had planned a two-hour rally in the park across the street from the Hilton Hotel, where Reagan was due to speak. The aroused workers were not interested in listening to speakers as much as they were in delivering an angry message to the President. They crowded around approaches to the hotel, standing sullen in the persistent soaking drizzle. Then, when it became apparent that Reagan must have made his way into the Hilton through an underground tunnel, the group rushed forward, breaking through police lines and screaming in rage. Police used dogs to force the crowds back.[22]

The President evidently got the message of their anger: "White House aides concede that the President's trip to Pittsburgh in early April was almost a total disaster. Jeers and complaints of several thousand jobless convinced officials not to send Reagan into a factory town again until employment figures improve."[23] Though it may have changed the President's travel plans, the demonstration—limited to Pittsburgh as it was—did little to change his mind about national policies.

Federal mortgage assistance did not pass,[24] but on Christmas Eve of 1983 the Commonwealth of Pennsylvania did pass such aid, becoming the only state to do so. Strong lobbying by the MVUC and groups of unemployed workers from Philadelphia and other communities around the state (at one point nearly 150 disgruntled unemployed steelworkers virtually shut the capital down) managed to turn back serious efforts by banks and mortgage companies to defeat the measure. The original funding of $5 million was supplemented by a more realistic provision of $25 million in May 1984.[25]

The state aid did not solve all the mortgage problems. In 1985 Sheriff Coon complained publicly that speculators were profiting from forced sales while those losing their homes often did not even recover enough from the sales to pay off their debts.[26] Bob Anderson, who had been actively involved in the MVUC mortgage protests, charged that the eligibility guidelines set by the state made it difficult for many in need

22. *McKeesport Daily News*, April 7, 1983; *Pittsburgh Press*, April 6, 1983.
23. *U.S. News and World Report*, April 1983.
24. Although a mortgage relief bill did narrowly pass in the House, 216–196, facing clear opposition from President Reagan, it was defeated in the Republican-controlled Senate, 55–39. *Pittsburgh Press*, June 30, 1983.
25. *National Unemployed News*, October 1984.
26. "Shuffle Sheriff's Sales?" *Pittsburgh Post-Gazette*, May 17, 1985.

to qualify. In fact, only 28 percent of those who applied were helped by the program.[27] Rather than resulting in a reexamination of program guidelines, the lack of qualified applicants led to a reduction in state funding for the program.

Anderson says Paul Lodico and Barney Ousler, key leaders in the committee, saw the state legislation as a major success and suggested moving on, but Anderson felt the need to continue the fight on the issue of mortgage problems, so he left the MVUC to start a separate Homestead Unemployed Center. He later charged that the reason the MVUC backed off from what he called "the mortgage struggle" was that funding for the MVUC was dependent on "cooling out demonstrations."[28]

In July 1984, when Anderson heard that a sixty-year-old handicapped widow had just been evicted from her home, he helped organize her neighbors to protect her possessions, which had been moved to the curbside. Two days later they moved her back into her house in defiance of the federal Department of Housing and Urban Development (HUD), which had insured her mortgage. HUD and Advance Mortgage felt they were justified in evicting her because she had not made a payment since 1981, when her husband was dying. Anderson responded to this reasoning with a leaflet whose logic reached well beyond this particular case. It read in part:

> In November of 1968 Helen Killinger borrowed $5,650 from Advance Mortgage. After 151 months of paying $134 per month, she had paid the bank, by May 1981, $20,234. *Where Is Justice For The Working People?* . . . This is why we are so poor and the rich rich. . . . The federal government gave $5–10 billion to the rich depositors of the Continental Illinois Bank in May when the bank got in trouble. . . . Where is the justice for us common people from our government? Helen should be given her home back and the bank told by HUD that they have had enough and to get off our backs.

Helen Killinger was never forced out of her home.

That was the last major drama on the mortgage front. The feelings of injustice expressed in the leaflet quoted above remained pervasive in blue-

---

27. "Renewal of Emergency Home Loans Called Likely," *Pittsburgh Press*, November 18, 1986.
28. Bob Anderson interview, Homestead, July 25, 1988.

collar Pittsburgh. The problem still continued, locally and nationwide. Claims for private mortgage insurance in 1985 had reached twelve times their 1980 level. In 1986, foreclosures seemed to level off but not decline.[29] Both Anderson's group and the MVUC continued to provide counseling to individuals with mortgage problems. Anderson also took the more aggressive approach of writing to everyone on the monthly list for sheriff's sales. In November 1986 the two groups joined with several other Pennsylvania groups to ensure the renewal of state mortgage aid.[30] According to Lodico, after the Thanksgiving fight won renewal, the mortgage program gathered enough bureaucratic momentum to sustain itself without further mobilization of outside support. After 1984, the issue moved out of the streets and became once again a problem that was dealt with primarily by isolated individuals confronting legal and financial institutions.

Working with the National Unemployed Network

If the MVUC had a slogan, it was "Jobs or Income!" Yet most of their efforts went into obtaining various types of government-supplied income, rather than addressing job-creation or job-preservation issues. Although their early statements had asserted a right to work and a right to survival income between jobs, they found it easier to appeal to government to gain the second right than to appeal to corporations to ensure the first. Realizing that winning concessions from government required that they be organized at more than a local level, members of the MVUC joined with the Philadelphia Unemployment Project to form the National Unemployed Network (NUN).

The organizational meeting, held in Pittsburgh in January 1983, drew eighty people from nine states. Representing a potential political base of 11 million unemployed workers, the group organized its first national action—the sheriff's sale of the White House—to be held in Washington in March. They also called NUN's first national conference for June of that year. It drew 250 people from forty communities in seventeen states. The group announced its goals:

1. To secure a decent living standard for all
2. To build a unified force of all workers, employed and unemployed

---

29. *Wall Street Journal*, February 18, 1986, p. 35.
30. *Pittsburgh Post-Gazette*, November 27, 1986, p. C2.

3. To change the government's budget priorities—money for jobs, not war—fund social services that help people not kill them
4. To fight the disproportionate effect of unemployment on women, minorities, and handicapped workers[31]

To achieve these goals, the National Unemployed Network announced a three-part political strategy of (1) pressuring candidates for election to take stands on employment issues (neither party had announced a serious jobs program); (2) staging local demonstrations the first Friday of every month, when the Bureau of Labor Statistics announced its unemployment figures (the first First Friday saw rallies in twenty-five cities); and (3) lobbying in Washington to preserve the Federal Supplemental Unemployment Compensation program, which was due to expire the following March.[32]

With Reagan trumpeting his "economic recovery," and Democrats cringingly accepting Republican and press efforts to describe labor as a "special interest," the unemployed won very little from the 1984 elections. Serious local conditions and serious lobbying by the MVUC and other Pennsylvania groups on First Fridays and on other occasions did convert most of the Pennsylvania congressional delegation into sympathetic allies. The MVUC joined in a major effort to save the Supplemental Unemployment benefits program they had helped win in 1982. Yet in March 1985, despite the MVUC's managing to send seven busloads of supporters to Washington to join with a thousand other NUN supporters, Congress voted to end the Supplemental Unemployment Compensation program.

The MVUC newsletter made sure that supporters realized their work had at least won something: Rather than simply ending the Supplemental Employment benefits in March, Congress agreed to phase them out. This provided an additional $160 million, or just under $500 for each of the 324,000 eligible unemployed workers.[33] MVUC members had helped make an important difference, but it was difficult not to taste the defeat. There was no third NUN annual conference.

Demobilization and Institutional Success

By the time of the first National Unemployed Network conference in 1983, the MVUC was already in trouble. A newspaper headline told the

31. *National Unemployed News*, July 1983, p. 1.
32. Ibid.
33. *MVUC Newsletter*, May 1985.

story: "JOBS RALLY—Crowd Missing This Time."[34] Even though the area's unemployment figures still stood at around 16 percent, only 250 people showed up for a major protest march called for downtown Pittsburgh—a mere 10 percent of the crowd drawn the year before, and a small fraction of a percent of the region's jobless.

Organizers had two explanations. One paper quoted MVUC leader Rob Toy: "When the jobless marched in Pittsburgh's streets last year they shared a feeling that their protests could spur action. This time people don't see that happening."[35] That statement neatly recapitulates my main thesis: Workers learn not to protest. Five years later, Toy offered an economic explanation as well.[36] People laid off in late 1981 and early 1982 had been eligible for one and a half to two years of benefits under a variety of programs. This gave them time to participate in demonstrations as well as other political activities. In the first two years of the downturn, people still hoped and believed (a belief U.S. Steel encouraged) that they might yet be called back to work. Yet by the summer of 1983, recovery seemed less and less likely and benefits were beginning to run out for most people.

Some moved out of the area in search of jobs. Others were busy holding down two part-time jobs and still scrambling to make ends meet. They were clearly not likely to attend demonstrations that seemed unlikely to produce the immediate benefits these workers needed. By 1985, when unemployment benefits were cut to a maximum of six months, most workers had little time to spend on political activities that seemed to bring few, if any, benefits.

Managers and planners throughout the Pittsburgh region frequently complained that workers were too attached to their past identities (see Chapter 6)—that they saw themselves as steelworkers, as union members, as members of specific neighborhoods and communities—and that this kept them from adapting to the new economic environment, as business deemed necessary for an efficient transition. In the minds of managers and planners interviewed in Pittsburgh, workers were merely "labor," a factor of production just like coal or cloth. Just as coal not converted to coke for steel production could be shipped to a power plant and burnt for fuel, so labor, responding efficiently, should shift to different vocations and different locations wherever markets found the best use for them.

34. *Tribune-Review*, July 28, 1983.
35. Ibid.
36. The following discussion is based largely on Rob Toy's comments in an interview conducted at his home on July 26, 1988.

Extended unemployment benefits presented a problem for this way of thinking. They allowed workers to continue, not as just labor but as humans with broadly defined identities and community ties. With unemployment falling in other parts of the country, it was no longer politically or economically necessary to provide workers with the means to subsist in their original communities. Cutting benefits helped convert the workers into the more efficient "factors of production" that the national economy seemed to require.

With benefits cut, workers were being forced to move into whatever slots the new economy offered them, regardless of the personal sacrifices involved. Many became salesmen, prison guards, nurses' aides, or short-order cooks. The fact that the media so obligingly repeated the Reagan administration's assurances that the economic recovery was well under way further undermined workers' sense that they were justified in doing anything but looking for work—wherever they could find it.

Bob Anderson added yet another explanation for the demobilization that became more obvious after the middle of 1983. In his opinion, "the antics of the DMS lunatic right wing burned people out. They made the whole struggle into a joke."[37] Many people believe that the DMS tactics, especially their attacks on church people in decidedly churchgoing Pittsburgh, alienated potential supporters from them and from other activist groups as well. Yet it is important to point out that, well before the DMS turned to its more dramatic tactics, most newspaper accounts of large MVUC events included a comment from a worker in the crowd like "These marches aren't going to find a solution"[38] or "This is not going to accomplish anything. . . . Reagan doesn't care."[39] It did not take long for those who had ventured into the streets in protest against the destruction of their jobs and their communities to let their sense of political futility drive them back into the isolation of their own individual situations.

Members of the DMS offer yet another explanation for the demobilization. They charge that by directing the attention of angry workers away from local corporations that workers could see both as causes of their misery and targets for their rage, groups like the MVUC—and Tri-State as well—defused workers' potential power. Furthermore, by attempting to create a respectable organization that could negotiate with powerful corporate and government bodies, they set themselves up for co-optation by their supposed adversaries.

37. Bob Anderson interview, July 25, 1988.
38. *Tribune-Review*, July 28, 1983.
39. *McKeesport Daily News*, April 7, 1983.

This progression toward demobilization is a classic pattern that many movements have followed and that two scholars make the central point of their book. Their analysis fits this case so closely that it is worth quoting at length:

> Whatever influence lower-class groups occasionally exert in American politics does not result from organization, but from mass protest and the disruptive consequences of protest. . . .
> Ordinarily, of course, elites do not support efforts to form organizations of lower-class people. But when insurgency wells up, apparently uncontrollable, elites respond. And one of their responses is to create those lower-class organizations which begin to emerge in such periods, for they have little to fear from organizations, especially organizations which come to depend on them for support. Thus, however unwittingly, leaders and organizers of the lower classes act in the end to facilitate the efforts of the elite to channel the insurgent masses into normal politics, believing all the while that they are taking the long and arduous but certain path to power.[40]

A good amount of evidence conforms to this pattern.

Rob Toy, a key MVUC organizer from the very beginning, is quoted in mid-1983 as being worried that the growing anger of the unemployed may turn to crime and destruction. "One of the things that we want to do," he said, "is take that anger and focus it on the political process, trying to get people to lobby their representatives."[41]

The DMS assertion that Mellon Bank would be happy to sponsor buses to carry angry workers from Pittsburgh to lobby government representatives in Washington or Harrisburg brings up the issue of co-optation by funding agencies. MVUC's Paul Lodico recalls that they got their first funding in 1983 from the elite Pittsburgh Foundation[42] and that they thought the best thing to do with the money was go out and spend it so they could show they needed more. Therefore, much of the money was quickly spent on signs and other expenses for their next demonstration. This caused the Pittsburgh Foundation to "come un-glued." The committee pledged to spend the rest of the foundation funds on paying staff rather than on demonstrations. Bob Anderson

40. Piven and Cloward, *Poor People's Movements*, pp. xxii, 36.
41. *Pittsburgh Press*, June 30, 1983.
42. Lodico interview, July 25, 1988.

concurred that the funding for MVUC (which increased steadily as mobilization declined) was "dependent on cooling out demonstrations."[43]

Rob Toy dissents from the view that corporate funding resulted in the MVUC becoming more conservative. Toy, one of the first staff members paid by the Pittsburgh Foundation, recalls telling them: "We'll take your bucks, but don't count on pleasant statements,"[44] and he points out that after receiving funds from U.S. Steel Foundation they recommended that the Commonwealth of Pennsylvania not channel any job-training funds through U.S. Steel. Furthermore, putting Mellon on their "dirty dozen" list during the mortgage struggles did not keep Mellon from giving them money.[45]

By 1988, funding for the MVUC was well established at a level of approximately $150,000 a year. The associated Unemployed Council of Southwestern Pennsylvania had a budget of $200,000. Funds for both come from a variety of foundations, corporations, churches, the United Way, and, to a much lesser extent, from individual members and supporters. During their mid-1980s reorganization, MVUC leaders were invited to confer at the prestigious Duquesne Club (as Lodico put it, "If there's a power elite in Pittsburgh, that's where you'll find them"). Later, Westinghouse and Alcoa executives invited them to finalize plans at a country club.[46] This list of supporters also fails to prove a co-optative influence. What it does establish is that the MVUC—whose rally participants once struck fear in such corporate figures as Senator Heinz—was no longer seen as threatening to the establishment. If worker power comes from the ability to disrupt or to threaten disruption, then by the mid-1980s the MVUC had apparently lost some of its power.

By the early 1990s, much of the corporate support for the MVUC had faded. Organizers were proud to point out that approximately half their support came from workers who targeted their organization to receive their United Way contributions. Working on approximately $100,000 a year, they somehow managed to play an organizing role in sixteen counties scattered around the state.

43. Ibid., July 25, 1988.
44. Rob Toy interview, July 26, 1988.
45. Here Toy's logic does not support his point. One would want to know whether the MVUC continued to attack Mellon after they started giving money. In fact, Toy said in his interview that he thought it was poor strategy for the DMS to focus so much attention on Mellon Bank. This does not prove that Toy was co-opted, but it does show—with a sequential, not causal, linkage—that Toy stopped focusing criticism on them after receiving Mellon funding.
46. Lodico interview, July 25, 1988.

Reorganizing the Committee

Whatever the cause, the demobilization of unemployed workers in 1984 provoked a crisis within the MVUC, a crisis of organization as well as a crisis of purpose. They needed to decide not only what they should do next but who they were. Making the second decision would have a strong effect on the first. It would determine who got to decide. The group's initial organization model—small groups associated with but independent from Steelworkers locals—had evolved into an ad hoc arrangement in which some decisions were made by whoever turned up at membership meetings, and some decisions were made by the paid staff regardless of the membership. This was soon to change.

By mid-1984 the MVUC had accomplished much. They had helped pass the only state mortgage-relief measure in the country, and their pressure tactics had prompted utility companies to agree not to shut off services to anyone who was supported by a call from MVUC. Unemployment compensation levels were at a historic peak. The National Unemployment Network had been established. Yet despite these accomplishments and the fact that the "recovery" was under way, the real problems of unemployment remained. As members blamed leaders, and leaders could convince no one of a clear course of action, the Mon Valley Unemployed Committee approached paralysis.

Outside consultants were called in, and by May 1985 the MVUC had a new leadership structure with day-to-day decisions being made by the paid staff, and policy decisions being made by a newly created policy council. The council included some MVUC members and respected professionals and community leaders. It was chaired by a lawyer from Neighborhood Legal Services. The decision-making role of the membership at large was curtailed.

The policy council helped establish a new sense of purpose. One strength of the MVUC had always been its ability to organize. At the country club meeting, Westinghouse and Alcoa executives suggested money would be available to help establish a regional "Unemployed Council." That council would provide two paid staff to each of the four unemployed committees: the MVUC in McKeesport, the Beaver County Unemployed Committee in Aliquippa, the Mid-Mon Unemployed Committee in Monessen, and the newest chapter, the Central Westmoreland County Unemployed Committee in Greensburg. The whole council was eventually coordinated out of the MVUC office. As the pace of plant closings slowed and the region adjusted to higher unemployment and lower wages, corporate funding for these unemployed committees and the regional council faded out by the early 1990s.

The Mon Valley Unemployed Committee continued to provide assistance to individuals with survival problems. They kept up their hotline, and with funding from the United Way, Mellon Bank, the Steelworkers, and various churches and synagogues, they published in 1986 the *People's Guide to Human Services,* a booklet that provided advice on how individuals and families could cope with (not resist) a decline in their standard of living.

While it is important to recognize that the information in this booklet could make a real contribution to meeting the immediate needs of low-income individuals and families, its conservative political message was not likely to be helpful to unemployed workers as a group. The first page features a list of major donors and the logos of companies that made the publication possible. Prominent among them were the Lutheran Church in America and Mellon Bank, each of which had been frequently attacked by the DMS as insensitive to the needs of people. The booklet was an inexpensive way to help counter those charges. Its final section, "Get What You Need from Social Service Agencies," reinforces the message that workers should not be wasting their time demanding better jobs or a more just society—better they should count their blessings and learn to adapt to a compassionate system that is working for them:

> Western Pennsylvania communities offer a satisfying variety of human services—social resources—for people in need. Too often needs remain unsatisfied because the community's resources fail to connect with the people who need them. . . . If you need help with food, shelter, medical care, or finding a new job, there is someone or some organization named in this guide who will help you. . . .[47]

The crisis of organization and purpose in the MVUC had been resolved in a way that put the committee on a new and improved institutional basis. A crisis brought on by membership frustrations with the fundamental problem of continuing high unemployment was solved by insulating the MVUC's now quite respectable leadership from their impatient membership and by focusing on providing relief rather than political empowerment and decent jobs. With the aid of powerful corporations, the MVUC had been converted from a group that had effectively helped to mobilize angry workers who wanted jobs and a decent society, into a dispenser of quieting balm on troubled waters.

47. *The People's Guide to Human Services,* pp. 47–48.

Members of the Pittsburgh elite felt so positive about this reborn MVUC that they provided money to extend its calming influence throughout the region. Major contributors to the project made sure that local media mentioned them as benefactors of the unfortunate unemployed. Not long before, they had been vilified as destroyers of jobs and communities. Clearly they trusted that investing in the MVUC would be cost-effective.

Moving Beyond the Steel Crisis

By 1988 the committee's emphasis had moved to expanding federal support for job training through the Trade Readjustment Act and the Job Training Partnership Act. After years of fighting for survival issues, leaders of the MVUC were glad to be working on issues like retraining or "remaking one's future," as Rob Toy put it. Toy had recently become less active in the MVUC because he had decided to go back to school himself.

The MVUC found the Trade Readjustment Act (TRA) superior to the Job Training Partnership Act (JTPA) because the TRA provides cash benefits to keep the worker alive during training. JTPA funds cover only training costs, so many who could barely support themselves in jobs they held but found inadequate could not afford to take time to train for better employment. The committee had an ideological problem with the TRA: It required workers to blame their troubles on foreign competition rather than on the decisions of domestic management and the federal government, which MVUC leaders felt were really responsible. But they saw merit in taking the funds anyhow.

The MVUC believed its lobbying efforts were responsible for getting training funds to thousands of area workers. Committee efforts to expand TRA coverage were exemplified by the flurry of activity one could observe by visiting their office in July 1988. One worker was involved in telephone calls to different regional Unemployed Committee offices to finalize preparations for those who would ride the bus to Washington that night to lobby on provisions in the trade bill then being redrawn after President Reagan's earlier veto. A volunteer was copying pages out of a political almanac on who to lobby. Copies for reading on the bus would be handed out. One conversation revealed optimism, because Senator Bentsen of the Senate Finance Committee—who now had added leverage, having just been named the Vice-Presidential candidate of his party—wanted to expand TRA coverage to cover oil and gas workers in his state of Texas.[48] Meanwhile, on the individual level, one staff person was dealing with a state bureaucrat who seemed to be holding up training certification of some workers, and another was trying to grab a few moments to prepare for cases he would argue on appeal in Harrisburg within the next week. It was easy to sense an organization that had learned to work hard and intelligently with donors, with government, and with individuals on a variety of levels.

In the early 1990s, the MVUC still responded to its hotline for individual assistance. It continued its work assisting people to deal with job training, welfare, unemployment, and mortgage or utility problems, but it had shifted its organizing efforts away from responding to shutdowns in the Mon Valley to a statewide problem—the welfare lien. Pennsylvania was one of only three states to require that a homeowner applying for public assistance give the state a lien on his or her property as security for a promise to repay the welfare grant if the property is ever sold. Having a lien made it difficult for people to get normal loans if they ever needed to borrow to repair their homes. The committee was working with a variety of homeowners around the state to have the lien law repealed. Organizers were finding that the people they were organizing to pressure state government were eager to sense that they could actually have an influence. At this writing, the bill had passed the state House but still needed votes in the Senate. It was hard not to get the sense from organizer Paul Lodico that it was refreshing to get out beyond the stagnation of the Mon Valley and that the process of empowering people involved in the lien campaign was at least as important as changing state policy on welfare liens.

Conclusions

Goals

The Mon Valley Unemployed Committee did not, in any fundamental way, challenge the decision-making process that was transforming their community. It never sought to. From the very beginning, the individuals involved in the various layoff committees attached to union locals were

48. It was perhaps more than an interesting coincidence that Republican Vice-Presidential candidate Dan Quayle claimed as his major legislative accomplishment the less favored JTPA.

concerned with large issues of social justice, yet their activities always focused around the immediate issue of survival. Though they could eloquently denounce the system that showed such callous disregard for the workers who had provided the basis of Pittsburgh's wealth, their actions were focused not on stopping that process but on seeing that most of those workers could at least survive it.

Compared with the other groups in this study—the Network/DMS and the Tri-State Conference on Steel—the Mon Valley Unemployed Committee had the least-radical goals. The goals stated in its 1983 brochure were relatively modest: "to change government and company policies to recognize that everyone has a right to work and survival income between their jobs." This statement can be broken up into four distinct goals:

1. To change corporate policies to guarantee workers' right to work
2. To change corporate policy to guarantee workers' right to survival income between jobs
3. To change government policy to guarantee workers' right to work
4. To change government policy to guarantee workers' right to survival income between jobs

This case study makes it clear that, regardless of such a statement of purpose, the committee chose to work almost entirely on the fourth goal. One cannot fault them for their choice. Though limited, the goal of obtaining concessions from government to ensure survival was clearly urgent. It was also the goal they could most realistically hope to achieve.

Elite Response

The elite's response to the MVUC was multifaceted, but to analyze it we must be clear about who the relevant elite are. The MVUC literature mentions both corporate and government targets for their challenge. We are concerned with an elite that had and exercised power to reshape the economy of Pittsburgh and the nation in the 1980s. This elite in Pittsburgh included, primarily, top corporate executives. At the national level, it also included key players in the Reagan administration and in the Congress. In this case, intermediate actors—local politicians such as Sheriff Coon and Judge Papadakos—also played important roles, but they should not be confused with the elite. Their actions, however, can tell us much about intermediate actors who must maintain their base of support in both elite and mass constituencies.

Elites were visibly concerned by the anger and potential danger from workers who attended early events organized by the MVUC. Both elite and intermediate actors responded to the power of mobilized workers in a variety of ways. When danger was greatest, the federal government extended unemployment benefits. As mobilization declined, benefits were withdrawn. Local and state politicians responded to mobilization with mortgage relief. The most significant of the elites (locally based, transnational corporations) responded by giving money and encouragement to the MVUC for its work in helping unemployed workers cope with—not resist—unemployment.

In terms of the first three of the MVUC's goals, the response of the elites was one of complete but invisible resistance. Using what we have called the second dimension of power through ignoring, through redirection, and through co-optation, they quickly defeated all but one of the challenges. The elite interpreted the fourth goal in terms of a concession they had made long ago: In order to maintain elite control, the welfare functions of the state must be activated to manage the demands of disgruntled underclasses. The level of the relief is adjusted up or down according to the degree of threat to elite control.[49]

State and local politicians accountable both to the elite and to the mass electorate did briefly require some limited concessions from local financial corporations when they declared and supported a moratorium on sheriff's sales. The local media quickly acted to limit the ideological damage inflicted by the moratorium's apparent message that a worker's right to shelter might sometimes take precedence over a corporation's right to profit. State politicians then acted to provide mortgage assistance, which would displace the financial cost of compassion from the banks to state taxpayers while at the same time reestablishing the apparent legitimacy and normalcy of mortgage payments from the unemployed to corporations, like Mellon Bank, which had participated in decisions to put them out of work.

The generous sponsorship the MVUC eventually received from local corporations was an indication not so much of the compassionate nature of Pittsburgh's elites as of their recognition that the work the MVUC was doing was a necessary part of the economic transformation of Pittsburgh. To a certain extent, the apparent success of the MVUC as an organization is a testimony to the continuing triumph of elite control over Pittsburgh's working classes.

49. James O'Conner makes this point especially clearly in his *Fiscal Crisis of the State* (New York: St. Martin's Press, 1973).

Mobilization

The first significant innovation of Pittsburgh's unemployed committees was their determination to keep people organized, through their union locals, after they had been laid off. Their initial efforts did keep many workers from becoming immediately isolated in their unemployment. However, they never did succeed in creating unemployed committees that acted to maintain the collective strength of the tens of thousands of laid-off workers. The bureaucratic resistance of USWA leadership had much to do with this failure.

Early rallies, called for specific purposes, often drew more workers than MVUC organizers expected. Workers seemed eager for any forum in which they could voice their outrage at what was happening to them and their communities. Through statements at rallies and through the hotline, workers moved the focus of MVUC efforts beyond unemployment compensation efforts to include mortgage relief—the most radical phase of MVUC activities. At the rally called to protest Reagan's visit, workers ignored MVUC speakers altogether to follow their own agenda: confronting, violently if necessary, the embodiment of the nation's economic-policy-making elite, Ronald Reagan.

At these times, the thousands of workers who showed up to MVUC-sponsored activities seemed in many ways far out in front of their would-be leaders. MVUC organizers were unable or unwilling to operate to facilitate the far-reaching goals of this proto-insurrectionary movement. Rather, they sought to minister to some of their survival needs and to direct their energies into more traditional appeals to various government agencies. This allowed them to be leaders rather than merely facilitators. It allowed them to create a stable and—within defined limits—quite effective organization. Most important, it allowed them to transform mobs of angry workers into petitioners to the state and into clients of the MVUC and other welfare organizations.

For many reasons already discussed, the masses of workers in the streets (never more than a very significant minority of the unemployed) demobilized. The organization lived on and prospered. Some groups of workers maintained contact with the MVUC and were occasionally mobilized to pressure government agencies.

Accomplishments

Compared with the other groups in this study—the Network/DMS and the Tri-State Conference on Steel—the MVUC's goals were the least challenging, the least ambitious, and the most nearly obtained. The MVUC accomplished a series of successes—each limited, yet each significant in its own right.

The very existence of the early layoff committees provided an example to all labor unions that it was both possible and necessary to maintain an organization of and provide services to workers after they had lost their jobs. Work in the MVUC provided education and empowerment to several dozen workers who moved out of the mills and into active political work on a variety of levels. Both Tri-State and the Network to Save the Mon-Ohio Valley grew out of the early discussions carried on in the layoff committees. Members and staff developed a surprising degree of expertise in matters dealing with organization, media manipulation, fund-raising, and relations with government bureaucracies and with elected officials at the local, state, and national levels. And they helped to win real benefits worth thousands—sometimes tens of thousands—of dollars for thousands of workers through their work on unemployment compensation, mortgage relief, health care, utility shutdowns, and job training. They also helped win the right of unemployed workers at least to have their needs listened to by local government, community, and corporate bodies.

In certain aspects, the committee also failed. From many of their early statements and from their efforts with the National Unemployed Network, one gets the clear impression that at least some of the MVUC leaders hoped to inspire a fairly militant national movement of the unemployed whose radical goals and resolute demonstrations might help catalyze a larger movement for social change. This did not come about. Yet it is possible to hypothesize that—worse than their failure to achieve the unlikely goal of broad social change—they may have helped undermine some of the movement's political potential by their choice of tactics and/or by underestimating the readiness of their constituents to appreciate a political perspective that addressed more than the concerns of their own situation of unemployment.[50]

We know that the anger of the workers, which so frightened Senator Heinz at the hearing held in August 1982 and was reported by journalists

50. Cynthia Deitch, "Grass-Roots Community Mobilization and the New Structural Unemployment," in Zdenik Suda, ed., *Structural Unemployment and the New Perspectives on the Social Meaning of Work* (Pittsburgh: University of Pittsburgh, 1983). Deitch says the leaders might have underestimated MVU members, because members voted to endorse a "Jobs with Peace" resolution even though the leaders sensed an unwillingness to vote against military spending. There is also evidence of underestimation at early demonstrations discussed above, where workers' expressed goals went much beyond those of the organizers.

covering the early marches and rallies called by the MVUC, was not merely a demand for specific relief services. It was a broad indictment of the entire system that had treated them so callously. The MVUC's tactical decision to focus on obtaining relief from existing government, corporate, and church institutions led it to become less of a mass democratic political movement promoting outraged challenges to the system and more of a bureaucratic organization capable of delivering goods from the system. Their political estimation of the workers' political potential must have influenced their tactical decisions. It focused that potential in specific, limited, and seemingly practical directions. In the process, the MVUC did more to legitimate Pittsburgh's corporate decision-making structure than to challenge it.

It would be inappropriate for me to judge the political consciousness of workers who initially responded to the MVUC's calls. I was not there; the MVUC leaders were. This discussion should not be taken as a judgment that the MVUC should have attempted a revolutionary insurrection to redirect the course of Pittsburgh's economic transformation. Such an effort would have been absurd and futile, given the broader context of class relations in the United States. But I do conclude that, when workers were prepared to take broader and more disruptive actions, the MVUC organization operated as a conservatizing influence.

Paul Lodico is sensitive to the charge that all the MVUC has done is provide band-aids, instead of trying to stop the monster causing the wounds. He accepts the charge but adds, "If you don't provide band-aids, a person could bleed to death." It would be unfair to end this assessment of the MVUC's accomplishments without pointing out that the MVUC provided more and better band-aids than any other organization of industrial workers in the United States during this time.

In the early 1990s, Lodico said the group's name—the Mon Valley Unemployed Committee—had become outdated but that they would keep it because it worked for them. Their campaign to remove welfare liens involved some unemployed steelworkers, but it had become a statewide organizing effort, and Lodico was most interested in organizing people who had never been involved in politics before. He was especially proud of involving people who previously had been powerless—even frightened women whose only involvement beyond their homes had been their churches. He enjoyed sensing their new sense of empowerment, seeing them look at their communities with new eyes.

Over the years, Lodico said, the MVUC had come to speak less in terms of ideology, "But the core belief—real democracy—is still the same. In the early years we demanded jobs. But when were we actually working on that? Then the big ideas were principles, but we didn't fight for them. They were 'happy thoughts.' We still have them. We just don't put them on the masthead as much."[51]

The MVUC's more recent accomplishments have been on two levels. They have chosen practical goals that could be accomplished by mobilizing their clientele around specific political demands. "Our black and gold [hats and tee shirts] have become well known at the Statehouse," claimed Lodico. The second level of personal empowerment goes hand-in-hand with these practical efforts. According to Lodico, "Most of these people have no other institutional way to feel empowerment." With one eye always on larger issues of social change, Lodico was encouraged by the rapid pace of change in Eastern Europe in 1989. From those events, and from the MVUC's political work, he has become further convinced that "when people take it into their mind to do something, they can. What it takes to get that going—who knows? On a small scale that's what we do—fight against the notion that you can't fight city hall."

Worker-Elite Interaction

Much like the case of the Tri-State Conference on Steel, how one judges the interaction of the MVUC with Pittsburgh's elite depends on one's definition of both "elite" and "organization." If the relevant elite is defined as the leaders of Pittsburgh's major industrial and financial corporations, and if one defines the MVUC as industrial workers demanding secure jobs and secure income between jobs, it is easy to trace their path through the matrix of elite-worker interaction (Figure 6): Individuals confronting layoffs in 1980, 1981, and 1982 chose to organize unemployed committees rather than remain unmobilized (A). They moved quickly to confrontation with the elite (B). In this phase, their rallies, demonstrations, and angry testimonies gained them some limited concessions from the elite. We could say they edged slightly into cell 1, our model of effectively working pluralist democracy (C). By 1984, however, many of these benefits had been withdrawn, and most workers were demobilized (D) and looking for their own individual solutions to life in postindustrial Pittsburgh. The elite no longer looked facilitative.

If we define Pittsburgh's elite more broadly, to include most politicians as well as representatives of foundations and churches, and if we define the MVUC more narrowly, as an organization serving the needs of Pittsburgh's unemployed industrial workers, we get quite a different picture (Figure 7). In this interpretation, by skillfully mobil-

51. Paul Lodico interview at MVUC headquarters, March 15, 1992.

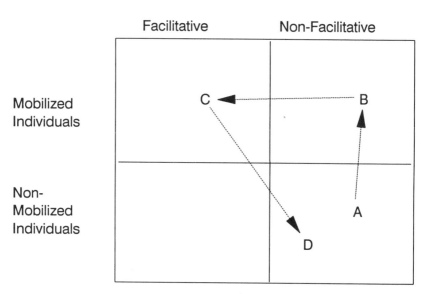

Fig. 6. MVUC-Elite Interaction Matrix 1

izing workers the MVUC moved from point *a* to point *b*, where, through a series of confrontations with the elite, the committee gained benefits for the workers and acceptance for itself as an organization (*c*). Its success thus leaves it in the ideal cell 1, where it interacts with a facilitative elite (*d*1) while its clients reside in cell 3 (*d*2), gaining benefits from a variety of benign bureaucracies whose generosity is guaranteed by the occasional return of its worker/clients to confrontational lobbying (*d*3).

The most accurate description is probably a composite of the two. In 1985, when the MVUC underwent its reorganization, the committee formalized its split from its mass base. By winning some bureaucratic concessions for its largely demobilized base, it gave some (mostly Pittsburgh's middle-class onlookers) the illusion that workers had moved to the relatively benign cell 3. In terms of the challenge of managing Pittsburgh's social transformation, the importance of this illusion—held by the sincerely concerned churchgoers who channeled money to the MVUC rather than to the DMS—should not be underestimated. Regardless of this illusion, most laid-off industrial workers found themselves stuck in cell 4. The few bureaucratic handouts they received did not

Elite Orientation

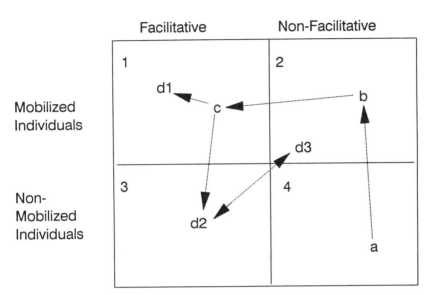

Fig. 7. MVUC-Elite Interaction Matrix 2

substantially change the impression that they had lost and were individuals confronting a world characterized by elite hegemony.

In 1988, when Paul Lodico was asked what he thought about the prospects for the Monongahela Valley's economic recovery, he responded that there were no serious developments there and that there would be none for quite some time, "not until the unions are crushed." He saw this sad result of deindustrialization already beginning to take hold. "Scabbing is up," he said, referring to recent events in local grocery stores and hospitals. He noted that the fire had gone out of local workers. Surviving had not become comfortable, but it had become easier. Most of those who lost steel jobs had found at least some job, and their spouses were now working too. Housing costs had declined, and workers who were over the age of fifty-two when they were laid off in 1981 had become eligible for social security and pensions. He predicted the end of the MVUC in the not-too-distant future. Soon all the important information will have been passed on to the people, "or they will have gone away or gone on welfare."

Asked whether he thought the efforts of the MVUC may have changed the political consciousness of the workers in the Valley, he replied no—

because there was no serious debate about the underlying cause of their community's collapse. There was no serious debate, he argued, because the socialist wing of the labor movement got wiped out in the 1950s, because there was no recollection of an alternative view, no left to draw on in communities.

He accepted that Pittsburgh is finished as a steel center, and brought up the example of Poughkeepsie, New York, which was once the barrel-making capital of the world. "Now that's all gone," he recalled. "People get wiped out. Do they like it? No. But if they work together they get some benefits. We live in a capitalist system. Most people like it, so they accept the lumps that go along with it."

MVUC leaders worked with people on that level. They accepted the system. They complained about the lumps but accepted them, organized, accepted that after 1983 they could only organize small groups, and won some benefits that made real differences in the lives of thousands of people but that did not change the world in which they lived. Yet, inspired by small, tangible successes, and by faith in something intensely democratic, MVUC organizers continued the work of showing ordinary people that by organizing they could gain more power.

5

WHO DECIDES?
Uncovering Hidden
Decision-Making Environments

In 1892 Andrew Carnegie created the Carnegie Steel Company Ltd. It included the Edgar Thomson, Duquesne, and Homestead mills and was the largest steel company in the world. That summer, Carnegie and Henry Clay Frick, Carnegie's partner and manager of the mills, determined to rid the Homestead mill of the Amalgamated Association of Iron & Steel Workers, then the strongest union in the country. The technology of steel production had advanced to a point that made reliance on the skilled craft workers that composed the Amalgamated Association no longer necessary. Carnegie and Frick were determined to use this technological change to their advantage in reshaping both production and social relations in the Monongahela Valley.

The Homestead strike was long and bitter, climaxed by a major gun battle on July 6 that left sixteen dead and scores of others injured. Strikers held firm until late November, when cold weather and hunger delivered victory to Carnegie and Frick and destroyed the Amalgamated Association.

Alexander Berkman was an anarchist sympathetic to but not directly involved with the strikers. On July 23, 1892, shortly after the bloody battle of Homestead, he entered Frick's office and fired at him with a pistol at close range. However, Berkman's poor aim deprived us of an adequate test of whether the Pittsburgh elite of that era was compact enough to have been deterred from its goals by removing one key actor.

What we do know is that in 1892 a few very visible people held the reins of economic power quite closely.

"Who Can I Shoot?"

Today Pittsburgh's elite is more diverse. Although it includes many powerful people, no one person holds such decisive power as Carnegie or Frick did nearly a century ago. The current Pittsburgh elite more nearly resembles that which confronted the 1930s Oklahoma tenant farmer described in Steinbeck's novel *The Grapes of Wrath*. When a bulldozer arrived to demolish the man's home and plow up his fields, the farmer threatened to shoot him. The conversation that ensued could well have occurred in the Mon Valley in the 1980s. The driver begins:

> "It's not me. There's nothing I can do. I'll lose my job if I don't do it. And look—suppose you kill me? They'll just hang you, but long before you're hung there'll be another guy on the tractor, and he'll bump the house down. You're not killing the right guy."
>
> "That's so," the tenant said. "Who gave you orders? I'll go after him. He's the one to kill."
>
> "You're wrong. He got his orders from the bank. The bank told him 'Clear those people out or it's your job.' "
>
> "Well, there's a president of the bank. There's a board of directors. I'll fill up the magazine of the rifle and go into the bank."
>
> The driver said, "Fellow was telling me the bank gets orders from the East. The orders were, 'Make the land show profit or we'll close you up.' "
>
> "But where does it stop? Who can I shoot?"[1]

Similarly, one might ask who is responsible for the destruction of the Mon Valley. Pointing to U.S. Steel's CEO David Roderick would be a simple beginning, but Roderick would answer that he is merely doing the bidding of the whole corporation, including its shareholders. He might also point the finger at the federal government for its policies on taxation, environmental regulation, and steel imports. Others might point to Mellon Bank and other regional banks for failing to provide sufficient capital for local investment. Many would blame foreign com-

---

1. John Steinbeck, *The Grapes of Wrath* (New York: Random House, 1939), pp. 51–52.

panies and governments for unfair competition. A discerning individual might point to the planners or academics who have paved the way for Pittsburgh's high-tech future. Some would blame the unemployed workers themselves for having demanded unrealistically high wages.

The fact that those involved in the decisions that have shaped the economic transformation are diverse does not mean we cannot understand something about the process that has led to that transformation, or about certain people and institutions that have played major roles in that process. We will not be able to answer the question "Who can I shoot?" but we will be able to answer questions such as How did it happen? Who was involved? and Who was excluded? Answers to these questions must be found before we can fully answer the question "Why so little protest in response to deindustrialization?" or, finally, "Can workers have a voice in shaping the economic transformation of their communities?"

As we begin this chapter on Pittsburgh's decision-making process, it is important to recall that this study is primarily concerned not with the details of what goes on within that process but rather with how people are excluded from the process of making important decisions that dramatically affect their lives and the lives of their communities. The thesis is, in general, that Pittsburgh's economic decision-makers are a group of corporate elites who succeed at minimizing participation by outsiders so frequently that outsiders rarely consider challenging the process. In our specific case, this means that certain elite actors in Pittsburgh made decisions that led to abandonment of the area's steel industry as a major source of employment, that they did this with very little input from the workers and communities affected, and that they did so with little overt opposition because of their ability to punish, co-opt, or distract those who were bold enough to assert their right to participate in the decision-making process.

The economic transformation was a response to many factors, many of them external to Pittsburgh (see Chapter 1). Chief among these were technological change and international competition. Of the many possible responses to the forces driving change only some were chosen. Within Pittsburgh, a small group of people had the most ability to make those choices. This group could appropriately be referred to as a "class" in the Marxist sense, because their ability to make decisions derived from their positions as capitalists—owners and/or major managers of the region's key industrial and financial corporations. Members of this class sometimes worked in close coordination, sometimes in competition, and sometimes in isolation. Yet, throughout it all, in formulating their decisions, they shared a number of assumptions that gave coherence to

their choices, chief among which was an agreement that they, Pittsburgh's corporate elite, had the right to make the choices that would
shape the future of the region. There was also agreement that ensuring
corporate profitability should take priority over such considerations as
stabilizing employment or improving the community. So it is in this
regard that one can talk about a reasonably coherent capitalist elite that
shaped Pittsburgh's economic transformation. As we shall see, there are
a number of other more specific indications of this elite's coherence,
coordination, and domination of Pittsburgh's decision-making process.

Decision-Making: Two False Models

The process of decision-making in Pittsburgh and throughout the nation
is masked by two rhetorical models, one of "free markets," the other of
"democracy." People assume that economic decisions are made in a
realm characterized by free-market capitalism. The gospel of Adam
Smith taught in U.S. high schools and colleges assures us that free-
market capitalism leads to the greatest good for the greatest number of
people. Thus, it is good, and thus our process of private economic
decision-making is assumed to be good. By this theory, corporate leaders
have no need to worry about levels of employment or quality of community. The theory suggests that the private decisions of entrepreneurs
will ultimately lead to optimal levels of employment and the best material
conditions for the community.

In the political realm, we are said to have a representative democracy,
through which process society supposedly protects the rights of all
individuals and ensures that their interests will be respected when social
policy is formulated. This is seen as fair and good and legitimate.

Unfortunately, such notions about how decisions are made do more
to hide the real decision-making process than they do to reveal it. As
such, they constitute part of the third dimension of power, which isolates
elite decision-making from challenge.

Most of the decisions that shaped the economic transformation of
Pittsburgh in the 1970s and 1980s were made as a part of processes that
can be characterized as neither free-market capitalism nor representative
democracy. Free-market capitalism would require more firms, each
having far less power than the behemoths that dominate today's economic landscape. While we can still apply the term "capitalist" to the
firms we are concerned with, we must refer to them as engaging in
corporate capitalism rather than free-market capitalism. Mammoth cor-

porations conduct major portions of their transactions internally—that is, in an economic environment devoid of real markets. Most of their other transactions are conducted in realms characterized by oligopolistic coexistence rather than competition. This allows corporate managers much more room for strategic decision-making than they would have in a free market.

For representative democracy to be effective in the issue areas here discussed, elected government bodies would have to have much more power in order to affect the future of the communities they supposedly govern, but we shall see that their powers are actually extremely circumscribed. Because markets and democracy are two of the most powerful legitimating myths of our society, the decisions we observe are often justified by the rhetoric of the free market, and many are at least articulated by bodies that seem somewhat representative.

One major illusion existing at the intersection of the false notions of free-market capitalism and representative democracy is that of shareholder democracy. According to this notion, any citizen with enough resources to buy stock in a corporation has some degree of control over that corporation.[2] Managers of corporations are legally obligated to manage corporations in the interests of their shareholders. In fact, so it goes, it is their fiduciary obligation to manage their corporations so as to maximize shareholder profits. This legal requirement legitimates many distasteful decisions management makes, such as laying off 30,000 steelworkers to maximize shareholder profits. Management can claim they had no other choice because of their fiduciary obligations to shareholders.

In the reality of corporate management, this is just one more screen over real decision-making procedures. Corporate size gives managers many more options than they would have if they were competing in truly free competitive markets. Studies on managerial capitalism have found that corporate managers often pursue goals other than profit maximization—goals such as market share, corporate prestige, and career advancement, which often serve the interests of managers more than those of the shareholders.[3]

In a decision disallowing an attempt by Paramount to take over Time Inc. before Time could take over Warner Communications, a federal judge endorsed the notion that the fiduciary obligation to maximize

2. For a discussion of shareholder democracy, see Neil H. Jacoby, *Corporate Power and Social Responsibility* (New York: Macmillan, 1973). In a slightly different twist, Peter Druker argues that corporations are broadly controlled by citizens through their pension funds in *The Unseen Revolution* (New York: Harper & Row, 1976).

3. See Introduction, note 18.

returns to shareholders could be subordinated to other strategic objectives. He ruled that Time's and Warner's management could proceed
with their planned merger even though a Paramount merger would have
rewarded stockholders more handsomely ($200 a share, as opposed to
the $141 the stock hit when this ruling was announced).[4] Evidently, all
that is required is that satisfactory profits rather than maximum profits
be achieved. This logic would seem to allow corporations to preserve
jobs as a managerial goal, but one should not expect managers to leap to
this conclusion without tremendous pressure. In the meantime, corporate managers can claim the defense of "fiduciary responsibility" within
this "shareholder democracy" when they "have no choice" but to lay off
workers.

The false models of decision-making discussed above are important
aspects of the third-dimensional power of a capitalist elite. By focusing
citizen attention on such notions as free markets, representative democracy, and shareholder democracy, the corporate elite is spared the
scrutiny that their important strategic policy decisions should have. The
remainder of this chapter looks behind the veneer of these illusions to
provide insight into the nature of the actual decision-making process in
Pittsburgh.

The environment in which Pittsburgh decisions are made bears scant
resemblance to the rhetorical models discussed above. Rather, it can be
characterized as a network of powerful and interrelated corporate elites.
(Many of Pittsburgh's corporate elites are listed in Table 2.) In free-
market capitalism as described by Adam Smith or Milton Friedman,
firms make independent decisions in response to signals from a market
over which they have no control.[5] In Pittsburgh, many firms are quite
powerful, exercising substantial influence in the markets in which they
participate. Many face international as well as national or regional
markets. In the 1980s, all steel-makers in the noncommunist world faced
market pressures because world steel production was greater than current
demand. But for corporations like U.S. Steel, the decision to shut down
production in the Monongahela Valley was largely an internal strategic
decision rather than a strictly market-driven decision. That is, there were
a variety of other strategies available for responding to the steel market
in the 1980s (see Chapter 1). U.S. Steel's choice of strategies was guided
largely by internal factors, such as the decision to shift corporate attention and assets to Marathon Oil.

    4. New York Times, July 15, 1989, p. 1:1.
    5. Adam Smith, An Inquiry into the Nature and Causes of the Wealth of Nations (1776;
reprint, New York: Modern Library, 1965). Milton Friedman, Capitalism and Freedom
(Chicago: University of Chicago Press, 1962).

The large corporate firms are interdependent, not independent. Members of the Pittsburgh elite sit on boards of directors of several corporations. They also sit on boards of the area's educational institutions, churches, and charities, are members of the regional planning organizations, receive major loans (and thus financial oversight) from common banks, such as Mellon Bank Corporation and PNC Financial Corporation. In many cases, they are represented by common law firms—Reed Smith Shaw & McClay, which serves Mellon Bank, being the most obvious.[6] All these links provide a network of communication and coordination that is out of the public view. It is through this network, more than through competitive markets, that the corporate elites interact, and it is through this network that they develop a consensus about what the Pittsburgh region needs—while at the same time paying significant attention to what the firms need as well. However, the decisions that grow out of this network are made public through individual corporations, government bodies, or planning agencies.

Three Realms of Decision-Making

Few of the actual decisions that have transformed and continue to transform Pittsburgh can be neatly and accurately described as occurring in either of the arenas discussed above. Free-market capitalism and representative democracy have little to do with the reality of this case, and it is also impossible to separate the economic and political realms so neatly from each other. I here suggest a different approach, encompassing three realms, each containing political and economic elements (see Table 1). These realms—the private, the semipublic, and the governmental—are first defined here and then explored more fully.

The Private Realm

It is in the private realm that corporations make decisions that determine investment and employment. It is here that the decisions are made to invest in Pohang, Korea, rather than Duquesne; to loan money to

6. Reed Smith Shaw & McClay was ranked as the forty-eighth largest law firm in the country for 1985, based on its gross revenues of $53 million. The firm has 223 lawyers and 100 partners. The partners averaged a quarter of a million dollars profit each for the year. *Pittsburgh Post-Gazette*, July 14, 1986, p. 25.

Table 1.   REALMS OF DECISION-MAKING

First Realm (Private)	Second Realm (Semipublic)	Third Realm (Governmental)
Hire & fire	Plan	Maintain order
Invest	Coordinate	Provide relief
R&D	Solicit funds	Offer incentives
Select product	P.R. for plans	Do infrastructure

Sumitomo Corporation rather than Mesta Machine; to develop robots rather than high-speed rail transport. It is here that decisions are made about how many workers to hire or fire, about whether to negotiate with a union, about whether to hire full-time or part-time workers. In terms of number of people directly affected, and in terms of determining the shape of Pittsburgh's future, decisions made in this realm are most important. In this realm, only the interests of managers and stockholders are considered to have a legitimate bearing on decisions.

The Semipublic Realm

In Pittsburgh, more than in most cities, there is a strongly developed semipublic realm charged with coordinating business and public plans. In this realm, professional planners, politicians, corporate executives, and representatives of community organizations and interest groups meet to share information and to set priorities for the region's development. While few of these plans are considered binding on any participant, many of their components are actually put into practice. The process also helps shape community understanding and expectations, which can be important factors in encouraging or discouraging resistance to decisions made in the private and the governmental realms.

The Governmental Realm

The governmental realm as it relates to the transformation of Pittsburgh can best be characterized by fragmentation. Relevant policies are set by the City of Pittsburgh, by Allegheny County commissioners, by the various municipalities of the Mon Valley, by judges and law-enforcement officers at various levels, by various agencies of the Commonwealth of Pennsylvania, and by the different branches of the federal government. None of them has the jurisdiction or the responsibility or the power to approach the issue of economic transformation in a holistic manner. This lack of coherence and power in the governmental realm leaves more power to be exercised in the private realm. In part, this is the intention of the U.S. Constitution, but it is also a problem that negates the potential for democracy in communities like Pittsburgh.

In trying to address problems raised by deindustrialization, government bodies have adopted numerous policies. They have provided relief, retraining, basic education, and funding for research. They have provided money for planning. They spend vast sums of money in support of certain sectors of the economy. Since World War II, most federal support has gone to militarily related industries, but money can and does go for such projects as highways, dams, bridges, and sanitation systems. (The possibility of redirecting money tied up by the military sector should now be an important topic of public debate in the decade of the 1990s.) Governments regulate imports, exports, pollution, mergers, and so on. They can offer grants or tax breaks to corporations to influence certain decisions. In short, government tries to encourage certain types of economic activities, and it must often clean up the mess—whether social or environmental disruption—caused by certain private decisions.

This overview of the three realms of decision-making makes it clear that, in relation to the transformation of Pittsburgh, the most important decisions are made in the first realm, the private realm. Initiative for change lies there. Decisions made in the second and third realms attempt to influence those made in the first realm. The third realm is responsible for responding to decisions made in the first realm, primarily for minimizing the social disruption caused by the negative effects of many of those decisions. While actors in the private realm have great autonomy, they also have important influence in the semipublic and governmental realms. In this regard, they constitute an elite that has had the most influence and that is most responsible for reshaping Pittsburgh.

The Decision-Makers: The "Limited Polity" Model

For a model of the overall polity—that body of people organized to make decisions in society—I draw on a model of what Charles Tilly has called "The Limited Polity." In Tilly's model (see my adaptation in Figure 8),[7]

7. From Charles Tilly, *From Mobilization to Revolution* (Reading, Mass.: Addison-Wesley, 1987).

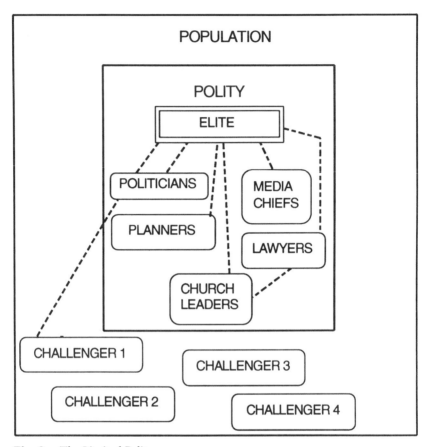

Fig. 8. The Limited Polity

the polity contains only the members of society who have significant influence on decisions. Those with less influence—most ordinary citizens—are considered outsiders in relation to the polity. Within the polity is an elite who make decisions, as well as numerous other intermediate actors, who exercise various degrees of influence on the decisions of the elite.

In our case, the elite are the economic elite of Pittsburgh. They are recognized by their positions of control in one or more of Pittsburgh's major economic institutions. They have final say in most economic decisions of consequence in Pittsburgh. Pittsburgh's intermediate actors include major politicians, as first among equals, followed by media chiefs, top union leaders, some planners, lawyers, academics, top church leaders, followed by minor politicians. Most other residents of Pittsburgh are outside the polity and have only indirect ways of influencing intermediate actors, whose influence on the elite is likely to be limited. They are the outsiders who are not even heard by the elite unless they attempt to break into the decision-making process in such ways as our three groups have tried. Only occasionally is the government process an effective avenue of influence for outsiders.

Decision-making in the three realms of Pittsburgh's polity bears little resemblance to the model of free-market capitalism and representative democracy that serves both to hide and to legitimate it. Access to the decision-making process, and accountability for decisions, are strictly limited. While democracy offers the fairness of majority rule with protection of minority rights, and free markets offer efficient production and distribution as their theoretical advantages, there is no analytical reason why we should expect decisions made in this process of three realms to be either efficient or fair. We now look more closely at each of these realms.

The First Realm: Private Decision-Making

Some of the decisions that led to the destruction of industrial employment in the Monongahela Valley (see Chapter 2) were made for very rational reasons within the confines of specific corporations. That is, (a) they were made within the corporations and without decisive participation of people outside the corporations' legal boundaries, and (b) their rationality was confined to the bounds of those corporations. If one were to consider the costs and benefits to all those affected by the decisions to eliminate nearly all steel production in the Mon Valley, some of those decisions might not appear so rational. But the reality of decision-making in the first realm is that, legally, only the interests of managers and shareholders need to be considered. What is perhaps most interesting about the work of both the DMS and Tri-State is that they sought ways to force social considerations into the private decision-making process— the first by injecting a moral component, the second by giving workers and community organizations a stake in the ownership of corporations.

The operations of individual firms, by themselves, are not so interesting at this point. What we turn our attention to now is some of the ways these individual firms and the corporate elites who dominate decisions within those firms work in coordination with one another to create or foreclose options for other actors in the region.

The key members of Pittsburgh's elite and their most significant corporate affiliations, as of 1985, have positions of substantial power in at least four of Pittsburgh's private or semipublic organizations (see Table 2).[8] For this group of men, membership in one or more of the semipublic planning agencies is quite important. From the twenty-three men listed, we can find forty-six affiliations to such bodies. The second most common link is that through banks. We can observe twenty-two links to banks at the level of executive or director. Mellon Bank alone has nine directors in this group. While these links prove little, they do show a network available for communication, coordination, and influence.

One revealing factor is that, in the elite of this erstwhile steel city, only two of these men have links to U.S. Steel. This suggests what we know from other sources—that U.S. Steel did not place tremendous importance on Pittsburgh. In 1985 the corporation not only continued reducing employment in the Pittsburgh region but also sold its sky-scraper headquarters building to Rockwell International. Many of the planners and business people interviewed for this study said they were glad that the presence of U.S. Steel was lessening. One spoke of lessening the "stranglehold" it had had, while another rejoiced that "the back of U.S. Steel had finally been broken."

The best-connected industrial firm in Table 2 is Allegheny Interna-tional, a company with one-tenth the assets of U.S. Steel that has diversified itself entirely out of its original steel business and gone transnational. The elite of Pittsburgh are ready to move to a new era in which steel will play a much smaller contributing role than the leading role it had played for well over a century.

While the elite have apparently shared a consensus about the desir-ability of steel's diminished role in Pittsburgh for quite some time, many of them were surprised at the speed of steel's demise in the 1980s. It is worth noting that their long-standing agreement favoring steel's decline was not reflected in plans for helping the Mon Valley survive the transition. Evidently they did not see this as their concern.

Power is a dynamic force, not a static force. The chart of Pittsburgh's elite merely suggests potential power. We can observe power best when it acts. Although the elite often act through the decisions their individual firms make about investment and employment, they also work together to achieve and to protect their common interests. I offer two views of

8. Names and associations in Table 2 are gathered from *Corporations Review 1985* (Pittsburgh: Herdick & Held, 1985). The table was originally compiled by the Allegheny Conference on Human Development (ACHD), a research subgroup of the Network to Save the Mon-Ohio Valley.

Table 2.   CORPORATE PITTSBURGH'S ELITES

JOHN ARTHUR
Duquesne Light–Chm
Mellon Bank–D
Joy Mfg.–D
Mine Safety Appl.–D
ACCD–Mem
RIDC–Chm
Penn SW–Chm
Robt. Morris College–Tr
Univ. of Pbg.–Tr

J. DAVID BARNES
Mellon Bank–Chm
Fed. Res. Bank (Clev)
Diamond Shamrock–D
Girard Bank–D
ACCD–Mem
RIDC–Mem
Penn SW–Pres. & CEO
Allegheny College–Tr
CMU–Tr

ANTHONY BRYAN
Allegheny Int.–D
Copperweld–Chm
Koppers Co.–D
Chrysler Corp.–D
Hamilton Oil Corp.–D
Federal Express–D
IMetal–D
ACCD–Mem
Penn SW–Mem
Pbg. Nat. Bank–D
CMU–Tr
Pbg. Ballet–Chm

ROBERT BUCKLEY
Allegheny Int.–D
Mellon Bank–D
Bell Telephone Pa.–D
Mellon Stuart Const–D
Wilkinson Match–D
ACCD–Mem
CMU–Tr
Duquesne Univ.–Tr

ALEXANDER W. CALDER
Mellon Bank–D
Joy Mfg.–Pres.
ACCD–Mem
Penn SW–Mem
CMU–Tr

RICHARD CYERT
Allegheny Int.–D
Copperweld–D
Am. Standard–D
Koppers Co.–D
H. J. Heinz Co.–D
First Boston–D
White Consol. Ind.–D
ACCD–Mem
RIDC–Mem
Penn SW–Mem
CMU–Pres.

ROBERT DICKEY III
Dravo Corp.–D
Joy Mfg.–D
Gulf Oil–D
Pbg. Nat. Bank–D
ACCD–Mem
RIDC–Mem
Penn SW–Mem
CMU–Vice-Chm
Pbg. Theological Sem.
United Way of Alleg. Cty.

DOUGLAS DANFORTH
Pbg. Nat. Bank–D
PPG Ind.–D
Westinghouse Elec.–D
Whirlpool Corp.–D
ACCD–Mem
Penn SW–Mem
CMU–Chm

Table 2. (*continued*)

THOMAS FAUGHT JR.
Dravo Corp.–Chm & CEO
ACCD–Mem
Duquesne Univ.–Tr
CMU–Tr

H. KROME GEORGE
Alcoa–D
Mellon Bank–D
Todd Shipyards
Intl. Paper–D
Norfolk S. RR–D
TRW–D
Intl. Exec. Serv. Corp
ACCD–Mem
Univ. of Pbg.–Tr

THOMAS GRAHAM
Mellon Bank–D
Hammermill Paper–D
US Steel–D
Intl. Iron & Steel Inst.
ACCD–Mem
RIDC–Mem
CMU–Tr

HENRY HILLMAN
Hillman Co.–Chm
Pbg. Nat. Bank–Chm
Cummins Engine–D
Chemical Bank NY–D
General Electric–D
ACCD–Mem
Penn SW–Mem

MILTON HULME
Equitable Gas–D
Fed. Res. Bank Pbg.–Chm
Koppers Co.–D
Mine Safety Appl.–CEO
Pbg. Brewing Co.–D
ACCD–Mem
Penn SW–Mem
CMU–Tr

ROBERT KIRBY
Allegheny Int.–D
Mellon Bank–D
ACCD–Mem
Univ. of Pbg.–Tr

WILLIAM KNOELL
Cyclops Corp.–Pres.
Duquesne Light–D
Fed. Res. Bank (Clev)
Koppers Co.–D
ACCD–Mem
Penn SW–Mem
CMU–Tr

JAMES LEE
Joy Mfg.–D
Pbg. Nat. Bank–D
Gulf Oil–D
ACCD–Mem
Penn SW–Mem
Robt. Morris College–Tr
CMU–Tr

RICHARD K. MEANS
Equimark–D
Ryan Homes–D
ACCD–Mem
CMU–Tr
Robt. Morris College–Tr

ANTHONY O'REILLY
Allegheny Int.–D
H. J. Heinz Co.
Bankers Trust Corp.–D
Mobil Corp.–D
ACCD–Mem
RIDC–Mem
Univ. of Pbg.–Tr
Duquesne Univ.–Tr

Table 2. (*continued*)

DAVID RODERICK
US Steel–Chm
ACCD–Mem
RIDC–Mem
CMU–Tr

WILLIAM P. SNYDER
Mellon Bank–D
H. J. Heinz Co.–D
Salem Corp.–D
Shenango Furn.–Pres. & Chm
Snyder Mining–Pres. & D
Whitney Nat. Bank–D
ACCD–Mem
RIDC–Mem
CMU–Tr

KONRAD WEISS
Cyclops Corp.–D
Dravo Corp.–D
Mobay Chem.–D
Euro-Amer. Bancorp–D
ACCD–Mem
Penn SW–Mem
CMU–Tr

L. STANTON WILLIAMS
Corning Corp.–D
Dravo Corp.–D
Mellon Bank–D
PPG–D
Prudent'l Ins.–D
Rubbermaid–D
ACCD–Mem
RIDC–Mem
Penn SW–Mem
CMU–Tr
United Way of Alleg. Cty.

JAMES WILCOCK
Copperweld–D
H. H. Robertson Co.–D
Joy Mfg.–D
L. B. Foster–D
Mellon Bank–D
Pogo Prod. Co.–D
Harris Corp.–D
Michael Baker Corp.–D
Pace Indus.–D

Source: Data from *Corporations Review 1985* (Pittsburgh: Herdick & Held, 1985). Originally compiled by the Allegheny Committee on Human Development.

Key: ACCD   = Allegheny Conference on Community Development
     RIDC   = Regional Industrial Development Corporation
     D   = Director
     Mem   = Member
     Tr   = Trustee of the College
     Penn SW = Penn Southwest Assn
     Chm   = Chairman
     Pres.   = President

their power in action. One view, from below, is from a food bank that offended members of the elite. The other view is quite literally from above, from an economist at Mellon Bank who is involved in envisioning a changing Pittsburgh.

The View from a Homestead Food Bank

From a dingy food bank in decaying Homestead, the network of the powerful appears decidedly paternalistic and stingy. In the words of a food bank worker, the corporate elite seemed to be saying, "We'll feed the people, but not if they're going to fight."

An incident involving the YMCA-1397 food bank made both the existence and the efficiency of the elite network clear. The food bank was set up in 1981 by steelworkers employed at or recently unemployed by U.S. Steel's Homestead Works. As such they were members of USWA Local Number 1397. It was one of the first efforts of what would soon become the Mon Valley Unemployed Committee. When the group approached the United Way for funding, United Way asked the YMCA to handle the group's finances and to provide a channel for contributions through the Y as a nonprofit organization, hence the name "YMCA-1397." The food bank raised its own funds through contributions, raffles, a fish fry, concerts, and so on, including a boost from rock star Bruce Springsteen whenever he did a local concert.

The food bank's organizers included Jay Weinberg and Mike Stout, who later devoted most of their energies to the Tri-State Conference on Steel. It also included Local 1397 president Ron Weisen and Dale Worton, who both became active with the Network to Save the Mon-Ohio Valley and the DMS. Worton continued as the food bank's manager.

In 1986, apparently as a cost-cutting measure, Worton allowed the Network/DMS to send out a mailing using stationery from the food bank, with the name "YMCA-1397" in the return address. The letter was sent to several Pittsburgh executives, some of whom happened to sit on the YMCA's board of directors.

The response of these directors was swift and effective. It demonstrated the cohesiveness of corporate elites, the network of communication and control, and two of those mechanisms of control: contact through boards of directors, and bank finance. According to Ron Flanders, head of accounting at the YMCA, the letter contained "very uncomplimentary statements about executives at U.S. Steel and Mellon Bank." Upon seeing the letter, Flanders explained, the board members "told my boss—the chief executive of the Y—to end support for the food bank." The Y promptly complied. Flanders noted: "We have a very large construction loan from Mellon. That could make things difficult for us."[9]

At the time of his interview, Dale Worton was uncertain how the Y's move would affect the long-term viability of the food bank. In the short run, it was quite disrupting, as loss of Y sponsorship meant bookkeeping and nonprofit status arrangements would have to be redrawn if the ability to receive tax-deductible funding was to be preserved.

The View from Mellon Bank

Mellon is the chief banker for many of the local corporations, and its influence extends far beyond limited banking matters. The commanding view from high up in any of Mellon Bank's new office buildings that tower over the Golden Triangle gives one a sense of vision as well as an ability to detach oneself from the details of the lives of sordid individuals far below. It offers a perspective from which powerful executives boldly chart the future of the region arrayed below them.

The thoughts of a senior Mellon Bank economist provide insight into how the business community at large sees the issues confronting the economic transformation of Pittsburgh.[10] The statements of this businessman were often echoed by other business, academic, and political figures interviewed, but no one else drew the threads together quite so succinctly. The fundamental premise of the economist—one might call it his cosmic viewpoint because of its all-inclusiveness and the nearly mystical quality of the voice with which it was intoned—was "You can't fight the world economy. Our rising standard of living is being challenged by low wages elsewhere." The rest of the interview was largely an elaboration of the Mellon strategy of how to adapt to this challenging world economy. It soon became clear that corporate strategy was at least as important as market forces in reshaping Pittsburgh.

"The region's steel market has been in decline since 1955," he asserted. In 1979 it began "its latest and final death rattle," he added without apparent remorse. He explained that steel moved out of Pittsburgh to places with a "better climate." It was clear he was not talking about Pittsburgh's frostbelt location when he went on to say that corporations

9. Dale Worton, telephone interviews, July 17, 1986; Ron Flanders, July 30, 1986.

10. The senior economist did not want to be identified by name because "I don't want this to come back to haunt me." Interview conducted at Mellon Bank headquarters on July 29, 1986.

view unions in Pittsburgh as "aggressive and antimanagement." In his view, unions had "sealed the doom of steel and other industries. Corporations don't want to overcome adversarial relations." When asked what he meant by adversarial relations, he responded tersely, "It means you don't go there." Union attitudes, he said, were "a major problem for the city to overcome."

Part of the strategy for overcoming the "problem" of labor militancy became clear when he added, "This will change over time as the percentage of unionization falls." How to reduce unionization? Speaking as an economist who knows that the Phillips curve (the negative correlation of rates of unemployment and wage increases) is enforced as much as it is observed, he answered, "You can't get high wages in a high unemployment environment."

He was clear that such changes may take time. "I see no quick turnaround for the Mon Valley. There's a need to thin it out some in terms of population." As steel declined from 1980 through 1984, Allegheny County (home of both the city of Pittsburgh and many of the steel towns of the Mon Valley) lost 40,000 residents. The *Pittsburgh Post-Gazette* called this population decline "a blessing that should be accepted and built upon."[11] The economist felt that more people needed to leave the Valley, and faster, but that they were constrained by an unfortunate "mind-set . . . this cultural thing." He explained: "With several generations in the mills, they developed a community feeling of strength, stability." As he eased back in his leather chair, he noted with obvious disdain "the level of income these people had" and suggested that they remember the problems of their ancestors. "They too may have to move on and struggle like in the old country." He wanted them to get the message that they should hold out no hope for the return of high-wage industrial employment. Pittsburgh's elites are pursuing high-tech industry. There will be no new smokestack jobs, he insisted. "We've got to replace them with another kind of worker."

In the delicate process of rebuilding the economy of the Mon Valley, it is clear that those making decisions are concerned not only with finding the appropriate types of businesses to establish, but also with the type of social relations and expectations established in the process. Government plays a crucial part in this process. The Mellon economist suggested that government can help by retraining workers and giving incentives such as tax breaks for business and free access to a rebuilt commercial infrastructure, but government must be "careful not to do too much or it will give the people the impression that it is government's responsibility to help them."

11. *Pittsburgh Post-Gazette*, "No Growth a Blessing," lead editorial, May 29, 1985, p. 8.

In summary, the Mellon economist indicated that the demise of steel is welcomed as a way to reduce the social and political power of the Pittsburgh work force as well as wages. To do so, wages must be driven down (through periods of extended unemployment if necessary), unions must be weakened or eliminated, and the culture of working-class communities must be crushed if it gets in the way of "progress." Business will lead the way in this process. The proper role of government is to reduce what the transformation will cost business without raising the expectations of the public at large. This is the vision of Pittsburgh's elites, a vision that reflects how much confidence they have in their power. It is a vision that consciously seeks to weaken the role that workers and their communities will play in shaping their futures. At the same time, it carefully allows only a limited role for government in the process.

The Second Realm: Semipublic Planning Agencies

Pittsburgh is one of the country's most advanced metropolitan areas with regard to nongovernmental planning bodies. The oldest of these bodies is the Allegheny Conference on Community Development (ACCD), started in 1943 by banker R. King Mellon, according to one chronicler, "to save Pittsburgh from ruinous decline."[12] Park H. Martin, the ACCD's first executive, describes the Pittsburgh Renaissance, its first project, as "the story of enlightened, unselfish teamwork."[13] The renaissance program did show that with sufficient coordination business and government could move decisively to reshape the city. However, in the words of another chronicler, "the issues are defined and the programs established largely in response to business objectives."[14] The result was "a dramatic expansion of public enterprize and investment to serve corporate needs, . . . a welfare state in reverse."[15]

There are several more recently formed planning groups, spin-offs of the ACCD. These include the Penn's Southwest Association and the Regional Industrial Development Corporation of Southwest Pennsylva-

12. Roy Lubov, *Twentieth-Century Pittsburgh: Government, Business, and Environmental Change* (New York: John Wiley & Sons, 1969), p. 106.

13. Park H. Martin, "Narrative of the Allegheny Conference on Community Development and the Pittsburgh Renaissance, 1943–1954" (Typescript, Carnegie Mellon University Library, 1964), p. 70.

14. Lubov, *Twentieth-Century Pittsburgh*, p. vii.

15. Ibid., p. 106.

nia (RIDC), the Ben Franklin Partnership and the Milrite Council (both founded by the Commonwealth of Pennsylvania to channel funds to projects favored by other planning agencies), and the Western Pennsylvania Advanced Technology Center (sponsored by Carnegie-Mellon and the University of Pittsburgh with funding from the Commonwealth through Ben Franklin). Other smaller but similarly linked agencies exist as well.

How do these planning groups affect the ability of working people to have a say in the decisions that shape their communities? In theory, they may either facilitate that process or work to discourage it. We can determine the facilitative or nonfacilitative nature of these groups by examining, first, the economic interests of many of their key participants and, second, some of the planning reports they produced during the 1980s as they attempted to define the future of the Pittsburgh region.

Each of these agencies is controlled by members of Pittsburgh's corporate elite, who make up their boards of directors, serve as executive officers, and provide major funding. Pittsburgh's corporate elite are nearly unanimous about the importance of participating in these planning bodies (see Table 2).

The corporate affiliations of leaders of these three planning agencies give an idea of some of the corporate links facilitated by these agencies. David Barnes is president and chief executive officer of the Penn's Southwest Association. He is also the chairman of Mellon Bank, a member of the ACCD and the RIDC, a trustee of Carnegie Mellon University and Allegheny College, and a member of the board of directors of Diamond Shamrock and Girard Bank, as well as governor of the Federal Reserve Bank of Cleveland. John Arthur serves as Chairman for both Penn's Southwest and the RIDC. He is also chair of Duquesne Light (the area's major supplier of electrical power), a director of Mellon Bank, Joy Manufacturing, and Mine Safety Appliances, a trustee of the University of Pittsburgh and Robert Morris College, and of course a member of the ACCD. James Lee, president of the ACCD, like John Arthur, sits on the board of Joy Manufacturing. He is also a director of Pittsburgh National Bank and Gulf Oil, a member of Penn's Southwest, and a trustee for Carnegie Mellon University and Robert Morris College.[16] A study of the ACCD's leadership from 1968 through 1985 shows that the offices of chairman, president, and first vice-president were all held by directors of either Mellon Bank or Pittsburgh National Bank, with Mellon holding more than two-thirds of the slots.[17]

16. See Table 2 and note 8 above.
17. David Rosenberg, "Did the Collapse of Basic Industry Really Take the Allegheny Conference by Surprise?" *In Pittsburgh*, March 21–March 27, 1990, p. 19.

The prevalence of corporate elites within the planning bodies as sources of both leadership and funding suggests that these organizations are likely vehicles for advancing corporate interests. At the very least, one could infer that they would never oppose fundamental concerns of the business community. These organizations do provide a way to coordinate the economic environment of the region in ways that markets cannot. They deliberately help to shape the region's future.

One of the key presumptions of this planning process is that progress will come through the growth of private business. Given this presumption, the role of nonbusiness participants in the planning process is that of facilitator to business. They may offer coordination, incentives, concessions, and various other gifts. Within this corporate-subsidized framework, they can offer very little, if any, control.

The fact that these bodies include participation of representatives of state and local governments as well as local labor and civic organizations does not guarantee that their proposals will democratically address the hopes and needs of the constituencies they symbolically represent. Rather, it allows the planning bodies to present their recommendations as though they were in the best interests of the community at large. Furthermore, the consultative, consensus-building process in which the nonbusiness representatives engage often has the effect of co-opting them into compliance with the business-dominated agenda. Thus, these groups not only coordinate business planning but also help eliminate resistance to it. They also preempt efforts to plan on a more democratic basis.

If we judge this process in relation to how well it has served the people of the Monongahela Valley, this nondemocratic nature is apparent in the results of its work. Most people of the Valley wanted to preserve jobs at union wages. They expressed this through their unions, civic gatherings, letters to the editor, and so on. What they got, as a result of decisions made in the private sector, was devastation. They also got a series of reports from these planning groups that sought to address the problems of the changing economy and to chart the course of the region's future.

A brief review of four of these reports, in chronological order, will provide insight into the way these groups plan the region's future. Our examination will pay particular attention to what the working people of the Mon Valley did or did not get out of this planning process.

Reports of Four Planning Groups

On June 1–3, 1983, the University of Pittsburgh sponsored a conference on "Regional Development Strategy for the 1980s and 1990s." Those in attendance included leaders from business, universities, churches, media, and labor organizations. Seven locally based corporations and the ACCD sponsored the event.

Out of this conference came a report with thirty-five recommendations, only six of which mentioned labor issues. The first of those six addressed the fundamental question "Will the real standard of living for large groups of people in the region decline in the years ahead?" and recommended that the ACCD *study* it—a classic nondecision. The second endorsed the concept of "enterprise zones," a Reagan-endorsed proposal to create zones where tax and minimum-wage laws were suspended. The third and fourth both recommended that labor and management cooperate to reduce even the appearance of tensions between them. The fifth suggested an increase in "opportunities for employee-ownership." And the sixth urged labor to make its views known in the "design and implementation of training and retraining programs."

There is no suggestion that wages should be protected or jobs be increased, or even that training programs be expanded. Except for the vague statement about employee-ownership opportunities, workers are given only studies, a chance to talk, a chance at still-lower wages, and a suggestion that they stop complaining and get along if they ever hope to lure new jobs to the region. On the other hand, it is recommended that business have lower taxes, management support, subsidized financing, infrastructure improvements tailored to business needs, and help with technology transfer.

In November 1984 the ACCD issued its glossy, multicolor, two-volume report, *A Strategy for Growth: An Economic Development Plan for the Pittsburgh Region.* The report begins with a frank and illuminating discussion of its own premises:

1. Change is inevitable. The forces at work are irreversible. Steel will not come back.
2. Future development should emphasize diversity.
3. Policy-makers should seek long-term solutions, not quick fixes. Fundamental adjustments are necessary. It is not possible to create massive numbers of new jobs in the near future.
4. Strategy should be private-sector-oriented and market-driven, . . . with strong public-sector support.

The report proposes a nine-point program. Five of the points are "in the area of business and job development." These mention provision of capital, technology, and technical support as well as recruitment of new firms. They do not mention anything about the workers who will hold the jobs or what sort of wages they will get. Two points do refer to workers: They suggest training and retraining, as well as the need to "improve the labor climate by addressing [i.e., eliminating] both the perception and the reality of the current situation [i.e., labor militancy] in the region."

It is not surprising that the program does not provide a list of workers' needs. The task forces that helped generate these recommendations had little labor participation. The manufacturing task force had eighteen members, one from labor; the task force addressing the burgeoning service sector had thirty-three members, none from labor; the task force on improving the business climate had seventeen members, two from labor.

In June 1985 the City of Pittsburgh, along with Allegheny County, produced a report called *Strategy 21: Economic Development Strategy to Begin the Twenty-First Century.* In addition to the city and county, the report is nominally co-authored by the presidents of the University of Pittsburgh and Carnegie Mellon University. We have already seen some of the ways these two universities are connected to the network of corporations and planning agencies in Pittsburgh.[18] Developed as a request for funding from the Commonwealth of Pennsylvania, the report describes how planners believe business should be helped with taxpayer-financed capital improvements. It asks for approximately $425 million. Priorities expressed, in terms of declining funding, are highway development, airport development, university–advanced technology research, tourism, and last, as well as least, "Mon Valley Redevelopment."

In February 1987 the Mon Valley Commission, a group organized by the Allegheny County commissioners, issued its *Report . . . for the Economic Revitalization of the Monongahela, Youghiogheny, and Turtle Creek Valleys.* It found: "Clearing prime riverfront properties of rusting steel mills to make them attractive to new development is a crucial early step." This commission also draws on the work of task forces that are similarly skewed to underrepresent labor—for example, its seventeen-member Education and Labor Task Force includes only one representative of organized labor. The fact that it includes twice as many (two) representatives of organizations providing relief services to the unemployed may suggest something about the group's dismal view of the future. It recommends possible reopenings of parts of two abandoned steel mills.

18. Of the two presidents, Richard Cyert is decidedly better connected. Not only is he a member of the ACCD, the RIDC, and Penn Southwest, but as of 1985 he was also on the board of directors of Allegheny International, Copperweld, American Standard, Koppers, H. J. Heinz, First Boston Bank, and White Consolidated Industries (*Corporations Review 1985*).

Some of these would provide employment in steel, others would provide jobs in lower-wage light industrial enterprises.

This Mon Valley Report is distinct in that it does call for at least a demonstration-size public-employment jobs program, as well as prior notice of major layoffs or plant closings. Inclusion of these more "radical" programs reflects the fact that the local government, local bank, and local business officials who dominate the commission's membership are more dependent on former steelworkers for votes, for tax payments, and for patronage of their businesses than are the elite of the region as a whole. Thus, they have more need to do something for unemployed steelworkers and for their common communities than do the corporate executives that dominate the previously discussed studies.

While there are still economic and social differences between the local business leaders who wrote this report and the workers suffering most directly from unemployment, they have something important in common. They are both rooted in the same community in a way that gives them shared interests that are different from those pursued by globally mobile capital. It is not that local business people are more liberal or more moral than their counterparts in the corporate skyscrapers, but that they face different structural incentives, some of which are identical to those of the workers of their communities.

This review of studies shows a number of things. While it does not show a distinct conspiracy to attack the position of labor further, it does show that those who view themselves as in charge of planning the region's future see need for only token representation of labor in that decision-making process. As a result of labor's virtual exclusion, there is little to suggest that key assumptions such as "the best way to increase employment is to improve the climate for business profits" were ever challenged. In the case of the Mon Valley Report, we have seen that changing the composition of commission task forces can change the sort of recommendations generated. One can imagine that a task force that is even more representative of the region's affected population would come up with still different recommendations. Just as the Steel Valley Authority argued that it is important that the interests of workers and neighborhoods be embedded in the ownership and decision-making structure of City Pride Bakery, we can here see a reason for structurally ensuring that interests of local communities are represented in the planning process. Representing the interests of all classes in that process is similarly important.

Studies that attempt to guide the future accomplish at least two sorts of things. First, they may actually produce plans that lead to new investment decisions—either public or private—that shape future development. As such, the issue of who is involved in producing those plans is politically quite significant. Second, such studies may also work as "nondecisions." That is, when groups of people demand some sort of action, they may sometimes be temporarily placated by the announcement that studies about what to do to help them are under way. If mobilized groups can be put off long enough, they may demobilize, or at least lose steam. Groups such as the Tri-State Conference on Steel or the Mon Valley Unemployed Committee were formed in outraged response to steel shutdowns. Leaders of these groups were often invited to participate in discussions leading to these reports. It is more likely that they were influenced to see the corporate leaders they met with less antagonistically, as a result of working with them in abstract discussions, than that they significantly affected the outcomes of those discussions. Furthermore, the recommendations of some of these reports included occasional concessions to the interests of unemployed workers, such as calls for a public employment program. If these proposals were made in the knowledge that they would probably never be implemented, they were merely another form of nondecision, fine tools for discouraging future citizen participation.

Regardless of the work invested, the at least symbolic inclusiveness of the task forces, and the public attention focused on the generation of these planning reports, final decisions on investment and employment remain in the first realm of the decision-making process, that of the private firms. Because the difference between planning documents and what gets accomplished is often quite large, the planning bodies' function as agents of social control may be at least as important as their actual planning function.

The legitimacy of these planning bodies is established by their appearance of being forward-looking visionaries representative of diverse community interests or, at the least, of being composed of those who will seek "the public good" or some such undefined but much revered concept. They are most vulnerable to charges that they actually do not represent the community's best interests. Generally, their aura of respectability as well as their defensive tools of co-optation and endless delay serve as adequate protections for their legitimacy. In that these planning bodies sometimes do become a focus of public anger, they can also serve as a first line of defense for the corporations whose interests they most fully represent.

The Third Realm: Government

In a democracy, citizens have a formal expectation that elected politicians will make decisions of major consequence for society. Already we have seen that businesses and planning bodies make a great many of the decisions that shape Pittsburgh's social and economic development. Politicians and the governments they manage also play an important role.

Before describing the role government has played in relation to Pittsburgh's economic transformation, it is useful to clarify the role government can reasonably be expected to play. With respect to economic affairs, we can distinguish a spectrum of possible roles for government ranging from the command economy of a totally centralized and socialized society to the completely laissez-faire economy of a society governed by a classic liberal state. We can imagine that either of these governmental arrangements can be democratic—which we can define to mean, at least, serving the expressed will of the majority of the people.

As discussed above, the political order of the United States describes itself as a free-market capitalist society governed by a representative democracy—that is, closer to the liberal than the socialist end of the spectrum. The theory of the capitalist state evolved during the time of capitalism's emergence in seventeenth- and eighteenth-century England. It asserted that economic affairs were best left entirely unregulated by the state, that the aggregate result of individuals pursuing their own economic goals and interacting through free markets was the best way to maximize and distribute society's production.

The socialist alternative assumes no such benevolent outcome of market competition and charges government with the responsibility of regulating both production and distribution. The legitimate functions of the liberal state were strictly limited to ensuring national and personal security. Personal security has been interpreted to include not only protection of one's body and possessions from physical assault, but also provision of basic common services, such as those having to do with sanitation, education, and transportation. That is, while economic production was left to individuals, the state was charged with maintaining an environment in which individuals could safely work and live.

Economic production in the late twentieth century bears little resemblance to that of eighteenth-century England. It is hopelessly anachronistic to characterize most economic activity as that of individuals. Early in this century, the government of the United States was forced to admit that markets would not guarantee socially desirable outcomes, and it gradually took on at least nominal responsibility for ensuring that products were safe to use, fairly advertised, and produced under safe conditions, that workers were paid a minimum wage, that all had the right to at least a certain level of income, some health services, and education, and that the environment be protected from the worst ravages of economic activity. All this can be taken as recognition that government must ensure some level of common good that market competition does not provide and that market competition may actually affect adversely. This expansion of government intervention in economic activity has not been without controversy. One way of understanding that controversy is to recognize what has happened to the concept of the "individual" in the market. As the size of economic producers changed from that of individual artisan to transnational corporation, it became clear that not all "individuals" were equal. Government gradually limited the power of some "individuals" (corporations) to damage other individuals—workers, consumers, and, one might add, other corporations. Here an element of class conflict enters the political arena. (It is important to note the limited nature of the conflict, as most relevant legislation was written in consultation with—if not by—the regulated corporations.) Corporations have carefully sought to limit the damage done to them by government's entrance into the marketplace, and governments have usually been sympathetic to corporate concerns.

At present in the United States, it is reasonable to expect that government will be reluctant to interfere with what it regards as internal decisions of businesses, but it is also important to note that citizens now expect government to assume the responsibility of providing for the common welfare in ways that may require some intervention. Thus, in evaluating the role of government in Pittsburgh's economic transformation, we can hold it accountable to the standards of a twentieth-century liberal democracy. That is, we can ask: (1) Is government providing personal security and basic common services? (2) Is it involved in providing for the common welfare? and (3) Is it serving the expressed will of the majority of the people?

When we examine the role government has played in Pittsburgh, we see that it has had difficulty in meeting even the first of these criteria. Furthermore, rather than serving as an active focal point for social decision-making, it has taken a primarily reactive role—responding to major decisions reached in the private realm.

Given these major constraints on the political process, politicians, along with various charities, are left to deal with the aftermath of the sometimes devastating decisions Pittsburgh's corporate leaders make. They must do so in order to fulfill their obligation to keep order in society and in order to get reelected. Generally, politicians interpret their role in a very limited way that allows them to make only some decisions. Given budget constraints, they may allocate money for relief, for job training, for planning, and for incentives to business. They may also prohibit certain activities. That is all they feel they may do.

It is reasonable to assume that the decisions of politicians are motivated by some generalized sense of what is "good" for "the public," as well as by a desire to get reelected. Getting reelected requires keeping a sufficient number of constituents reasonably satisfied. Constituents include not only workers but owners of businesses as well, and owners and workers may have differing interests when it comes to planning a region's economic future. Since owners are more likely to be able to make campaign contributions, it would be reasonable to assume that, on a per capita basis, it is more important to keep owners happy than it is to keep workers happy, but since there are many more workers who vote than there are owners, we might expect this to balance out, except for two factors. First, we know that money plays a tremendous role not only in influencing elected officials but also in choosing who will be selected to run for elected office and how those selected will present themselves to the voters. Second, once politicians are elected they are influenced in an additional indirect way, described by Charles Lindblom:[19] They must maintain the "confidence" of business, or business will not invest. In the extreme case, there is the threat that business may "vote with their feet"—substantially reduce production or shut down completely in favor of another location. If business does not invest, all constituents will suffer, and they may well blame any politician who has offended business confidence. Thus, when politicians think of "the public interest" they tend to include in that a healthy respect for the desires and aversions of business. We have already seen that, despite the free-market fantasies of Adam Smith, we have no reason to believe that the aggregate results of business desires will equal the public welfare. While the sensitivity of politicians to corporate concerns does not give business the unfettered ability to write its own checks from the public coffers, it does give business a strong influence over what programs will be favored, and a strong veto over programs it opposes.

The Politicians' View

It is neither possible nor necessary here to present a full study of the ways Pittsburgh's politicians make their decisions. What is helpful, however, is an overview of how some of the region's politicians view the issues of Pittsburgh's economic transformation, of their responsibilities and abilities with regard to that process, and a review of some policies implemented by government at the national, state, and local levels in

19. Charles Lindblom, "Market as Prison," *Journal of Politics* 44 (1982), 324–36.

response to the changing economic environment. Many of the insights reported here were obtained through a series of interviews conducted with Tom Foerster, Allegheny County commissioner and Democratic party chair; Edward P. Zemprelli of Clairton, minority leader of the Pennsylvania State Senate; Charles Martoni, mayor of Swissvale; Leo Zabelski, mayor of Duquesne; and from remarks of three local U.S. Congressmen who spoke at the USWA's "Save American Industry and Jobs Day" in June 1986.

With the exception of the two mayors, all these politicians could be lumped into the category of traditional, New Deal Democrats—that is, they are concerned about their labor constituencies, but they accept as given the rights of private business to make its own decisions about levels of investment and employment.

Zabelski of Duquesne departed to the right of the group. He saw unions as the cause of their own troubles, blaming high wages and rigid work rules for causing the demise of local steel. Although Duquesne was the site of a major U.S. Steel mill, at the start of the 1980s only one-sixth of the mill's work force lived there. The rest had moved to newer suburban housing as their standards of living rose, leaving him with a constituency composed mostly of welfare recipients, retirees, and small-business people such as himself. He was angry that efforts to reactivate the Duquesne mill's Dorothy Six blast furnace were delaying his efforts to bring in light industry that would offer employment, albeit at much lower wages. He believed the few hundred jobs that might be salvaged in the effort to save Dorothy would not go to local residents, so he opposed the project. He was largely ignored by the more powerful county commissioners, as well as by U.S. Steel and the Steelworkers Union.

Across the river from Duquesne, Mayor Charles Martoni of Swissvale departed slightly to the left. Martoni was a college administrator and professor who was more apparently sympathetic to the rights and needs of labor. Swissvale is uphill from the Edgar Thomson works of Brad-dock. It has gained residents from Braddock, just as Duquesne lost them. It had also been the home of a major railroad equipment factory, American Standard's Union Switch & Signal Company, which shut down in 1987, eliminating 1,200 jobs. A strong proponent of the Steel Valley Authority, Martoni worked closely with both the Tri-State Con-ference on Steel and the fairly militant United Electrical Workers union Local 610 on efforts to encourage and/or compel the plant to stay open. He was convinced that both the workers and the community had a right to better treatment than they were getting, but he had little power to compel it. He and his worker-allies turned to the state court system for relief. They got none.

Except for Zabelski, none of the politicians had a simple explanation for the demise of the local steel industry, yet all agreed that the Reagan administration had made a bad situation worse by acting too slowly to curb imports and by cutting the types of federal aid they needed to help rebuild and retrain. As a solution, all favored stronger restrictions on imports, while Zabelski, County Commissioner Foerster, and State Assemblyman Zemprelli all spoke of various incentives they had tried to provide to induce new business investment. Foerster and Zemprelli also talked about increasing job-training programs. Foerster, Zabelski, and Zemprelli all agreed that major efforts would be needed to overcome what they called the "negative image" the region had as a result of its history of labor militancy and recent demonstrations, especially those of the DMS. Without successfully addressing this image problem, they felt they could not expect business to move into the Valley.

While all three congressmen were willing to speak about the "right" of workers to employment, only Martoni and Foerster showed a willingness to use government power to ensure this right. The importance of Martoni's willingness is diminished by his nearly total impotence. Foerster, the region's most powerful politician, had provided money for retraining displaced workers; he was pressing the state to fund at least a pilot public works program; and he said he had been willing to use the county's powers of condemnation to seize the Duquesne Mill from U.S. Steel if feasibility studies had been more favorable. Foerster's asserted willingness to use the county's power to seize property is interesting in light of his initial refusal to have the county support the creation of an independent Steel Valley Authority, which theoretically could also have seized the property. One can only speculate about whether this reflects merely a bureaucratic tendency to preserve one's own powers intact, or whether it might gain extra impetus from an unwillingness to have a more community-based agency derived from grass-roots political insurgency wielding such power.

Assemblyman Zemprelli also made a gesture that, on the face of it, might seem to challenge the prerogatives of business. He introduced a bill requiring that all businesses opening in the Mon Valley with government assistance pay a minimum wage of $7.50 per hour. The argument was that one needed not only jobs, but jobs that could pay a living wage for family people. The bill was not Zemprelli's idea. It had been pushed on him by one of his local constituents, the Rev. Douglas Roth of the DMS. Rather than say no to this group that might skunk-bomb or otherwise disrupt his office, he chose an overtly responsive action, confident it would lead to a nondecision. He carried it to the State Assembly, where he let it die. In the Assembly, he said, the bill met opposition, some on its merits and some because it derived from the controversial DMS, and then there was the "silent opposition." The silent opposition, he explained, came from the business and industrial interests. Because they know how difficult it would be to pass such a bill, they remain silent unless a major effort is being made on behalf of the bill. Their silence, however, communicates.

All these politicians have believed that the issues raised by Pittsburgh's economic transformation were at the top of their list of priorities. What is common about all of their experiences is that they have been able to do little to affect the course of change or even to lessen the misery of their dislocated constituents.

Government Policies Adopted

A review of some of the major policies adopted by government at the national, state, and local levels helps confirm the conclusion that government has little initiative in shaping Pittsburgh's economic transformation. All three levels of government are involved in providing various types of relief to workers who have lost their jobs (see Table 3). These levels of relief vary according to the amount of pressure workers are able to apply to government. When unemployment was at its highest nationally in the early 1980s, workers were able to win mortgage relief and increased unemployment benefits. As the numbers affected decreased— not individual need—relief was cut back.

One major difference between local and national actions is the level of specificity. While local government can address very specific issues, the national government is primarily involved with policies that affect the economy as a whole. This has not always helped Pittsburgh. Both the Carter and the Reagan administrations sought to reduce inflation by driving up interest rates and unemployment just as the steel industry was facing intensified international pressure. This made the investment required to save regionally important steel jobs less likely and made reemployment almost impossible. Furthermore the Reagan policy of encouraging attacks on organized labor weakened the area's work force even more, when it most needed to defend itself. The policy of restricting steel imports—seen as too little and too late by many—did not stop U.S. Steel from closing domestic plants and importing steel from abroad.

Local government does have the ability to stand up to corporations, either by pressuring them or by taking their property (see Table 3), but it has done this only very rarely and, with the exception of the Nabisco case, with very limited consequences for the corporations or the com-

Table 3. GOVERNMENT RESPONSES TO CHANGING
ECONOMY

Level of Gov't	Policy or Action
National	Macroeconomic adjustments. Interest rate, money supply, level of spending. Investment tax credits. U.S. Steel used theirs to buy Marathon Oil. Encourage union busting. Destruction of air controllers union, antilabor appointments to NLRB, antilabor policies of NLRB and federal courts. Regulate imports. Voluntary restrictions on imports of steel and autos, subsidies for some other goods. Unemployment compensation. Increase then decrease period covered, as needed, to respond to workers' challenges.
Commonwealth of Pennsylvania	Retraining programs. Fund at low levels. Welfare. In conjunction with national and local gov't provide AFDC, food stamps, etc. Aid to bankrupt communities. Provide police services, intervene in schools, etc. Mortgage relief. Provide funds to banks to prevent some foreclosures. Planning. Fund planning groups (ACCD et al.). Development. Fund infrastructure improvements to encourage business development.
Local: Pittsburgh Region	Maintain order. Enforce mortgage foreclosures and evictions, police protests & jail some protestors, arrange moratorium on foreclosures. Reemployment. Fund some local training programs, conduct job fairs. Development. Plan new development, develop infrastructure for new private investment. Tax incentives. Offer tax breaks to encourage private development. Pressure corporations. Pressure Nabisco not to leave town, Mellon to release paychecks during Mesta bankruptcy, U.S. Steel to delay demolition of blast furnace. Create Steel Valley Authority. Has power to take over industrial properties to encourage new enterprises.

munity. The most common means of attempting to get a corporation to respond to government is through incentives. Incentives are used at all three levels. One of the problems with incentives is that they are very imprecise, often because legislators are unwilling to take responsibility for formulating them precisely enough that they accomplish specific policy objectives. They are also imprecise because they are merely incentives—that is, they leave the final decisions up to private executives operating in the first realm of decision-making.

One can find numerous examples of incentives failing to accomplish their objectives. Management of U.S. Steel lobbied the federal government for tax relief very strongly. It claimed the savings were needed to modernize its steel mills, but then it turned around and used the money to buy Marathon Oil. Similarly, local governments may build industrial parks to attract new business, but the investment is lost if business does not respond to the incentives. As states and localities offer corporations tax relief to attract new investment, they compete against one another. Communities at large lose and the corporations gain, as acceptable tax rates are driven down.

The fragmentation characteristic of our federal system of government further limits the power of government to act effectively and the ability of citizens to hold their representatives accountable for the state of their communities. No one branch or level of government has the ability to deal in a holistic manner with the diversity of issues raised by economic transformation. Therefore, no one can be held accountable, so many politicians do as little as necessary to keep their constituents happy. As a result, the prerogatives of the private realm of decision-making are left less disturbed than they might otherwise be.

For a number of structural reasons, the national government would be the appropriate branch of government to intervene in the problems experienced in the Monongahela Valley and in other regions afflicted by industrial shutdowns. Steel corporations are national or international in scale and thus often beyond the effective reach of state and local governments. The vast amount of investment capital required to address problems like those facing the Mon Valley could be raised most easily by the national government. (In fact, during World War II the federal government invested in expanding the steel capacity of the Mon Valley. After the war, those new facilities were turned over to private steel corporations, such as U.S. Steel, often for a mere 10 percent of the government's cost.) State or local governments that seek to raise capital by raising taxes might well lose corporate patronage to other states, because intrastate competition leads to lower, not higher, taxes. State and local governments that attempted to require greater corporate permanence would face this same problem of intrastate competition and a possible constitutional hurdle (article 1, section 10) as well. Only Congress has the power "to impair the obligation of contracts." By implication, Congress could explicitly reinterpret "fiduciary obligation" to require a greater measure of community responsibility.

Yet there are more compelling political reasons that make it unlikely that Congress would take such action. James Madison made some of these clear in his Federalist Paper No. 10, a fine defense of the U.S. Constitution as a guarantor of elite rule. He notes that the size of a large republic can make it very difficult even for groups representing the concerns of a majority to direct government policy:

> Extend the sphere, and you take in a greater variety of parties and interests; you will make it less probable that a majority of the whole will have a common motive . . . or if such a common motive exists, it will be more difficult for all who feel it to discover their own strength and to act in unison with each other.

In the early 1980s, when steel communities were suffering their greatest declines, other parts of the nation, especially the sunbelt, were still basking in the glory of their oil-induced triumph over the rustbelt. For this reason, steel's problems were seen as isolated and regional. Yet when employment in the sunbelt plummeted in the mid-1980s, the industrial Northeast had begun a modest recovery. Both regions suffered from the same problem of unfettered capital mobility in a shifting global economy, yet differences of region and time made it unlikely that they would discover their "common motive" or "their own strength and to act in unison with each other."

The increased foreign competition that led to the declines in industrial employment also led business to organize itself more effectively in order to secure its class interests at the national level. (They had far less trouble with Madison's obstacles.) In the late 1970s, they waged an effective campaign against the federal government's "interference" with their ability to "compete." This led to the wave of deregulation that began in the late 1970s, to the weakening of agencies designed to protect workers, such as the National Labor Relations Board (NLRB) and the Occupational Safety and Health Administration (OSHA), to a decline in federal funds available for local economic development projects, and to the establishment during the Reagan administration of an ideological climate hostile to the sort of solutions necessary even to begin to reverse the decline of communities such as the Mon Valley. The ascendance of unreconstructed free-market rhetoric in Washington meant that while appeals to state and local governments were structurally unrealistic, appeals to the federal government were nearly pointless. It is instructive to ask what is missing from Table 3. In response to economic decline, we might expect to see programs that have been tried and proven in other times or places. Other nations invest heavily in worker retraining and relocation while maintaining the worker's income at a level required to provide for his or her family. For example, laid-off steelworkers in France were eligible for up to two years of retraining with full benefits and at least 70 percent of previous salary. In Britain, steelworkers were supported for only one year of retraining, but if the resultant job paid less than their former wages they would receive supplemental benefits to lift their income to 90 percent of what it had been.[20] We see no comparable programs here. In the 1930s, federal investment in the Tennessee Valley Authority vitalized a region mired in economic collapse and provided the basis for decades of economic growth. In the same period, federal employment programs, such as the Works Progress Administration (WPA), not only channeled income to some families in need of assistance, but also made major cultural contributions, in the arts and in community buildings and parks, that have served the public since then in ways that merit emulation.

If those programs were successful in meeting short-term economic needs and providing long-term benefits, why were they not repeated in the 1980s? The answer lies in their ideological impact. They are reflections of social responsibility and community vision expressed through government rather than through the private market. They resulted from pursuing the common good rather than the private good. As such, they challenge the legitimacy of the corporate elite's decision-making process. That is the reason federal programs were opposed in the 1930s, and that is why they have been attacked since then too. In all practical terms, they were remarkable successes. Their absence in the 1980s is evidence of an increase in elite hegemony since the 1930s.

This survey of various local politicians and government policies sheds light on the limitations of the political decision-making process. All the actual responses discussed are either reactions to harmful decisions of business leaders, or enticements aimed at eliciting positive business decisions. No programs embody a pursuit of the common good—except as it may be hoped to result from encouraging activity by private firms. Real initiative lies with the corporate community. Politicians have little power to act creatively and decisively in the interests of their communi-

20. Everett M. Kasslow, "Four Nations' Policies Toward Displaced Steel Workers," *Monthly Labor Review* 108 (July 1985), pp. 35–39.

ties except as purveyors of inducements to business. Such inducements also include efforts to reduce labor militancy—that is, to reduce the already small likelihood that workers will try to influence future decisions made in the private realm of decision-making. In this project, politicians collaborate in increasing the autonomy of the corporate elite to set the course of their community—in restricting both political participation and the scope of government action.

When Commissioner Foerster, clearly the most powerful of all the politicians surveyed, was asked whether he thought government should have the power to affect levels of private investment and employment, he responded eagerly, "I only wish we did!" He seems to feel frustrated at his inability to convince U.S. Steel to modernize its facilities in the Mon Valley. Yet corporate hegemony remained intact. With his next breath, he once again recited: "The proper role of government is to provide inducement, a favorable climate, and expenditures for infrastructure."

The survey of politicians and policies only reinforces what we have seen in the decision-making process in the fields of private business and regional planning bodies—what Gramsci called "the ideological hegemony of capitalism." That hegemony permits consideration of how to alleviate the suffering of workers and communities ravaged by the decisions of major corporate actors. However, because it considers private capitalist decision-making to be entirely legitimate, it does not permit consideration of a different basis of decision-making—one that might produce quite different adaptations to the changing economy by giving the health of communities at least as high a priority as that of the profitability of private corporations.

The Decision-Making System of the Elite

It is of little value to look for. individuals to blame, to try to pinpoint whom to shoot or whom to praise for the decisions guiding Pittsburgh's economic transformation. It is essential, however, to understand the kind of system that allowed and even encouraged certain individuals to make the types of decisions that led to the devastation of the communities of the Mon Valley.

The complex and often interrelated decisions that helped determine the character of the still-evolving but significantly transformed Pittsburgh region were many, and the choices were not inevitable—there were a variety of options. But a privileged few who held positions of power in Pittsburgh's major industrial corporations and financial institutions made the choices, sometimes with the assistance of key politicians and planners, and they were made strategically, to achieve the goals of that elite group. Those choices determined who gained and who lost in Pittsburgh in the 1980s.

It is necessary to recognize that the elite made and carried out the policies to reshape the region. These policies were just as significant and just as political as previous government decisions to create a Tennessee Valley Authority or to tear down low-cost housing for "urban renewal," for example. The fact that the decisions were made and carried out primarily in the realm of private business obscures but does not fundamentally change the decidedly political nature of the decisions. Hiding these policy decisions as "economic" rather than "political" is one of the most effective ways to preclude popular input.

If we stop even briefly to consider alternatives suggested to us by logic or by comparative cases, we realize that defining the economic decisions that transform whole communities as somehow "private" rather than "political" is an odd convention. Yet it is a convention widely observed in the United States. One of the most significant ideological accomplishments of the modern corporate elite of the United States has been the application of eighteenth-century notions of liberalism—which enshrine the individual producer as the source of society's wealth—to the twentieth-century reality of mega-corporations with budgets that often exceed those of the states in which they operate. Clearly this anachronistic protection of business decisions as private and thus not within the purview of government operates to the advantage of corporations and to the detriment of the public. This ideological sleight of hand prevents most of the public from even imagining that they have a right to influence decisions that shape the economic future of their communities. These well-established and reinforced cultural assumptions work to preserve and extend the hegemony of an economic elite over the day-to-day life of communities. This is an example of the third dimension of power—extremely effective, but because people accept it as "the way things are" it is also almost entirely invisible.

The policies that devastated communities in the Mon Valley while transferring the Valley's wealth to other areas were carried off fairly smoothly, considering the amount of damage done. This can be attributed to the pervasiveness of elite influence throughout the three realms of decision-making. So these decisions were made in an environment that precludes popular input in most areas of significance.

The most economically powerful individuals were directly present in both the first and the second realms, and their influence was expressed in both the second and the third realms in a variety of ways. These include overt financial influence, whether through contributions or, as in the case of the YMCA-1397 food bank, through loans or other types of financial control. It also includes less-visible influence—Assemblyman Zemprelli spoke of it quite clearly as "the silent opposition," and Lindblom spoke of it as the need to retain business confidence. The planning studies we reviewed called it the "need to improve the business climate." Legally it hides behind the obligation of "fiduciary responsibility." Bachrach and Baritz have called it "the mobilization of bias" or simply "the rules of the game."

It all adds up to the cultural hegemony of capitalism—elite influence in the affairs we are discussing is accepted as the way things are and the way they should be. Few can imagine even suggesting that it should be otherwise, and those who do, do so against the current of cultural norms.

The system of decision-making in Pittsburgh is structured to give overwhelming predominance to the wishes of the corporate elite. But we know that Pittsburgh's elite is not monolithic in its desires; many were clearly relieved to see U.S. Steel playing a less-dominant role in their community. U.S. Steel—now USX—is content with becoming a still more diversified and international corporation. It does not want to be very involved in Pittsburgh's difficulties.

Yet while this elite group is not entirely harmonious, it shares numerous goals. The decline of steel has caused certain traumas, but it has helped promote many important elite objectives. As the Mellon economist pointed out, it has helped drive down wages and reduce the power of unions—or, as elites more politely but repeatedly insist in their planning reports, it has helped "improve the labor climate." Corporate elites agree too that they need to reduce not only labor militancy but also what the Mellon economist called "this cultural thing . . . a community feeling of strength, stability." The traumatic decline of the Mon Valley has certainly gone a long way toward injuring the sense that stable communities are both desirable and a necessary and natural component of a healthy society, but it did not totally eliminate it.

It is not enough to say that Pittsburgh's elites are managing the problems caused by the decline of steel and the challenges of a high-tech future. We must recognize that their vision of a new Pittsburgh includes the destruction of many aspects of working-class culture and working-class power. Once we understand this common goal, we can see that the elites are determined to use the strategic advantages afforded them in the three realms of Pittsburgh's decision-making process to resist any non-elite input that would tend to defend the cultural, economic, and/or political power of the industrial working classes. In so doing, they seek to make Pittsburgh's decision-making process even less democratic.

While this indictment may suggest a sinister conspiracy, it does not require one. Most of the elite act this way out of the sincere belief that they are doing what is best for their region, that they are promoting progress, that while there may be some difficulties on the road of progress, all are better off in the end. As long as they believe this, the third dimension of power protects their dominance even from the possible challenge of their own moral or democratic qualms.

The Denominational Ministerial Strategy, and to a lesser extent Tri-State and the Mon Valley Unemployed Committee, appealed to the moral sensibilities of individual members of the Pittsburgh elite. It is important to recall that although the elite is made up of individuals, many with particular styles and varying degrees of compassion or social consciousness, each of those is much like Steinbeck's tractor driver: If he didn't bump the farmer's house down, someone else would be found to do the job. The structural dynamics of capitalism in late twentieth-century America—with its peculiar blend of cultural and political opportunities and constraints—drive corporations to shift assets without regard to community needs or moral niceties. Thus, focusing on the moral or democratic sensitivities of individual members of the elite is unlikely to have a lasting effect if the structural incentives and political constraints facing the elite are not changed.

The problem with elite dominance of decision-making in all three realms is not merely that it is antidemocratic, but that by being anti-democratic it fails to provide a means for important inputs into the community's decision-making process. The corporate elite make decisions based on the needs of their own firms, not on the needs of the communities in which they operate. They are ever more concerned with opportunities and threats on a global scale. Both the legal obligation of "fiduciary responsibility" and the personal interests of managers require that of them. We should not expect them to do otherwise.

Yet citizens are not required to cede all power in the policy process to the corporate elite. If citizens are able to break out of the thrall of elite definitions of "the way things are," they can act to shape their own futures. It is possible for nonelite citizens to insist—as members of our three challenging groups have tried to do—that there is a community responsibility, which is at least as important as fiduciary responsibility. It is simply insane—suicidally so—for a society to continue to trust the future of their communities to elites who see strong community ties as a problem rather than a goal. Unless ordinary citizens challenge elite hegemony, they will have no way to take the initiative in determining the type of community they want to have as they enter a new economic era. And without more popular input, there is no reason to expect that future elite decisions will not be as catastrophic as the decision to nearly eliminate steel production in the Mon Valley.

6

CAN WORKERS HAVE A VOICE?

It is now time to answer the question that is the title of this study: In the politics of deindustrialization, can workers have a voice? Based on what we have observed in Pittsburgh, the answer must be that workers can have only a very limited voice and that they will have to fight to get that much.

In Pittsburgh, elites deliberately made a series of decisions that changed the basis of their economy and their community. The transformation began in the late 1940s with the effort to clean up the air. It continued with the Pittsburgh Renaissance, which replaced older commercial buildings and low-cost housing with the high-rise corporate headquarters of the Golden Triangle. It accelerated rapidly in the 1970s and 1980s, driven largely by technological change and the globalization of markets. Its most dramatic turning point was the virtual abandonment of its traditional economic base, the steel industry of the Monongahela Valley.

Throughout the decades, the goal of Pittsburgh's elite was to transform the region's economy from one dominated by industry to one structured to serve the needs of its corporate headquarters and its high-tech medical, research, and manufacturing sectors. That goal was pursued without regard for the effect it would have on tens of thousands of workers.

During this process of transformation, elites faced a variety of policy choices. One of the principles guiding those choices was to lessen the role played by the region's traditionally strong base of organized labor. This entailed attacking unions, driving down wages, and getting rid of what the Carnegie-Mellon robotics designer called "totally unnecessary humans" through a combination of technological change and economically driven out-migration.

The new Pittsburgh, voted most livable city by Rand McNally in 1984, is no longer tarnished by the smoke of industrial operations. Its new image is that of its high-rise office headquarters, its supercomputer, its world-leading medical transplant center, and its fine music. The downside of this transformation is that Pittsburgh, even more dramatically than the rest of the nation, has become much more a house divided against itself. The industrial middle class has been considerably diminished. The new service sector includes very few middle-income jobs. The entire Mon Valley, once a key component of the region's economic life, has been left to decay until the residues of unionized labor are sufficiently dissipated that it can attract new employers.

The transformation of Pittsburgh was inherently political. One sector of the population, responding to external economic pressures, decided on a series of policies that served its own interests at severe cost to another sector. Other policies could have been chosen. It is not at all clear that the policies selected were those that were best for the region as a whole. Some elite decisions provoked protests, but those protests were too late and too limited to alter the direction of change the elites had already chosen. Pittsburgh may be an extreme example of this transformation process, but it is not unique. Many other regions have been similarly transformed, with workers similarly absent from the decision-making process.

Why have so few workers tried to have a voice? This question has been answered by our study of Pittsburgh. The answer is that workers have been systematically excluded from decisive roles when they tried to participate in shaping the future of their communities. But even more, workers have been systematically excluded by the lesson taught to them in so many ways: that they have no need, no right, and no hope of gaining anything from trying to join the region's exclusive polity. Elites do not want to hear their voice.

For anyone concerned about democracy as something more than a rhetorical device or a collection of periodic rituals for placating a subject population, this exclusion of a region's work force from having a say in shaping the future of their community must be of great concern. It takes place both because of and in spite of the citizenry's belief in democracy as the governing principle of their society.

Oligarchy through democracy requires careful sleight of hand. It is accomplished by keeping the actual exercise of power as well hidden as possible. Our three groups in Pittsburgh, by pressing against the rules that excluded them from decisions, have exposed many aspects of that power. They have forced people to pay attention to a decision-making process that sought to operate without scrutiny. They have also shown how that process manages to discourage challenges to its decisions.

This exposure of Pittsburgh's policy-making process as antidemocratic should not be interpreted as a simplistic and stubborn defense of steel-based employment or of coal-smoke-fouled air. Rather, it is an attempt to direct attention to the *process* by which some policies were chosen and others excluded.

Is there any alternative explanation for the elite behavior shown here to be antidemocratic? That is, if the challengers were presenting no reasonable alternatives, but merely being disruptive, then it would be wrong to conclude that the elite were being unfairly exclusive in rejecting the challengers. So, let us look once more at what our three challenger groups did propose and how the elite responded.

Policies Proposed, Policies Rejected

The goals of Pittsburgh's corporate elites clearly included the reduction in the power of the working class. While this goal was not new to the 1980s, it was given added impetus by increased global competition. Elites chose to respond to that competition by reducing wages and removing constraints imposed by unions and by government regulations.

Reducing the power of the working class was a goal shared by economic elites throughout the nation and championed by the Reagan and Bush administrations. Elite decisions routinely attempted to exclude policies that would defend or expand the power of the working class. To understand the decisions of the 1980s, we must realize that policy decisions were made not solely in terms of economic costs and benefits but also as part of a contest between competing political blocs. This makes it possible for us to understand not only why none of the policies proposed by the challenging groups has been implemented, but also why the challenger proposals have been given little or no consideration by elite decision-makers.

The following review of policy options proposed but not chosen is not an attempt to prove that the challengers' proposals are superior to the policies adopted by Pittsburgh's elite. It is intended to show that the policies chosen were not the only options available, and not indisputably the most rational and desirable choices for the region as a whole. It also shows a pattern of choice that is consistent with maximizing elite power at the expense of working people.

Reindustrialization

The Tri-State Conference on Steel proposed a reindustrialization of Pittsburgh and other regions of the country based on rebuilding the nation's crumbling infrastructure. This proposal is not supported merely by anachronistic industrial romantics. Financiers such as Felix Rohatyn and others supported it because it made sense to them. It made sense because preserving an industrial base is essential for long-run viability of the national economy, something short-run investors and investor-pleasing managers are structurally unable to consider. And it made sense because a healthy economy of any sort requires good transportation, good water supplies, and good sanitation if it is to survive.

The federal government could support such a reinvestment program. It is no stranger to the idea of promoting the interests of certain sectors of the economy through purchases. Despite the end of the cold war, it continues to support the military sector of the economy, largely as a jobs program. Eventually, after enough bridges collapse and enough water systems fail, the government will act to respond to the crisis. With deficits high, and crisis still at bay, such spending will be put off. Early indications are that the Clinton administration's efforts in this direction will be modest. As Rohatyn points out, rebuilding our infrastructure "cannot be financed without changes in our priorities."[1] A policy of reindustrialization through rebuilding basic infrastructure could benefit the Pittsburgh region enormously in terms of direct improvements and employment. The economic stimulus from such a program would probably be quite significant.

Yet this proposal got virtually no support from Pittsburgh's decision-makers. Elites who were working more and more in financial manipulations, electronic impulses, and the exploitation of a highly bifurcated but primarily low-wage service sector did not deem it necessary, but they also saw it as undesirable because it would tend to strengthen the economic stronghold of Pittsburgh's unionized labor.

---

1. Felix Rohatyn, "On the Brink," *New York Review of Books*, June 11, 1987, p. 3.

Support for Workers in Transition

Another rational policy option is generous government support for workers making a transition to new careers in a changing economy. Such support would maintain the economic base for local businesses and government services and provide social stability. And it would allow for a well-trained, highly motivated work force. Such policies are relatively common in social democratic nations of Western Europe, where they are seen not only as humane policies toward workers but also as promoting a highly productive economy in which workers are active proponents of change.

Without adequate support during transition periods, the interests of workers in the United States lead them to resist many socially desirable options. In the Monongahela Valley, this means they had little choice but to try to cling to jobs in antiquated mills. With adequate support, it would have been in their interest to be real advocates of redevelopment of the region. Again, the point here is not to change the psychology or morality of various actors, but to change the structural incentives they face. The performance of Sweden, which has very generous programs of support and retraining between jobs, compares very favorably with that of the United States during the economic turmoil of the 1970s and 1980s.[2]

The Mon Valley Unemployed Committee campaigned for various parts of such a policy, yet it failed to adequately articulate such policies as part of an industrial policy; they articulated them only as survival assistance. Whether this failure is the result of lack of information and imagination or the result of a sense of what was realistic to ask for, it is yet another silent victory achieved through the third dimension of elite power. The most the MVUC obtained in this regard was temporary relief at low levels of survival. Federal policy continued to favor Dan Quayle's meager Job Training Partnership Act over the more supportive but narrowly available Trade Readjustment Act program.

The corporate elites of Pittsburgh, and of the United States as a whole, do not favor a policy of generous support and retraining between jobs because they are seeking to reduce the wages, the organization, the morale, the political power, and the community basis of its work force

---

2. For a brief discussion of Sweden's active labor-market policies, see Gregory Hooks, "The Policy Response to Factory Closings: A Comparison of the United States, Sweden, and France," *Annals of the American Academy of Political and Social Science* 475 (September 1984), 110–24. For data on comparative wages and unemployment, see International Labor Office (ILO), *Yearbook of Labor Statistics,* Geneva.

in order to compete better internationally. Thus, unemployment benefits were extended only during the period when unemployment was most widespread and political pressure was most severe. Benefits were cut back when unemployment became primarily a regional and sectoral problem, the logic being that unemployed workers would then move from their home communities to where the jobs were, or that they would take locally available jobs at lower wages. Although driving down wages in the United States is not the only way to compete internationally, it is the way that maximizes, rather than reduces, the power of corporate elites. Because these elites have enjoyed tremendous influence in setting national and state policies on job retraining and relocation, the resultant policy choices are not surprising.

Worker and Community Ownership

Another policy option promoted by Tri-State and eventually by the Steel Valley Authority is the idea of worker and community ownership of major economic enterprises. Proposals for workers and community-based groups to buy and operate LTV's South Side plant were blocked by LTV's refusal to sell at an affordable price. LTV's subsequent decision to sell the plant for scrap at a fraction of the SVA's offer showed that price was not the reason the deal fell through.

The potential success of a plan of employee and community ownership at the City Pride Bakery is a different story. Here local political elites recruited support from Mellon and other banks for a project to empower unionized workers and their working-class neighborhoods. By the early 1990s, Tri-State had convinced elites not tied primarily to globally oriented corporations that preservation of some industrial employment was necessary for the local economy and that employee ownership was one way to preserve jobs. In this case, elites with local ties were willing to oppose a transnational corporation and ally with workers. In this case, in contrast to the LTV South Side case, they could also help find sufficient funds.

In a world where most capital is ever more mobile, communities need to find some mechanism to ensure that policy-makers of locally active firms have incentives to preserve local employment. Control through ownership by local employees and community groups is the most likely short-term candidate. A dramatic example of this principle in operation is the worker-owned cooperatives of Mondragon in the Basque region of Spain. This confederation of internationally competitive industrial and service co-ops met the uncertainties of the 1970s and 1980s by retraining and reassignment and by research and innovation, but not by unemployment and not by moving operations abroad.[3]

Local ownership provides incentives for adaptation and stabilization. Absentee owners, who are constantly scanning the globe for investment alternatives, will always be more willing than workers to cut and run. The difference is not one of compassion but of structural incentives. (The potentials and problems of this approach are the subject of an extensive literature that cannot be further addressed here.[4])

The policy of economic stabilization through promoting worker and community group ownership gets mixed responses from Pittsburgh's elites because it deliberately challenges the primacy of private capital. While the *Wall Street Journal* is willing to praise Employee Stock Ownership Plans as sources of new capital and increased productivity, business has been willing to collaborate only with ventures that are still primarily controlled by traditional sources of private capital. Even the successful and frequently noted case of employee-owned Weirton Steel was structured to give nearly complete control to bankers during its first ten years.[5]

The Morality of Community

Finally, it is difficult to imagine that elites would adopt the policy recommendation of the clergy of the DMS—that they would let moral concern for fellow human beings temper their pursuit of profits and power. We are not accustomed to thinking in terms of morality when we consider macroeconomic policy, but philosophically the concept has

3. Hank Thomas and C. Logan, *Mondragon: An Economic Analysis* (Winchester, Mass.: Unwin Hyman, 1983). Roy Morrison, *We Build the Road as We Travel Mondragon: A Cooperative Solution* (Santa Cruz, Calif.: New Society Publishers, 1990).

4. For a good discussion of the problem of extinction and of efforts to weaken its appeal, see Jaroslav Vanek, "The Basic Theory of Financing of Participatory Firms," in his *Labor-Managed Economy*, pp. 186–98. On the important concept of a "supporting structure," see Vanek's introduction to *Self-Management: The Economic Liberation of Man* (New York: Penguin Books, 1975). On the political consciousness of workers in self-managed firms, see Edward Greenberg, "Context and Cooperation: Systematic Variation in the Political Effects of Workplace Democracy," *Economic and Industrial Democracy*, May 1983, pp. 191–223.

5. "Joining the Game: Some Workers Set up LBOs of Their Own," *Wall Street Journal*, December 12, 1988, p. 1. Albert Crenshaw, "Looking at the Reality Behind the ESOP Fable," *Washington Post Weekly Edition*, January 30, 1989, p. 20.

much merit. If a society is to apply moral consideration to anything, surely it should do so in deciding the means and ends to which it will apply its productive abilities—to the consideration of its very basis of organization.

Adam Smith, who billed himself as a moral philosopher rather than an economist, beguiled us into thinking that moral consideration in economic affairs was no longer necessary, that an invisible hand working through perfect markets would convert selfish impulses to the common good. Because this capitalist gospel has been accepted by our society regardless of the facts, we are left with no means of exercising social judgment in these affairs. We have surrendered such judgment to the corporate elite.

The clergy of the DMS have insisted that, in a world where markets are not perfect, society requires something other than an invisible hand if selfish impulses are to be harnessed to serve the common good. They have suggested accountability to a Christian moral code as one effective means. Workers in Western Europe have used another mechanism— political organization—to force their corporate elite to adopt some of the policy options discussed above. Such options force employers to treat workers in ways that appear more compassionate. But these options came about through political struggle, not moral conversion. Pittsburgh's elites are struggling to maintain or increase their power in a competitive world, and they don't want moral constraints to get in the way.

Most of the goals our three challenger groups proposed were rejected or ignored. Meeting the MVUC's demands for adequate income and retraining between jobs with demeaning, subsistence-level handouts was largely a rejection. Yet it also worked to blunt further demands. Support by some local elites for the idea of worker-community ownership at City Pride Bakery showed some interesting divisions in elites. It is too soon to tell how deep support for this model of local control will go. All the policy rejections are consistent with the corporate elites' goal of reducing the power of the organized working class. However, goals that constitute an attack on the cultural cohesiveness and political influence of erstwhile steel-making communities cannot be stated overtly, so they are reshaped and expressed in a variety of respectable ways. Universities announce new efforts in robotics and supercomputers while they advance the technological means of further reducing the need for industrial workers. Mellon Bank announces charitable contributions to assist the MVUC in helping impoverished workers find ways to cope, while simultaneously breaking the union of its janitors and driving them into poverty. Planners announce the progress of new modern highways for the Mon Valley without explaining that workers will have to leave their local communities and travel much farther to work.

It is not surprising that decision-makers prefer to speak of progress rather than destruction. What is surprising is that people are apparently beguiled by such talk. The deception is helped by the fact that the real decision-making process is hidden behind the false front of the assumed decision-making process—that of free-market capitalism and representative democracy.

The Role of Democracy in Economic Transformation

In relation to the issues involved in the economic transformation of Pittsburgh, representative democracy has a very small role to play. Decisions that are most important in reshaping the Pittsburgh economy are made in the first realm, that of private enterprise. The most democratic realm, that of government, makes the least transformative and thus least important decisions.

Furthermore, nearly all government policies recognize the supremacy of the private decision-making realm. They are limited primarily to offering incentives to private decision-makers or to making amends after private decision-makers have created social dislocation by eliminating employment opportunities. In the governmental realm, decision-makers must accommodate the interests of the economic elite as much as possible, so that a favorable business climate will be maintained and investment will take place. The needs of working people hold no such structural advantages. Working people have only their votes, and that is rarely enough to ensure that their interests will also be considered.

Even if the economic influence of the capitalist elite were not sufficiently strong to skew government away from what can reasonably be called representative democracy, there remain two other barriers between ordinary citizens and their ability to participate democratically in shaping the future of their communities. The first of these is the fragmented nature of government in the United States. Fragmentation makes it impossible for local governments to deal with international economic phenomena. It makes it unlikely that the national government will deal with local economic problems. And it makes it nearly impossible for citizens to hold a particular politician accountable for any of the concerns we are addressing. It should not be surprising that the fragmentation of government is an obstacle to citizens trying to affect economic policy. That was one intent of the authors of the Constitution, who feared "excessive democracy"—such as that exhibited by farmers who, through elections, gained control of Rhode Island's legislature and adjusted the money supply to favor them rather than bankers. Their construction of a fragmented government was consistent with an idea expressed so bluntly by John Jay: "Those who own the country ought to govern it."[6]

Tri-State and the Mon Valley Unemployed Committee had impressive but very limited successes using democratic influences to stop home foreclosures and to create the SVA. But even these successes showed the limits of what can be accomplished for working people. Mortgages still had to be paid. The SVA was limited by access to capital. Having won victories through democratic influence on local governments, these workers saw that they were still relatively powerless compared with the economic elites.

The Role of Free-Market Capitalism

The other major limitation on the ability of citizens to use the mechanisms of government to influence their changing economic environment is the second half of the illusion—the notion that economic matters are determined by the principles of free-market capitalism, principles that are held sacrosanct in U.S. society.

One of the key principles of capitalism is competition, and competition is a force driving Pittsburgh's transformation. The Mellon economist recognized this when he intoned, "You can't fight the world economy." Even U.S. Steel is forced to respond to international competition. Yet for competition to produce optimal results, it must be competition among equals, none of whom has the power to influence market conditions. Competition in the international marketplace is heavily influenced by the policies of government as well as those of producers and consumers. Real competition in the local market is often impossible, as U.S. Steel made clear when it said it would drive a reopened Dorothy Six out of business, along with any clients that proved too helpful to it. If workers are willing to produce steel at a lower price than that which U.S. Steel requires, then the gospel of free-market capitalism would insist that they be given the chance to try. However, imperfect capital markets make workers unable to get access to the capital required to compete.

6. Cited in Edward S. Greenberg, *The American Political System*, 5th ed. (Glenview, Ill.: Scott Foresman, 1989), p. 58.

Free-market capitalism does not describe the principles guiding Pittsburgh's evolution from the domination of steel to the domination that is developing. What we see, rather, is a competition of the powerful and the exploitation of the powerless. Although this is nothing new in human history, the current exchange among nonequals masquerades as progress. It is justified by the principles of free-market capitalism and representative democracy. These principles ensure the populous that what is going on is not only inevitable but just and efficient too.

As long as the residents of Pittsburgh and other cities fail to see how the power of the elite is exercised, that power is greatly amplified. As long as the biases built into the three realms of the decision-making process continue to operate, the same process will continue to be used in selecting options for Pittsburgh's future—the process that favors the interests of the elite regardless of the costs to some parts of the region's citizenry. If citizens disadvantaged by certain policy choices don't like their new opportunities, they are urged to abandon their anachronistic sense of community and move somewhere else.

How the Decision-Makers Respond to Challengers

We postulated in the first chapter that Pittsburgh's relatively closed decision-making process would respond to challengers according to the degree of their challenge. This has been borne out by our study. The Network/DMS, in challenging the legitimacy and the very basis of the private decision-making process, posed the most fundamental challenge. While not directly rejecting the right of corporations to make decisions based on private property and profitability, they asserted that a moral obligation to one's fellow humans must be allowed to temper those rights. In this regard they placed social rights—embodied in Christian morality (Love your neighbor as yourself)—as equal to private rights. Network/DMS members were most severely repressed. Several of them lost jobs, or were forcefully opposed in union elections, or were fined or jailed. Some of them received many of these reprisals.

The Tri-State Conference on Steel challenged specific decisions on the basis that they were not rational if one considered the economic impact on the entire community, not just the immediate economic impact on managers and shareholders. They sought to use the structures of government to embody the rationality of the community's economic interest and to overcome corporate decisions they deemed destructive of that interest. This too was a daring and important challenge, but it was limited by its failure to challenge the sacrosanct nature of private capital. That is, it accepted the limitation that the community interest could prevail over the corporate interest only if the community could buy out the corporation.

The acceptance of this limitation is a reflection of corporate power. Restated somewhat, it concedes that the transient phenomenon of private ownership confers rights to economic decision-making that are superior to those accorded workers or community at large. As long as this hierarchy of rights is accepted as one of the rules of the game—as the way things are, or as not worth challenging because everyone else accepts it as natural—it prevents effective challenges. This is power exercised in the third dimension. In this case, the third-dimensional power was acting within the minds of the challengers from Tri-State. Whether for lack of imagination—a conditioned effect—or as a result of the strategic judgment that challenging property rights as defined by corporations would be futile, the result was the same.[7] Tri-State did not challenge the game rule that said it takes money to be able to decide what happens to industrial plants. This left their corporate opponents with obvious advantages.

Because the challenge of Tri-State was potentially serious, it had to be confronted. When the limitation on Tri-State's challenge became clear— that is, when the elite saw where their power was still working quite effectively—the strategic elite response became clear. Judge McCune put it bluntly in his decision not to grant the new Steel Valley Authority the injunction it wanted to prevent Switch & Brake from leaving town: The agency had legal authority but no capital, so it was powerless. Tri-State could be tolerated as relatively harmless as long as they could not get their hands on sufficient capital to play in the big leagues.

Thus, U.S. Steel did not tear down the Dorothy Six blast furnace when it wanted to. It could have used its overt powers to demolish the plant and thus make further discussions about its future entirely moot. However, popular mobilization spearheaded by Tri-State had focused enough public attention on the issue that a decision to do so would have been costly. Therefore, instead of using its first-dimensional power to win a quick but costly victory, U.S. Steel saw it could rely on less visible power. It knew it would win a contest of second-dimension power based on the rules of the game. It let Tri-State continue with further feasibility

---

7. I suspect it was a strategic choice, because Staughton Lynd, an advisor to Tri-State, had previously written about losing such a battle in court while trying to stop a steel shutdown in Youngstown. For the dramatic statements of the judge in this case concerning community rights and property rights, see Staughton Lynd, *The Fight Against Shutdowns*, pp. 164–66.

studies, confident that Tri-State would lose when the challenge shifted from challenging corporate policy to finding capital. The failure to find sources for capital willing to take on U.S. Steel as a hostile competitor meant the end of the Save Dorothy campaign. And the failure of this campaign meant the loss of Tri-State's mass base and its ability to threaten real change. The decision to play by U.S. Steel's rules—a reflection of third-dimensional power—led directly to the end of Tri-State's challenge. It is still too early to know the long-term response to the more recent, small successes of the Steel Valley Authority.

The Mon Valley Unemployed Committee initially generated more fear from the local and national elite than the other two groups did. They mobilized threatening groups of angry workers and tapped into community outrage against the inhumane treatment many displaced workers received through no fault of their own. Yet it soon became clear that they were not challenging the decision-making process, but merely insisting that decision-makers be more compassionate about those they had dispossessed *after* they had implemented their decisions to dispossess them. Quite early, this group gave up any efforts to stop the process that was generating unemployment. They focused instead on making unemployment more bearable, so this group turned out to be the least threatening. They were given corporate grants to direct their protests toward government in Washington and Harrisburg. As we have already seen, this meant moving away from confronting elites that had decided to lay off workers, and shifting instead to cleanup activities, as that is all governments were doing in relation to Pittsburgh's transformation. When the group reached its crisis of purpose and finance, corporations stepped in with financial and organizational assistance. Of the three groups we have studied, only the MVUC was openly received. Corporations evidently found their work of humanizing unemployment to be quite useful.

In the Introduction we considered a hypothesis—derived from John Gaventa's research on coal-mining communities—that workers are generally quiescent about major economic decisions because they see that realm of decision-making systematically closed to them. A matrix of citizen-elite interaction (Figure 1), which provided four possible ways to categorize the environment in which decisions concerning the economic future of a community are made, was proposed. We assumed, based on historical precedent and the theoretical starting points of both pluralists and Marxists, that workers would want to have some say in determining their futures but that they could be either mobilized or nonmobilized in pursuit of influence. Based on objective analysis and a near consensus in the literature, we assumed that a class of elites played the primary role in determining which options would be pursued with a community's economic resources. We said that their attitudes toward nonelite participation in those decisions could range from facilitative to nonfacilitative. Cell 1 of Figure 1 (pluralist democracy) would correspond to the rhetorical description most commonly applied to U.S. society, while cell 4 (elite hegemony) would correspond to the world consistent with our hypothesis.

If we take the goal of groups to be that which is central to this study—having a voice in the decisions that shaped the economic transformation of Pittsburgh in order to keep their communities alive—then it is clear that all groups end up in the cell corresponding to elite hegemony. If we disaggregate the groups, separating out leaders from grass-roots constituencies, and if we allow the groups' goals to become survival rather than gaining influence, we are able to chart the course of marginalization or even co-optation. The leaders of each group manage to stay more mobilized than the followers. The more successful groups of leaders are those who become most separated from their base. In the process, they become less threatening and thus less capable of mounting significant challenges to elites.

In terms of our analysis, we must adopt the first of these goals—having a voice in the economic transformation of Pittsburgh rather than organizational survival—to be the relevant standard. The path of marginalization is part of the process of elite hegemony, rather than the way to pluralist democracy. The projects Tri-State and the MVUC pursued in the latter half of the 1980s were dependent on elite funding and/or elite cooperation if they were to be carried out. They did not threaten the elite's monopoly on decision-making power. If anything, they further legitimated it.

The matrix analysis leaves us with the conclusion, consistent across the three groups, that in relation to the major decisions that work to transform the region, Pittsburgh's economic elites are nonfacilitative and that they preserve their hegemony by achieving the demobilization of workers bold enough to have temporarily overcome their conditioned quiescence. The stagnant economic conditions of the 1980s also contributed to workers' sense of hopelessness. They had few apparent choices, other than scrambling to find whatever means of survival they could in Pittsburgh's postindustrial society.

The Rationality of Quiescence

None of our three groups succeeded in penetrating the decision-making process sufficiently to stop or even slow Pittsburgh's deindustrialization.

To put it succinctly, they failed. This confirms the generally accepted wisdom that it is futile to fight decisions of the corporate elite. Their experience also serves as one more lesson in the rationality of quiescence for the working class of Pittsburgh. That is, if we can assume workers learn from the experiences of themselves and others like them, we can conclude that those who are even marginally involved with or interested in the experiences of these groups will have learned again that challenging elites is not likely to succeed. We can assume that this will affect their future behavior, just as we can assume many learned from past experiences the apparent folly of participating in the activities of these groups or of finding other ways to challenge elite decisions. As such, the experiences of these groups both confirm and reinforce elite power.

Reinstructing workers in the rationality of quiescence can be seen as good or bad, depending on one's normative position on democracy. Those who see democracy as a limited set of institutional rituals designed to obtain consent for governance by a select group will view this as positive. For this group, greater activity by workers in the 1980s would only have cluttered the decision-making environment with disorderly distractions and might have produced worse outcomes. For this group, order is the primary goal of democracy.

Yet this study is motivated by the opposite normative position—that the most important goal of democracy is justice, and that this goal is facilitated by expanding, not contracting, participation. In this light, finding that elite hegemony is intact in the 1980s, and that it is reinforced by the experience of these groups, is a dismal conclusion—too dismal to end with. Thus, let us consider an additional set of lessons we can draw from this study.

In the first chapter, we also mentioned the concept of dual consciousness: the simultaneous existence within workers of a coping, collaborationist consciousness consistent with a knowledge of elite hegemony, and a revolutionary consciousness clearly opposed to the continuation of that hegemony. One of the most important tasks of the third dimension of elite power is making sure that workers will always see it as in their interest to make the pragmatic choice of acting on the basis of their collaborationist rather than their revolutionary consciousness. The experience of our three groups has done much to show workers the wisdom of that choice, but it has also fed their revolutionary consciousness in a variety of important ways.

The Rationality of Challenge

Second- and third-dimensional power is most effective when it is invisible. The challenges of the groups studied here have made the existence, the character, the methods, and the goals of Pittsburgh's powerful elites more obvious. When workers' final paychecks were held up for months by Mellon Bank during bankruptcy proceedings at Mesta Machine, the callousness of that powerful institution was exposed for all to see. When DMS broke the news that Mellon's decision to loan money to Mesta's Japanese competitor, Sumitomo, rather than to Mesta was the event that had precipitated the bankruptcy, the bank's abandonment of the region's industrial base became painfully obvious. When sheriff's deputies broke down a church door to arrest Pastor Roth for his militant work in addressing unemployment, the attention of people around the nation was focused on a policy process that was clearly out of control. The initial feasibility study on saving the Dorothy Six blast furnace caused communities up and down the Mon Valley to question the very basis of U.S. Steel's "need" to shut down production. Furthermore, it suggested an alternate arrangement of power, one in which workers could manage investment decisions regarding the future of their mills. Because the third dimension of elite power relies on invisibility, on unquestioning acceptance, each of these small accomplishments was a major blow to the elite's monopoly on power.

Power exposed is power weakened. Mobilization fuels mobilization. Even small victories by challengers give lie to the notion of elite invincibility. They expose vulnerabilities. The efforts of these three groups exposed numerous elite vulnerabilities. The DMS exploited corporations' concern for their positive corporate image. While their dead-fish and skunk campaigns did not succeed in getting much of the community to adopt their proposed slogan of "Smellin' Mellon," their work helped destroy Mellon's preferred corporate identity, "Mellon: A Neighbor You Can Count On." Efforts of the Mon Valley Unemployed Committee and the Tri-State Conference on Steel demonstrated that the existence of formally democratic government procedures can be used to threaten the elite's hegemony. Because Sheriff Coon and Judge Papadakos planned to face reelection, they caved in to the demands of protestors from the MVUC to stop foreclosing on homes of unemployed workers. Tri-State used popular mobilization to force local governments to set up the Steel Valley Authority. At least in theory, the SVA has the ability to seize corporate properties not being used and to reemploy them to serve the community's good. In the early 1990s at City Pride, they gave their first significant example of being able to mobilize capital, to provide training and jobs, and to establish new patterns of ownership and control. These accomplishments begin to show that democratic institutions can be made to serve democratic ends if enough people insist on their rights to be heard.

Each of these groups began with quite limited resources, so it is not surprising that they accomplished only limited gains. Yet given the limited resources available, some of their gains are quite remarkable. Through grass-roots mobilization, laid-off steel workers and their allies created the Steel Valley Authority. While the importance of the SVA is only beginning to be felt, its potential is worthy of notice. On paper, the SVA may well be the most powerful industrial redevelopment agency in the nation. When it was created, Tri-State managed to see that its staff was composed of people supportive of their vision of industrial management—one accountable to, and possibly owned by, workers and their communities. The potential of the SVA still depends on its getting large amounts of capital. Yet its success with City Pride gives real hope. It tapped private, government, and socially based sources of funds. It led the Episcopal church to make its first investment in business development. In the future, it may be able to inspire major investments by worker-owned pension funds, currently the largest block of investment capital in the country. Working in projects that require smaller capital investments per job will likely prove to be a wiser strategy than its earlier efforts in heavy industry. Fully capitalized, the SVA and other institutions like it could become powerful tools for community-based redevelopment.

The MVUC's success in helping force the federal government to triple the period covered by unemployment benefits must be recognized as important in at least two regards. The first is direct and obvious: It channeled money to workers at a time of great need. The second is at least as important: It demonstrated once more that when enough workers mobilize and threaten to create social upheaval, the federal government can be frightened into making concessions to workers. The impression of impending social upheaval is exactly the impression workers gave in their initial Pittsburgh march, or to Senator Heinz when he came to listen to his constituents, or to President Reagan when he had to sneak in and out of the Hilton to avoid menacingly angry crowds.

The MVUC is now working at politicizing other groups of politically and economically disenfranchised people throughout Pennsylvania. Even Network activists, though now thoroughly demobilized, have not forgotten what they learned about the networks of Pittsburgh's powerful elites. Nor have they forgotten the research skills they gained. Like former shipbuilder Darrell Becker, who now claims to be miserable as "an activist without a cause," they and many others will be available for future challenges to the domination of their communities by the wealthy few.

The decisions that destroyed the steel-making communities of the

Monongahela Valley were set in motion well before workers began to mobilize to resist them. By then, they were too late to influence anything but the amount of assistance they would receive as they adjusted to the loss of their incomes. In the 1990s, both the SVA and the MVUC—successors to the mobilization efforts of the 1980s—have begun to work proactively: to initiate developments, to build political networks, to develop new models of community-centered economic development. Their past success at forcing democratic and economic institutions to work in keeping with a new rationality can be a powerful base to build on. The development of a new common sense that favors the needs and the hopes of common citizens over the bottom lines of elites is a challenge to elites' third-dimensional power. Successes here can make it possible for workers to have more voice in the future.

If three small groups of workers in Pittsburgh can accomplish this much with so few resources, then the revolutionary half of workers' dual consciousness should also digest the obvious lesson that more could be accomplished if more workers mobilized. Furthermore, preservation of the tactical successes of these groups constitutes a resource that can be drawn on by future groups, just as these groups drew on the experiences of groups before them.

Community and the Need for a Workers' Voice

Pittsburgh has been transformed and continues to be transformed as the result of choices corporate elites make in responding to pressures that are affecting communities throughout the world. The people of Pittsburgh have adapted to pressures they did not seek, and it is unlikely that these pressures will relent at any time in the near future. In fact, it is more likely that they will increase.

The principles that have guided Pittsburgh's elites in responding to changes are primarily principles relating to short- and medium-term profitability. These are abstract, mathematical principles applied by accountants, economists, and managers with no sentimental or moral attachment to the people of a given community. In a world characterized by rapid change, these principles are unlikely to produce stability. Community, on the other hand, requires nurturing over time. It requires commitment. It requires stability. Obviously there is a conflict between the needs of corporations and the needs of communities. In fact, many of Pittsburgh's elites see the workers' sense of community as a significant problem to be overcome.

If workers and the interest of the community at large had been represented as important factors in the decision-making process from the beginning, how differently might Pittsburgh have responded to the pressures driving its economic transformation? It is not likely that all the antiquated steel mills of the Mon Valley would have been saved, but if workers had been involved in the 1950s, 1960s, and 1970s, many of them probably would have been less antiquated when the world steel crisis hit. Research would have been conducted on how best to utilize the available resources of existing mills, of labor, and of the skills, knowledge, and technology available in the rich Pittsburgh region. Few areas in the country would have been better equipped to combine industrial, technical, and financial resources in innovative ways. It is likely that new enterprises would have been developed and that workers would have been trained or retrained for them. Resources for research and development, plentiful in Pittsburgh, could have been productively applied to this task. (As it was, the resources were applied, but for different ends.)

It probably would have been impractical to maintain all steelworkers in full-time employment. It might have been most practical to offer partial retirement to some older workers, some of whom might have been reassigned to understaffed segments of the human-service sector, such as education, day care, or parks and recreation. Workers in transition would have been given generous support both for their own good and for that of community members around them.

Such a scenario would embody all the policy recommendations of the three groups we have studied, especially the DMS recommendation to consider "your neighbor as your self." Change would be promoted in an orderly manner. Facilities would not be abandoned if they could still have useful economic roles. Workers would not be thrown out of their homes or left cold or hungry—for workers and families abandoned without resources become problems for their communities, but workers supported become valuable resources for building the future.

Compared to what did happen in Pittsburgh, the above scenario seems like a mere pipe dream, but it is not tremendously different from the way organizations of workers in Sweden or in Mondragon, Spain, responded to the same sort of pressures that drove Pittsburgh's wrenching transformation. The scenario above is offered neither as a blueprint nor as a utopian fantasy, but only to show how beneficial bringing workers into the decision-making process could be. Without workers involved in the process, community interests are not considered until the cleanup stage. Involvement earlier might prevent some of the mess. If communities are to survive and to prosper in an era in which economic

pressures rapidly sweep the globe, workers' interests must be incorporated into community decision-making processes from the beginning.

A Question of Democracy: Reclaiming What Is "Public"

If workers are to have a voice in the decisions that shape the economic
futures of their communities, they will have to fight for it. Although it
can be easily argued that participation in decisions so fundamental to the
nature of one's community is an essential ingredient in any political
process that claims to be democratic, the climate of assumption in this
country is otherwise. Thus, workers rarely consider it even remotely
within their rights or within their competence to have any say in such
matters. They are disempowered from the start by this effective exercise
of the third dimension of elite power. In effect, therefore, if workers are
to have a voice in shaping such public policies, they will first have to
fight to expand the accepted definition of the word "public." They must
reclaim as part of their province much of what corporations have claimed
to be their own "private" affairs.

The first battle in this fight will be within workers' own minds, where
elite power has invisibly succeeded in defining the very thoughtforms of
workers. Those who have overcome elite definitions of their own powerlessness and illegitimacy, and who have found ways to assert their
rights to have a voice in the decision-making process, have consistently
faced a variety of daunting obstacles. But we have seen that even with
limited resources, and even against the tide of community attitudes that
reinforce elite hegemony, groups of workers can make real gains. Within
the context of modern corporate capitalism, however, gains will be quite
limited.

In order to make community an important consideration in shaping
investment and employment decisions, the structural incentives facing
those making momentous economic decisions will have to be changed.
The policy-making process that currently maintains much of its antidemocratic autonomy by claiming not to be political at all will need to be
democratized and openly politicized.

Yet such thinking flies in the face of the "lessons" we are supposed to
learn from the collapse of Eastern Europe's Communist governments:
that socialism has failed, that planned economies serve the interests of a
select group of official functionaries while neglecting the needs of most

workers, and that free-market capitalism is the best of all possible systems.

However, in the rush of the U.S. corporate elite and their media allies to congratulate themselves, and to have the rest of us congratulate them too, an important part of reality is left out: The economy of the United States cannot be realistically described as a free-market economy, because most economic decisions are made within huge corporations, not within markets. The markets corporations do enter are generally characterized by unequal market power, by unequal information, by collusion, by government subsidy or sanction—that is, most decisions are planned. We live in a planned economy—a privately planned economy—not a free-market economy. As sectors of Eastern European economies are privatized, the invisible hand will not suddenly arrive like a Santa Claus in the night to bring new goodies to all. Already the pall of unemployment, hunger, and lack of health care has swept over Eastern Europe to an extent unknown since World War II. Instead of efficiently functioning, perfect markets, some new combination of corporations and governments will take over the region's economic planning. And unless enough people insist otherwise, they will do it for purposes that will serve their own ends first and foremost.

Just as in Eastern Europe, the important issue is not primarily elimination of planning, for planning will not be eliminated. Rather, it is Who will plan? What incentives and what constraints will the planners face? Whom will they serve? The critique of self-serving Eastern Bloc bureaucrats can and should be applied to the self-serving corporate planners of the United States. In Pittsburgh and in many other communities, economic elites—insulated from popular control—routinely make decisions that serve their interests, often at great cost to huge segments of their populations.

The champions of capitalism often boast proudly that their system of free enterprise has generated the standard of living that sets the United States apart from most of the world. In fact, "the American way" is a phrase that enshrines this accomplishment as its central aspect. What is less often trumpeted, but at least as important, is that many of the most important components of what Americans have come to accept as their way of life and as fundamentals of democracy were gained by struggles against the economic elites of the nation. These victories were won through means (some of them considered illegal) that were outside the bounds of institutionalized decision-making procedures because those procedures were controlled by nonfacilitative elites. These victories include the end of slavery, the elimination of property ownership as a requirement to vote, direct election of Senators, women's suffrage, the right to collective bargaining, the eight-hour work day, social security, the expansion of middle-class incomes to include many ordinary working-class people, civil rights legislation, environmental protection—and the list goes on and on. In each of these cases, victory came only after enough people refused to accept the elite's definition of the rules of the game. That which was considered a private affair was made public, and the public reality changed.

The plight of the communities of the Mon Valley should alert us again to the dangers of excluding working people from society's decision-making process. The creative response of groups of workers to the destruction of the Mon Valley can offer workers in other times and other places both inspiration and a chance to learn from mistakes. Such efforts also expose the tremendous antidemocratic forces that will oppose such efforts in a variety of subtle and overt ways—forces that work best when they are unrecognized. The experiences of these groups explain, tragically, why so few workers voiced opposition to the destruction of their jobs and their communities in the early 1980s.

The efforts of people in groups like those we have studied, as well as the efforts of people in some of the other important struggles mentioned above and of those in struggles yet to come, must be seen in two lights. Most obvious is that they seek specific gains in relation to specific needs, and so are part of specific policy struggles. Yet they are also part of a larger struggle that has vast historical dimensions—the struggle of ordinary people to gain control over their own lives in spite of the needs and desires of elites. That is nothing short of the ongoing, heroic, and life-affirming struggle for a fuller democracy.

Selected Bibliography

ARTICLES AND BOOKS

Alinsky, Saul. 1969. *Reveille for Radicals*. New York: Random House.

Almond, Gabriel, and Sidney Verba. 1963. *The Civic Culture*. Princeton: Princeton University Press.

American Iron and Steel Institute. 1987. *Statistical Highlights, U.S. Iron and Steel Industry*. Washington, D.C.: AISI.

Ansbury, Clare. 1986. "Laid-Off Steelworkers Find That Tax Evasion Helps Make Ends Meet." *Wall Street Journal*, October 1, 1986, p. 1.

Aronowitz, Stanley. 1973. *False Promises: The Shaping of the American Working Class Consciousness*. New York: McGraw-Hill.

Bachrach, Peter, and Morton Baratz. 1970. *Power and Poverty: Theory and Practice*. New York: Oxford University Press.

Bachrach, Peter, and Morton Baratz. 1962. "Two Faces of Power." *American Political Science Review* 56:947–52.

Beers, David. 1990. "Competing Conversions." *Mother Jones,* July–August, p. 32.

Bensmen, David, and Roberta Lynch. 1988. *Rusted Dreams: Hard Times in a Steel Community*. Berkeley and Los Angeles: University of California Press.

Bialer, S., and S. Luzar, eds. 1977. *Sources of Contemporary Radicalism*. Boulder, Colo.: Westview Press.

Bluestone, Barry, and Bennet Harrison. 1982. *The Deindustrialization of America*. New York: Basic Books.

Boggs, Carl. 1976. *Gramsci's Marxism*. London: Pluto Press.

Boyer, Richard O., and Herbert M. Morais. 1955. *Labor's Untold Story*. New York: Cameron Associates.

Brecher, Jeremy. 1972. *Strike!* Boston: South End Press.

Burnham, Walter Dean. 1970. *Critical Elections and the Mainsprings of American Politics*. New York: Norton.

Boulding, Kenneth. 1967. "The Basis of Value Judgments in Economics." In S. Hook, ed., *Human Values and Economic Policy*. New York: New York University.

Cyert, Richard M. 1985. "The Plight of Manufacturing: What Can Be Done?" In *Issues in Science and Technology,* Summer 1985, pp. 87–100. Washington, D.C.: National Academy of Sciences.

Dahl, Robert A. 1961. *Who Governs? Democracy and Power in an American City*. New Haven: Yale University Press.

Daley, Anthony. 1989. "Challenge to Labor: Job Loss and Institutional Innovation in the French Steel Industry." Paper presented to the New England Political Science Association, Cambridge, Massachusetts, April 7, 1989.

Davis, Dave, and Tim Peek. 1984. "Pittsburgh Pastor Rallies Victims of Hi-Tech Visions." *In These Times,* December 19, 1984, p. 17.

Davis, Mike. 1980. "The Barren Marriage of American Labor and the Democratic Party." *New Left Review* 124 (November–December 1980), 43–84.

Deitch, Cynthia. 1983. "Grass-Roots Community Mobilization and the New Structural Unemployment." In Zdenik Suda, ed., *Structural Employment and the New Perspectives on the Social Meaning of Work.* Pittsburgh: University of Pittsburgh.

Domhoff, G. William. 1978. *The Powers That Be: Processes of Ruling-Class Domination in America.* New York: Random House.

———. 1967. *Who Rules America?* Englewood Cliffs, N.J.: Prentice-Hall.

———. 1983. *Who Rules America Now?* Englewood Cliffs, N.J.: Prentice-Hall.

Draper, Hal. 1977. *Marx's Theory of Revolution.* Vol. 2. New York: Monthly Review Press.

Druker, Peter. 1976. *The Unseen Revolution.* New York: Harper & Row.

Dubovsky, Melvyn. 1975. *Industrialism and the American Worker, 1865 to 1920.* Arlington Heights, Ill.: AHM Publishing.

Economic Report of the President, 1986. Washington, D.C.: Government Printing Office.

Estrin, Saul, and Jan Svenar. 1987. "Productivity Effects of Worker Participation: Evidence for Producer Co-ops." *Journal of Comparative Economics* 11, no. 1 (1987), 40–61.

Ezcuria, Ana. 1986. *The Vatican and the Reagan Administration.* New York: CIRCUS Publications.

Friedman, Milton. 1962. *Capitalism and Freedom.* Chicago: University of Chicago Press.

Fuechtmann, Thomas. 1989. *Steeples and Stacks: Religion and Steel Crisis in Youngstown, Ohio.* Cambridge: Cambridge University Press.

Galbraith, John K. 1967. *The New Industrial State.* Boston: Houghton Mifflin.

Gaventa, John. 1980. *Power and Powerlessness: Quiescence and Rebellion in an Appalachian Valley.* Urbana: University of Illinois Press.

Ginsberg, Benjamin. 1982. *The Consequences of Consent.* New York: Random House.

Goldfield, Michael. 1987. *The Decline of Organized Labor in the United States.* Chicago: University of Chicago Press.

Goodwyn, Lawrence. 1978. *The Populist Moment.* New York: Oxford University Press.

Gramsci, Antonio. 1971. *Prison Notebooks.* New York: International Publishers.

Greenberg, Edward S. 1983. "Context and Cooperation: Systematic Variation in the Political Effects of Workplace Democracy." *Economic and Industrial Democracy,* May, pp. 191–223.

———. 1989. *The American Political System.* 5th ed. Glenview, Ill.: Scott Foresman.

Greider, William. 1985. "They Had an American Dream." *Rolling Stone,* June 20, 1985, pp. 47–48.

Gross, Bertram. 1987. "Rethinking Full Employment." *The Nation,* January 17, 1987.

Gunn, Christopher. 1986. *Workers' Self-Management in the United States.* Ithaca, N.Y.: Cornell University Press.

Gunn, Christopher, and Hazel Gunn. 1991. *Reclaiming Capital: Democratic Initiatives and Community Development.* Ithaca, N.Y.: Cornell University Press.

Hamby, Alonzo, ed. 1981. *The New Deal: Analysis and Interpretation.* New York: Longman.

Hartz, Louis. 1955. *The Liberal Tradition in America.* New York: Harcourt Brace & World.

Hoerr, John P. 1988. *And the Wolf Finally Came: The Decline of the American Steel Industry.* Pittsburgh: University of Pittsburgh Press.

Hofstadter, Richard. 1948. *The American Political Tradition.* New York: Knopf.

Hooks, Gregory. 1984. "The Policy Response to Factory Closings: A Comparison of the United States, Sweden, and France." *Annals of the American Academy of Political and Social Science,* September, 110–24.

Huntington, Samuel. 1981. *American Politics: The Promise of Disharmony.* Cambridge, Mass.: Harvard University Press, Belknap Press.

Jacoby, Neil H. 1973. *Corporate Power and Social Responsibility.* New York: Macmillan.

Kasslow, Everett M. 1985. "Four Nations' Policies Toward Displaced Steel Workers." *Monthly Labor Review* 108 (July), 35–39.

Laslett, J., and Lipset, S. M., eds. 1974. *Failures of a Dream? Essays in the History of American Socialism.* Garden City, N.Y.: Doubleday.

Lawrence, Collin, and Robert Lawrence. 1985. "Manufacturing Wage Dispersons: An End-Game Interpretation." Washington, D.C.: The Brookings Institution.

Leff, Judith. 1986. "United States Steel Corporation and the Steel Valley Authority." Harvard Business School, 0-386-171.

Leuchtenburg, William E. 1963. *Franklin Roosevelt and the New Deal.* New York: Harper & Row.

Lijphart, Arend. 1971. "Comparative Politics and Comparative Method." *American Political Science Review,* September, pp. 682–93.

Lindblom, Charles. 1982. "Market as Prison." *Journal of Politics* 44:324–36.

Locker/Arbrecht Associates, United Steelworkers of America. 1986. *Confronting the Crisis: The Challenge for Labor.* Pittsburgh: United Steelworkers of America.

Long, Philip D. 1985. *The Book on Pittsburgh: The Other Side of the Story.* Pittsburgh: DMS/East Liberty Lutheran Church.

Lorant, Stephan. 1964. *Pittsburgh: The Story of an American City.* New York: Doubleday.

Lowi, Theodore. 1984. "Why Is There No Socialism in the United States? A Federal Analysis." *International Political Science Review* 5, no. 4, pp. 369–80.

Lubov, Roy. 1969. *Twentieth-Century Pittsburgh: Government, Business, and Environmental Change.* New York: John Wiley & Sons.

Lukes, Steven. 1974. *Power: A Radical View.* London: Macmillan.

Luria, Dan, and Jack Russell. 1981. *Rational Reindustrialization.* Detroit: Widgetripper Press.

Lynd, Staughton. 1983. *The Fight Against Shutdowns: Youngstown's Steel Mill Closings.* San Pedro, Calif.: Singlejack Books.

———. 1987. "The Genesis of the Idea of a Community Right to Industrial Property in Youngstown and Pittsburgh, 1977–1987." *Journal of American History* 74, no. 3, pp. 12–87.

MacAdams, Doug. 1985. *Political Process and the Development of Black Insurgency, 1930–1970.* Chicago: University of Chicago Press.

Mann, Michael. 1973. *Consciousness and Action Among the Western Working Class.* Essex, U.K.: Anchor Press.

Marris, R. 1964. *The Economic Theory of "Managerial" Capitalism*. New York: The Free Press.

Martin, Park H. 1964. "Narrative of the Allegheny Conference on Community Development and the Pittsburgh Renaissance, 1943–1954." Typescript, Carnegie Mellon University Library.

Mellon Economic Update: Pittsburgh. 1987. 4th quarter. Pittsburgh: Mellon Bank.

Metzgar, Jack. 1985. "Plant Shutdowns and Worker Response." *Socialist Review* 10 (September–October), pp. 9–50.

Mills, C. Wright. 1959. *The Power Elite*. New York: Oxford University Press.

Morrison, Roy. 1990. *We Build the Road as We Travel Mondragon: A Cooperative Solution*. Santa Cruz, Calif.: New Society Publishers.

Morse, David. 1986. "Surrender Dorothy." *In These Times*. February 19, 1986.

O'Boyle, Thomas. 1985. "Industry Seeks Radical Cures." *Wall Street Journal*, April 16, 1985, p. 1.

O'Conner, James. 1973. *Fiscal Crisis of the State*. New York: St. Martin's Press.

Olson, Deborah G. 1982. "Union Experiences with Worker Ownership: Legal and Practical Issues Raised by ESOPs, TRASOPs, Stock Purchases, and Cooperatives." *Wisconsin Law Review* 54:729–823.

Pateman, Carole. 1970. *Participation and Democratic Theory*. Cambridge: Cambridge University Press.

Piven, Francis Fox, and Richard A. Cloward. 1979. *Poor People's Movements: Why They Succeed and How They Fail*. New York: Vintage Books.

Polsby, Nelson. 1963. *Community Power and Political Theory*. New Haven: Yale University Press.

Przezworski, Adam, and Henry Teune. 1982. *The Logic of Comparative Social Inquiry*. Melbourne, Fla.: Krieger.

Reutter, Mark. 1988. *Sparrows Point: Making Steel—The Rise and Ruin of American Industrial Might*. New York: Summit Books.

Rohatyn, Felix. 1987. "On the Brink." *New York Review of Books*, June 11, 1987, p. 3.

Ross, Irwin. 1987. "Is Steel's Revival for Real?" *Fortune*, October 26, 1987, pp. 96–99.

Rousseau, Jean-Jacques. 1968. *The Social Contract*. New York: Penguin Books.

Salzman, Jack. 1967. *Years of Protest: A Collection of American Writings of the 1930s*. Indianapolis: Bobbs-Merrill.

Sartori, G. 1962. *Democratic Theory*. Detroit: Wayne State University Press.

Schlozman, Kay, and Sidney Verba. 1979. *Insult to Injury: Unemployment, Class, and Political Response*. Cambridge, Mass.: Harvard University Press.

Schumpeter, Joseph. 1943. *Capitalism, Socialism, and Democracy*. London: George Allen & Unwin.

Scott, R. H. 1969. "Avarice, Altruism, and Second Party Preferences." *Western Economic Journal* 7, no. 3, pp. 287ff.

Shannon, David A. 1960. *The Great Depression*. Englewood, N.J.: Prentice-Hall.

Shorrock, Tim. 1985. "A New Phase in Korean-American Relations: U.S. Steel's Pohang Strategy." *AMPO-Japan Asia Quarterly Review* 17, no. 3, pp. 2–13.

Simon, Herbert. "Theories of Decision-Making in Economic and Behavioral Science." *American Economic Review*, June 1959.

Smith, Adam. 1965. *An Inquiry into the Nature and Causes of the Wealth of Nations* (1776). New York: Modern Library.

Sombart, Werner. 1976. *Why Is There No Socialism in the United States?* Armonk, N.Y.: M. E. Sharpe.

Steinbeck, John. 1939. *The Grapes of Wrath*. New York: Viking.

Suda, Zdenik, ed. 1983. *Structural Unemployment and the New Perspectives on the Social Meaning of Work*. Pittsburgh: University of Pittsburgh.

Thomas, Hank, and C. Logan. 1983. *Mondragon: An Economic Analysis*. Winchester, Mass.: Unwin Hyman.

Tilly, Charles. 1978. *From Mobilization to Revolution*. Reading, Mass.: Addison-Wesley.

U.S. Catholic Bishops. 1987. "Economic Justice for All: Catholic Social Teaching and the U.S. Economy" (pastoral letter). *National Catholic Reporter*, January 9, 1987, pp. 1–44.

Vanek, Jaroslav. 1971. *The Labor-Managed Economy: Essays*. Ithaca, N.Y.: Cornell University Press.

———. 1975. *Self-Management: The Economic Liberation of Man*. New York: Penguin Books.

Yarrow, Mike. 1982. "How Good Strong Union Men Line It Out: Exploration of the Structure and Dynamics of Coal Miners' Class Consciousness." Ph.D. dissertation. Rutgers University.

INTERVIEWS

Anderson, Bob. Rainbow Kitchen. July 25, 1988.

Anonymous senior economist, Mellon Bank. April 4, 1985.

Becker, Darrell. Network to Save the Mon-Ohio Valley. April 2, 1985; November 8, 1985; July 15, 1986; July 31, 1986; September 24, 1986; July 6, 1992.

Benn, Jim. Tri-State Conference on Steel. July 24, 1985.

Erickson, Bob. Steel Valley Authority. March 16, 1992.

Flanders, Ron. Pittsburgh YMCA. July 30, 1986.

Foerster, Thomas. Chair, Allegheny County Commissioners. July 15, 1986.

Gilke, Arthur, Esq. Deacon, Shadyside Presbyterian Church. July 29, 1986.

Hebditch, Edward. Management consultant. April 4, 1985.

Higgie, David, and William Hoffman. Public relations, USX corporate headquarters. July 29, 1986.

Honeywell, Charles. DMS trainer. July 29, 1986.

Jones, Jim. DMS supporter. June 19, 1985.

Krien, Martin. DMS supporter. June 7, 1985.

Lodico, Paul. Mon Valley Unemployed Committee. July 25, 1988; March 15, 1992.

Long, the Rev. Philip D. DMS, East Liberty Lutheran Church. June 19, 1985.

Lynd, Staughton. Tri-State supporter. April 2, 1985.

Martoni, Charles. Mayor of Swissvale, Pa. July 26, 1985.

Prellwitz, Sam. Early retired metallurgist, U.S. Steel. April 2, 1985.

Robin, Jack. Allegheny Conference on Community Development. July 30, 1986.

Rosenberg, David. Network supporter, professor of history, and labor archivist at the University of Pittsburgh. July 31, 1986; July 30, 1988; March 16, 1992.

Roth, the Rev. D. Douglas. DMS. April 1, 1985; July 17, 1986.

Shortridge, John. Public relations, USX. June 1, 1987.

Smith, Ray. People's Natural Gas. June 5, 1985.

Solberg, the Rev. Dr. Richard. Director of Higher Education, Lutheran Church in America; father of DMS member Daniel Solberg.

Stout, Michael. Tri-State Conference on Steel. April 2, 1985.

Toy, Bob. Mon Valley Unemployed Committee. July 26, 1988.

Von Dreele, James. St. Matthew's Episcopal Church. DMS. April 1, 1985; June 18, 1985; July 24, 1985.

Weinberg, Jay. Tri-State Conference on Steel. July 26, 1988.

Weisen, Ron. Network to Save the Mon-Ohio Valley, and president of United Steel Workers Local 1397. July 18, 1986.

Worton, Dale. Network to Save the Mon-Ohio Valley and YMCA-1397 Food Bank. July 16, 1986.

Yedlicka, the Rev. John. Former member of DMS. July 24, 1985.

Zabelski, Leo. Mayor of Duquesne, Pa. April 3, 1985.

Zemprelli, Edward P. Minority Leader, Senate of Pennsylvania. July 18, 1986.

Index